Scarecrow Resource Guide Series

Hearing All the Voices

Multicultural Books for Adolescents

Mary Ann Darby
Miki Pryne

Scarecrow Resource Guide Series, No. 2

The Scarecrow Press, Inc.
Lanham, Maryland, and London
2002

SCARECROW PRESS, INC.

Published in the United States of America
by Scarecrow Press, Inc.
4720 Boston Way
Lanham, Maryland 20706
www.scarecrowpress.com

4 Pleydale Gardens, Folkstone
Kent CT20 2DN, England

British Library Cataloguing in Publication Information Available

Library of Congress Cataloging-in-Publication Data

Darby, Mary Ann, 1954-
    Hearing all the voices : multicultural books for adolescents / Mary Ann Darby and Miki Pryne.
        p. cm. — (Scarecrow resource guide series ; no. 2)
    Includes bibliographical references and indexes.
    ISBN 0-8108-4058-8 (alk. paper)
        1. Teenagers—Books and reading—United States. 2. Reading (Middle school)—United
States. 3. Young adult literature—Bibliography. 4. Pluralism (Social sciences) in
literature—Bibliography. 5. Ethnic groups in literature—Bibliography. 6. Minorities in
literature—Bibliography. 7. Multiculturalism in literature—Bibliography. I. Pryne, Miki,
1946- II. Title. III. Series.

Z1037.A1 D18 2002
028.5'35—dc21

2001031380

∞™ The paper used in this publication meets the minimum requirements of American
National Standard for Information Sciences—Permanence of Paper for Printed Library
Materials, ANSI/NISO Z39.48-1992.
Manufactured in the United States of America.

This book is dedicated to all our students, without whose differences we might have never taken this journey.

To Janela -

This is dedicated to you - and my other students ☺ - because you are the ones who inspire me. Writing this book was something I wanted to do - so, I want you, too, to follow your dreams. Best wishes + love from
Mrs Darby

Contents

Preface

A book for every student: that sums up our goal.

What can be a better gift to any student we work with than to help that young adult discover the love and joy of reading? Reading takes us on journeys that help us find the way through personal anguish, through different lifestyles, through countries other than our own, through the maze of growing and changing. Unless teens have discovered books that speak to them in a special way, they tend to think of reading as a chore, a time-consuming task—and if that is how they see reading, they have lost something incredibly special and important. Yes, reading will foster success in school, as it builds vocabulary, writing, and thinking skills. But reading also fosters growth of character. It helps teens to know they are not alone in their struggles. Good literature offers ideas, worlds, and challenges to our students.

The book you hold is a work of love: We have read books and gathered these ideas for seven years, and have shared them with other teachers, librarians, counselors, parents, anyone who works with teens. At every turn we have been encouraged by our colleagues who tell us that what we have gathered here is useful, practical, and helpful. We have included in our lists only books we have read, so that we can share them and how to use them confidently. Young adult literature is some of the best being produced right now. Authors are writing about topics that matter to teens and are exploring ideas that need to be brought into the light. Our hope is that this book will be a springboard for those who work with teens to find books that match the interests of the young readers with whom they work or live.

Acknowledgments

Throughout our years of teaching, so many of the best ideas have emerged because of collaboration: surely sharing and borrowing ideas from one another is at the heart of innovation in the classroom. With that in mind, we would like to thank the following people who have inspired us, listened to us, shared their ideas with us, and encouraged us: Marcie Belgard, Cathi Dunn MacRae, Margaret Garrison, Debra Harris-Branham, Gordon Knight, Virginia Malmquist, the Nelsen Middle School Teachers as Readers group, Robin Russell, and Marilyn Wayman-Terry. And especially to our families, for their unending patience and support.

Part I

HEARING THE VOICES

CHAPTER 1

Why Listen to the Voices?

Try to imagine, if you will, that you are thirteen years old, sitting in a classroom, listening to yet another book your teacher has selected to read aloud. Your mind is half wandering to the things you are going to do that evening or next weekend. You are used to hearing stories about people who are not much like you and whose stories have little relevance in your life. Suddenly, you hear something that brings your attention fully back to the story. You discover that the main character is just like you. Maybe she belongs to your ethnic group. Maybe he has a brother with Down syndrome. Now the story holds you enthralled. Suddenly books take on a whole new meaning. Maybe you can find more books with characters like you. With this realization comes the almost certain knowledge that while others are learning about your culture, you can learn about theirs.

Students benefit from reading literature that reflects their own cultural background. Their lives suddenly are validated. Additionally, students increase their knowledge of the cultures around them. They become aware of the differences and, more important, the similarities between themselves and those perceived as different. Good multicultural literature helps students recognize the stereotypes that abound in the broader culture—and overcome them. It has also been our experience that when students are exposed to multiple points of view, their ability to analyze, evaluate, and make judgments improves. For all these reasons, finding literature on which to build a multicultural program has become a passion for us.

Selecting the right book for every young reader takes more than knowing the best new authors and the timeless classics. You also have to know about the young people you are working with, the things that make them happy, and the concerns they have about growing up today. Literature also has to compete with flashy video games and fast action movies to grab the young reader. The books you offer have to capture them from the first few words, and more important, they must be accurate and have central characters who share their life stories. As our population becomes more diverse, authors of books for adolescents are writing about this rich tapestry of cultures, reflective of us all. Young adult multicultural literature has come into its own.

Two things are constant in today's classroom: change and diversity. Every student weaves a new thread into the classroom tapestry. They bring different gifts, abilities, learning preferences, family backgrounds, and values. Each student brings pieces of his or her own culture—family, community, ethnic, religious, mental, and physical—to school every day.[1] Because of this rich diversity, we believe we need to regularly provide an equally rich background.

All too often, multiculturalism is taught as a separate entity. Black History Month means studying the life of Dr. Martin Luther King Jr. and reading the poetry of Langston Hughes sometime during February. Sometime in the spring, many schools have cultural festivals with songs, dances, and food from around the world. Multiculturalism does not have to be kept in a box, to be unwrapped and dusted off for these special occasions.[2] Using multicultural literature as a part of the regular reading program is a powerful and simple way to say you value the gifts and differences all your students bring to you.

We jumped at the chance to bring in literature written about the students we teach in our classrooms. We spent a lot of time talking with our students about culture and how important it is to learn about your own as well as the cultures of the people around you. We discovered that many of our Caucasian students did not believe they fit into any specific culture. We decided that if we wanted to find reflections of all our students in the literature we were introducing, we needed to go beyond the commonly used definition of multiculturalism, which is primarily multiethnic. The American Heritage Dictionary of the English Language defines *culture* as "The totality of socially transmitted behavior patterns, arts, beliefs, institutions, and all other products of human work and thought characteristic of a community or a population." As we began fitting all our students into this broader definition, we discovered an even richer tapestry in our midst.

With this broader definition of *multiculturalism* in mind, we began to look for books that included characters who were living in nontraditional families, or coping with major illnesses or other physical and mental challenges. We found books about young people living in cars or struggling with obesity or anorexia. Some of the newer books have protagonists who discover they or someone they love is gay or lesbian. We discovered authors who write about the deaths of people they love or the horror of being sexually harassed in the school halls. Family abuse, alcoholism, racism, and discrimination are all addressed in books written for young adults. We just had to seek them out.

We have chosen to focus on literature for the eleven- to fifteen-year-old for several reasons. First and foremost is that we really enjoy working with young people in this age group. They are both fun and challenging. They are also the hardest to reach, in many ways. They are dealing with so many changes, both physically and emotionally, that getting them to read anything other than glossy magazines is tough. These students are trying to separate from their families and find their new place in the world. This world is filled with powerful messages to conform to some unspecified norm and deviation from that norm results in derision and discrimination. They are teetering in a quandary between conforming to peer pressure and finding their own identities.

As we began reading young adult literature, we found that this adolescent angst is dealt with in compelling and provocative ways. The emphasis is on the day-to-day changes that are a part of these adolescent years and how these changes can become stepping stones for positive growth. Where it might have been okay to have parents who were mentally challenged when you were little, at thirteen it is hopelessly embarrassing. Kimberly Holt describes this change very well in *My Louisiana Sky*. When Tiger Ann was in elementary school, she thought it was great fun to have a mother who was such a great playmate. That all changed when her mother showed up to meet her at her middle school. Suddenly the bright, funny clothes she was wearing were a major embarrassment. In Holt's skillful storytelling, Tiger Ann comes through this crisis and becomes stronger. This kind of literature can help our students work through their own identity issues and empower them in unique ways.

Over the years, as we have presented our ideas at conferences, we have been asked the same question repeatedly, "Why should I worry about bringing multicultural novels into my classroom? I teach in a very homogeneous student population." With limited resources for books, this is an important question. The answer lies in the greater world outside the classroom. Even in a so-called homogeneous community, there are vast differences in family cultures. Forty-one percent of today's marriages are predicted to end in divorce.[3] Mental illness has increased dramatically, and funding to support families has dwindled. With advances in medicine, people are living long and full lives with physical illnesses and challenges that would have ended their lives at a young age only fifty years ago. Family violence has increased five-fold. Teen suicide has tripled, alcohol and drug use continues to increase, and eating disorders have become all too commonplace.[4] Our classrooms are filled with students who face one or more of these challenges or they know someone who does. One of the reasons we expanded our definition of multicultural is so we can reach these young people.

We have also made sure to keep multiethnicity at the core of our list. Each time we step outside our classroom, or our community, we meet people who are more different from us than similar. The population in the United States is growing ever more diverse. In California alone, it is estimated that Hispanics will become the majority population within ten years. On the Internet, our world neighbors have become our next-door neighbors. For our students to be successful competitors in the changing world market, they need to understand and value these new neighbors. Using multicultural literature is a positive way to develop empathy and understanding during a time when these commodities are all too rare.

We have worked hard to find titles from as many different cultures as we can. For some cultures, we have not found books in English by authors from within that culture. When we do select a book written from the outside, we are very mindful of possible stereotyping and the harm that can do. Before we started this project, we had to take a hard look at our own biases. Where did they come from? How have they been reinforced? What can we do to make sure our biases do not color our selections? We have both spent many hours talking about this issue with friends and colleagues. If we have a question about a particular title, we ask friends to read it and discuss it with us. We also follow the discussions on this topic in professional journals.

There is a lively discussion going on in the professional literature these days about the authenticity of a book written by an "outsider."[5] When Gary Paulsen writes about the American slave experience, critics celebrate his insight and sensitivity, but when Virginia Hamilton writes about a Caucasian protagonist, these same critics ask how she dares. A great way to have students engage in this debate is to assign readings from two books on a topic like slavery, one written by a person who has experience inside the African American culture and one written by a person who does not. *Wolf by the Ears* by Ann Rinaldi and *Clote: Diary of a Slave Girl* by Patricia McKissack are good examples. After reading primary documents about slavery and about Thomas Jefferson's attitude toward slavery, have the students read selected passages and discuss which picture they think is more accurate. Then have them debate the merits of each story. We don't know if this question will be resolved but we do believe that asking it and struggling with the answer is important. It will help our students become critical thinkers as they explore the rich diversity around them.

In the chapters and appendixes that follow, we describe the ways in which we have used this rich world of adolescent multicultural literature in our classrooms. Literary circles have been very successful for us. Not only do the students get to select their own books from a list chosen for the theme we are working on, but they have opportunities to interact with their peers about many books on the same topic. We have described ways in which our students have responded to the literature, both individually and in groups. There is a chapter on how to integrate multicultural novels across the curriculum and uses outside the classroom. We have also included a chapter on using science fiction/fantasy in the classroom. These works often deal with the same growing pains our students face and appeal to some of our more reluctant readers. And of course there is the annotated bibliography, which is at the heart of this book. As we continue to search for more adolescent multicultural novels, we are ever mindful that there are many books out there that are just perfect for each of our students.

NOTES

1. Mary Ann Darby, and Miki Pryne, "Multiculturalism in the Classroom: Using Literary Circles," *Washington English Journal* (Spring/Fall, 1995): 43.

2. Darby and Pryne, "Multiculturalism in the Classroom," 43.

3. Divorce statistics provided by Americans for Divorce Reform, http://www.divorcereform.org/rates.html, 2000 [accessed December 2000].

4. Statistical information on these problems can be found on the World Wide Web at http://dianedew.com/suistats.htm; www.instruct.nmu.edu/criminal, 2000; www.soundvision.com/domesticviolence/statistics.shtml, 2000; www.randomhouse.com/features/eatingdisorders/stats.html, 2000; and www.siu.edu/departments/coreinst/public_html/recent.html, 2000 [accessed December 2000].

5. Jacqueline Woodson, "Who Can Tell My Story?" *The Horn Book Magazine* (January/February, 1998): 34–38; and W. Nikola-Lisa, "Around My Table Is Not Enough," *The Horn Book Magazine* (May/June, 1998): 315–18.

CHAPTER 2

Using the Voices in Literary Circles

WHY LITERARY CIRCLES

How many times have you taken out the class novel set only to hear moans and groans all around? "Do we have to read that? Why can't we choose our own book?" Because we believe strongly that getting students to read fosters success in all areas of learning, we began brainstorming ways to bring student enthusiasm into the reading class. We had observed that when our students chose their own books, they tended to read more and become much more invested in their reading. However, in our classrooms, students usually picked books well below their reading levels and limited in subject matter and vocabulary. We decided to incorporate student choice in our reading program with an emphasis on encouragement toward the great adolescent literature we were finding and reading.

Choice is a powerful motivator for students: Being able to pick one title out of five or ten novels means students immediately become more invested in that book than in one that is simply required. Our chief means of incorporating the choice factor was by creating a basic framework for literary circles.

CREATING LITERARY CIRCLES

Literary circles, as we define them, are formed by choosing a theme, then selecting five to ten books that incorporate that theme. Because our students are from different cultures, and have different reading abilities and interests, we strive to include novels that feature both male and female protagonists, are of varying reading levels, and represent as many cultures as possible. Any core novel that a teacher has used can be the basis for a circle of books by choosing one of the core novel's themes to build around. For example, instead of the whole class of seventh graders reading S. E. Hinton's *The Outsiders,* we created a circle of books that dealt with the theme of adolescent struggles: Ponyboy struggles throughout the story with his authoritarian big brother, with the cross-town rivals, and with the idea that even different people must have similarities. Other themes we might have considered instead include living in a nontraditional family (Ponyboy's parents are dead), or dealing with prejudice (the Socs and Greasers judge each other by the labels they use), or finding similarities amid differences (Ponyboy and Cherry both watch the same sunsets).

Once a theme is identified, other books can be selected. If we use the adolescent struggles theme, the possibilities for other titles are vast. Again, within the possibilities, we want to include variety in reading levels, male and female protagonists, and cultural variety. Below is one set of choices, including how the titles meet different considerations.

The Outsiders: Caucasian American protagonist; below grade level; nontraditional family; gang conflict

Scorpions: African American male protagonist; on grade level; nontraditional family; conflict within a gang

Humming Whispers: African American female protagonist; above grade level; nontraditional family; family member with schizophrenia

Hannah in Between: Caucasian American female protagonist; below grade level; two-parent family; mother is showing signs of alcoholism

Buried Onions: Latino American male protagonist; on grade level; nontraditional family; barrio life and violence

Finding My Voice: Asian American female protagonist; above grade level, traditional family; struggle against prejudice

Dakota Dream: Native American male protagonist; on grade level; nontraditional family; struggle to find a place to belong

Homeless Bird: Indian female protagonist; on grade level; traditional family; struggle to find a place in society

By choosing this sort of variety, students suddenly have a number of factors to help them make their choices. As we booktalk each title we choose for a circle, we are honest about the pros and cons of each. We cannot emphasize enough how important it is that you read each book before including it in a literary circle, so you know what the book is about and whether it is appropriate for your students. If students have read the books, we include examples of their critiques as well. For example, we might share a comment such as, "Last year's groups complained that this book started slowly, but after the first four chapters, everyone agreed it went more quickly and was worth reading." If a book is panned by two or more student groups, we usually do not use it the following year. We might also add comments based on our own observations: "*Homeless Bird* is a relatively short book, but Koly uses many Indian words in the story. There is a glossary in the back of the book that is useful."

During the booktalk, we give students a preference sheet. This can be done several ways. We like to type out the title and author, and leave a space for students to write how many pages are in the book and other comments that will help them decide whether they want to read it. Students can also simply create their own list as the teacher presents the books, but they tend to focus on how to spell titles and names and sometimes do not listen as closely. However the list is created, students need to rank at least their top three choices. We urge them to consider their own interests and abilities, as they will be spending quite a bit of time and energy on the book. We invite them to make comments on the preference sheet as well. We tend to get comments like, "My brother said *Scorpions* is the best, so PLEASE let me read it," or "I will read anything but another book by (_____)."

Once we collect preference sheets, we stack them by the first ranked book. Because choice is such an important factor for the students, we try to give as many students as possible their first choices. When isn't it possible? If only one student prefers a particular title in a class, he or she has to get the second choice. An important aspect of circles is peer discussion about the shared book. Some teachers want only one group for each set of books, so if more than five students choose a particular title, they give other students their second or third choices. We see no real problem with having more than one group reading a book. Sometimes we get overly enthusiastic about a title, or a book's reputation has preceded it and we get many students selecting a single title. The other factor that might eliminate first choices is the number of any given set of books.

There are many ideas about literary circles in current literature. Some suggest groups should be made up of only three or four individuals, and that each individual must have a role assigned in that group, such as to be a facilitator, summarizer, or reinforcer for all group meetings. We have had consistently good results with groups of two to five students. Rather than assigning tasks to individuals, we allow roles to develop naturally, which in itself is an interesting process to observe. Inevitably there is a student who takes on the role of watch-dog, making sure that all group members keep up with the reading and do their share of the work. We simply create a packet of materials that each student must work through. Some of the exercises are for the group to work through, while others are for individual effort. The packets are a guide for students so that when they meet on a daily basis to discuss their progress, they have concepts to focus on, and can discuss, predict, question, and clarify, using the active reading process together.

CREATING A RESPONSE PACKET

Packets for students can be created in many ways. Below is a sample of what can be included in a literary circle packet that each student would receive and be responsible for completing:

1. **Vocabulary:** We challenge our students to find the words they do not know, and then list and define them. If students assure us they know all the words, we have lists that we have created for each book to hand them. We set a minimum number of words per book, and usually give extra credit for those who go beyond the minimum.
2. **Setting:** After discussing setting as a class by using short stories or a work we have all done together, we expect students in literary circles to be able to specify both the time and place of a story and explain the effect of the setting on the story. We encourage the groups to discuss this together.
3. **Conflicts:** After discussing conflicts and types of conflicts in earlier works covered in class, we expect students to be able to identify a minimum number of conflicts in a story, explain what type of conflict it represents, then point to a specific instance in the book that shows the conflict. For example, in Walter Dean Myers's *Scorpions,* Jamal has an internal conflict as to whether he should follow his brother's footsteps into a gang. Usually we ask students to identify at least five conflicts in the novels they read. Again, they may discuss this as a group.
4. **Main characters:** As students are reading, they are to identify those characters that are most important in the story. They also need to write a brief (one to two sentences) description of that character.
5. **Themes:** Even with our eighth graders, the concept of theme is challenging, and one we inevitably must talk with each group about during literary circles. We discuss themes as the ideas behind the story, the concepts we think about after we close the book. After a small-group discussion, we ask students to identify five themes from the book they read.
6. **Daily responses:** Each day that we give to students to read, we ask them to respond briefly in their packets. Responses can be of many varieties: summaries, individual reactions, predictions for what might

happen next, or questions about what they have read. We also ask students to point out something or someone they were able to identify with, or to explain a phrase or figure of speech that they found to be compelling. All of these responses are active reading strategies that not only ensure students are reading, but also to make sure they are digging below the surface for some of their responses. A variety of response options is usually most popular with students. Another form of response that works best with books dealing with emotionally charged issues is an interpersonal journal. The format we have chosen is to ask students to copy a short passage from a chapter, then respond to it in two ways: first, they must explain what is happening in the passage they chose and set it in context of the chapter; second, they must react personally to the passage. How did it make them feel? Why did they choose this passage? Did they identify with it in some way?

7. **Other ideas:** While the first six items are standard in all our packets, we tailor other portions of the packets to fit the themes of the books we are reading, to fit other concepts we wish to reinforce, or to incorporate more creative responses. With a nod to the multiple intelligences, we often ask students to create and depict a symbol that represents a favorite character, or draw a scene from the book. Sometimes we ask them to extend the story and explain what might happen next to a favorite character. Asking students to create character webs is another way to have students visually represent part of a story. We also make frequent use of an "I Am" poem format by having students write a poem from the viewpoint of one of the book's characters. We ask students to find figures of speech in books to try to illustrate the power of strong word choices and interesting language. We have also asked students to create metaphors or similes for the main characters in their stories. The packet assignments are usually brief and straightforward. We save more creative ideas for another important part of literary circles—the individual and group projects that are explained in chapter 3.

The benefits of literary circles are many. An immediate benefit is the increased motivation of the students to read when they are able to choose a book. The other benefits come with the number of books students are exposed to. When they hear their peers talking about a novel, they listen critically and closely. They ask questions of each other to make sure everyone really did read their novels, and are genuinely interested in each others' opinions of books. When students respond to the novels, many times we see that they are able to explore issues that are of personal importance to them. One of our favorite by-products of literary circles is having students ask us if it is possible for them to read a book from another circle: you can imagine that our answer is always positive! Exposure to good literature and interesting ideas are vitally important in creating students who want to read and want to learn. Literary circles are certainly one method that leads in that direction.

CHAPTER 3

Responding to the Voices

Once students have read a book, we want to see and hear their responses. What did students find in their books that opened their eyes? What struck a familiar chord? What questions did the books raise? What issues do they want to discuss further? What did they understand? What was confusing?

Rather than traditional tests, we have veered toward projects and creative responses. Usually, if students are able to fill out the materials contained in the packet we described in chapter 2, there is no question whether they read and understood the book. There have been times when we have incorporated tests or quizzes as one type of response, but we have found that projects can demonstrate a student's depth of understanding and spawn discussion of different dimensions of a book. Quizzes and tests may not evoke the response we are looking for and do not draw on the diversity of intelligences we find in our students. We have listened to other teachers' ideas, and we have listened to our students who often have very appropriate and creative ideas.

Our projects fall in to two categories: (1) individual projects for students to produce on their own; and (2) group projects, which are produced and presented by literary circle groups. We typically require one of each from our students when they read a novel. What follows are descriptions of the responses we have found to work well with middle school students. All these responses, individual and group, require the students to interact with their selected novel in more than a fact-collecting way. They need to analyze the theme, plot, and characters and synthesize this information into a coherent response that will demonstrate their complete understanding of the book. The bonus is that the students enjoy the opportunities to display what they have learned, using more than just their verbal-linguistic skills.

INDIVIDUAL PROJECTS

1. Creating **compact disc covers** is a project students enjoy. This four-part assignment requires a piece of paper the size of a compact disc

cover that folds like a book. On the front, students design an illustrated cover for a CD, which includes the name of the featured band or group. The lead singer of this group must be one of the major characters from the novel. One student named her group Kit and the Witches after reading Elizabeth George Speare's *The Witch of Blackbird Pond*. The CD *Howling at the Moon* featured Russel and the Sled Dogs for a student who read Gary Paulsen's *Dogsong*.

The inside cover is a biographical sketch of the lead singer, and should be written to show an understanding of the character and worded as if the character were singing about life as shown in the novel. One example we created is based on *Dogsong* by Gary Paulsen: "Russel wrote his first lyrics on a moonlit night in the frozen north as he and his dogs mushed across the snow to find a sense of what life was about. On his return from the sled trip, during which he encountered life and death challenges, he set his lyrics to traditional Eskimo style music. The result was his first CD, *Howling at the Moon*. He dedicates this CD to Oogruk who inspired the trip that changed Russel profoundly. He and the Sled Dogs are currently working on new material."

On the inside back cover are the original lyrics to a song that exhibits an understanding of the themes, protagonist, or conflict of the story. This may be the title song or any other song from the CD. If students ask how to write lyrics, we explain they should listen to the music they like and examine how the lyrics are written, or tell them it is simply a poem set to music. If we use the poem analogy, we hasten to add that the lyrics do *not* have to rhyme.

The back of the CD cover is the fourth and final piece of the project. It must list all of the songs on the CD. Each of the titles must clearly represent an event, theme, or character from the book. Examples from a *Dogsong* CD might include, "Where Am I Going?," "Oogruk and the Old Ways," "Icebergs and Sorrow," "Running on the Ice," and "Howling at the Moon." The back cover must also contain the name of the CD producer (the student), when the CD was produced (date of project), and any acknowledgments the producer wishes to make. Some students like to put their finished product into a CD case, although that is optional.

Alternatively, some students have asked if they could create a soundtrack with existing music they select to go with the characters, theme, setting, and plot of the novel. One student created a lovely sound track for *The Education of Little Tree* by Forrest Carter which included the John Lennon and Paul McCartney song "Blackbird." She explained that the song's images evoked a picture of the setting that Little Tree described, and also tied to Little Tree's growth. "Blackbird singing in the dead of night/ Take these broken wings and learn to fly . . ." depicts Little Tree learning the Way of the Cherokee from his grandparents after losing his own parents. Either of these projects asks students to stretch outside the box, responding to their novels in a unique way.

2. **Timelines** are a fun and easy response to literature. Our criteria for timelines are fairly straightforward: the timeline itself must be a symbol from the book, and students must represent a minimum of eight items from the plot on the timeline along with appropriate illustrations or enhancements, such as other symbols from the story. For example, students responding to Linda Crew's *Children of the River* frequently chose a river for their timeline. One student who created a timeline for Laurence Yep's *Dragonwings* created a kite with a long tale as the basis of his timeline.

3. A **storyball** can be made in many ways. Our basic formula is to have students cut three circles of the same size. Six-inch diameter circles work well for this project. Each circle depicts a different aspect of the story. The compositions for each circle can vary. Choose from the following ideas: an illustrated title page; an "I Am" poem (see format below); a symbol from the story; an illustration or symbolic representation of the main conflict in the story; a critique of the story; an illustration of the setting; or a map depicting the setting. The last step is to fold each circle in half and paste half of the first circle to the second, the other half of the second circle to half of the third circle, and the other half of the third circle to the remaining half of the first. We liked to punch a hole at the top, add yarn, and hang these from the classroom ceilings.

Example 1. I Am poem format

I am (two adjectives describing character)
I wonder (something the character is curious about)
I see (something the character wants to see)
I want (something the character would like to have)
I am (restate the first line of the poem)

I pretend (something the character might pretend to do)
I feel (a feeling the character has about something)

I worry (something that concerns the character)
I cry (something that makes the character sad)
I am (restate the first line of the poem)

I laugh (something that makes the character happy)
I dream (something the character would like to do or be)
I say (something the character believes in)
I hope (something the characters hopes for)
I am (restate the first line of the poem)

4. A **storycube** is similar to a storyball in that each surface gives the student an opportunity to depict some important aspect of a novel. Students will need heavy drawing paper and a pattern for creating the cube (Fig. 3.1). You may enlarge the pattern for the students or you may incorporate measuring and geometry skills into this project. We like this project because it can include artistic expression, verbal-linguistic and mathematical skills, and is very kinesthetic.

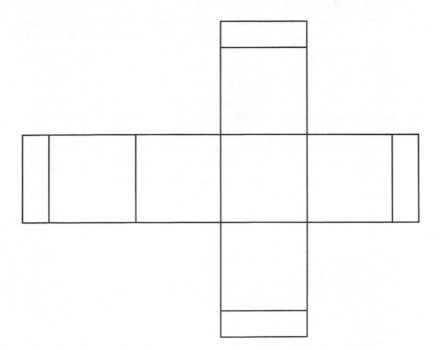

Figure 3.1   *The storycube pattern*

5. **Posters** have always been popular with our students. Whether it is a promotional poster for a film made from the novel or a "wanted" poster based on one of the main characters, students have shown a great deal of imagination and creativity. One student chose to depict a scene from the Chinese folktale told in Laurence Yep's *Child of the Owl,* which he turned into a movie poster, selecting favorite actors for the key roles. Another student created a wanted poster for Jesse in Will Hobbs's *Downriver.* She included all the vital statistics she could glean from reading the novel.

6. The **window shutter** project is a take-off of the traditional Advent calendar. Students select a symbol depicting some aspect of the novel they read. Good examples are the school bus from Mildred Taylor's *Roll of Thunder, Hear My Cry* or the whale from Herman Melville's *Moby Dick.* The symbol should be a fairly simple shape. The shape is then cut out of one piece of colored construction paper and one piece of white. It should be at least 8 inches by 5 inches. At least six "windows" should be created in the colored shape by cutting three sides so the "shutters" hinge at the side or on the top. Then the windowed piece is glued to the white background. Inside each window, the student writes either descriptions of main characters, pieces of the plot summary, or themes from the novel.

7. **Magazine covers** are a good way to incorporate writing as well as visual skills. Students select the cover of an old magazine with a recognizable format. *National Geographic, Time, Newsweek,* and *Rolling Stone* work well for this project. Students cut out the border and the title from the original magazine cover and glue them to the right half of a piece of construction paper. Using any artistic media, students then design a cover page depicting a scene or theme from their novel. Students then add the publication date which corresponds to the time in which the novel is set and a headline for their cover story. The paper is then folded in half and on the inside, students write the cover story and the table of contents. The cover story may be a critique of the novel, an in-depth character sketch, or a detailed summary. Publication information, such as student's name, date of project, class, novel title, and teacher's name, should go on the inside left page.

8. Another written response is the **character sketch.** Students select one of the main characters of the novel and write an in-depth profile. This response should include vital statistics: where the character was born, age, physical characteristics, occupation, education. It should also include major personality traits supported by events from the novel that

demonstrate each trait. For example, Omar S. Castaneda's Isabel in *Among the Volcanoes* showed her curiosity and willingness to accept new things when she sought out the Western doctor to help her mother even though the other villagers were superstitious and sometimes hostile.

9. **Character journals** are a good way to evaluate whether students have developed a good understanding of the characters in their novel. Entries are made for eight to ten events in the story from a main character's point of view. Students describe the event and the thoughts, feelings, and ideas the chosen character might have about the event. This response works best with novels written in the narrative or third-person voice; however, a way to use this with first-person or diary-style novels, is to have students write entries for events that could happen after the story ends. A student who has just finished *Don't You Dare Read This, Mrs. Dunphrey* by Margaret Haddix may want to pursue the results of Tish's disclosure of her tragic situation and how her life may have changed.

10. The traditional **diorama** is always a favorite project because it is a familiar format. Students are asked to create dioramas for science and social studies from early grades. Using a shoebox, or other small box, and any arts-and-crafts materials available to them, students create a three-dimensional scene depicting some event or theme from the novel. One student recreated Timothy and Phillip's home in *The Cay* by Theodore Taylor. She used twigs and sand along with construction paper and cardboard to create the compound and part of the surrounding landscape. It was very effective.

11. Most students are familiar with **cartoons** and enjoy creating four-panel cartoons of a favorite part of their novel. A sheet of drawing paper is folded into quarters, one for each panel. This project is very good for sequencing plot events. Many of our students are visual learners, and this project can help them develop a better understanding of the book they read. Students with limited artistic skills can complete this project using stick figures and still feel successful.

12. Another linguistic response to a novel is a written **editorial** about an issue raised in the novel. This response requires the student to think beyond the novel and connect it to events in their own lives. *Adem's Cross* by Alice Mead tells the story of an Albanian family living in Kosovo under the Milosevic regime. Students can research this time period using original sources and respond to the novel based on their

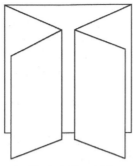

Step 1: *The fold*

Step 2: *The cover drawing*

Step 3: *The inside drawing*

Figure 3.2   *The tri-fold card*

research and their own thoughts about the events. This is a good response project to use when incorporating literature in the social studies curriculum.

13. One of the most creative responses we have used is the **tri-fold card**. This response requires some artistic talent and is best used as one choice among many. Students who are not strong in this area may be put off if it is the only choice. Students choose one important event in the novel to use as the central scene in this project. The first step is to fold a piece of construction or drawing paper into thirds. The top page is then folded in half, back on itself. The next page is folded the same way (Fig. 3.2). The drawing on the front of the card should be something fairly simple that is symbolic of the story, like the salamander in *Babcock* by Joe Cottonwood. As the card is opened, the lines of the front drawing become part of a more complex drawing taking up the entire inside of the card (see illustration). When it is

done well, the front drawing completely disappears into the larger drawing. Many students have risen to the challenge of this project and produced wonderful results.

14. **Songs** and **poems** elicit responses that are often deeper and more meaningful than many of the other projects we use. Upon finishing Maureen Wartski's *A Boat to Nowhere,* one seventh-grade girl wrote a moving poem about her mother's experience fleeing her homeland in Vietnam. Other students have written and performed songs using familiar tunes but new words that tell the story of the novel and how the reader responded to it. Biopoems in two voices are a good way to see if students recognize and connect with the protagonist and the antagonist in the story (see example 1).

The Biopoem

Adjective describing the person
Adjective describing the person
Adjective describing the person
Much loved by . . . . .
Sibling of . . . . .
Wishes to be . . . . .
Dreams of becoming . . . . .
Wants to . . . . .
Who wonders . . . . .
Who likes . . . . .
Who dislikes . . . . .
Who loves . . . . . (may be repeated)
Who plans . . . . . (may be repeated)

15. We were introduced to the **shoebox float** by a colleague who had been using them for biography reports. We adapted them to our fiction responses with good results. Students create a float, like the ones in large parades, from a shoebox. They use the sides and bottom as a base on which to build images representing the story as a whole. Unlike a diorama, which depicts one scene from the story, the float will have many symbols and objects that are tied together by the theme of the novel. A float based on Paul Fleischman's *Whirligig* might have a whirligig in the center with a Greyhound bus moving around the perimeter on a relief map of the United States. In each corner would be a symbol depicting Brent's moments of self-revelation.

16. A **collage** is another good way for students to demonstrate a thorough understanding of the theme of a book. Using a large poster board as a base, students search through magazines for pictures that represent important aspects of the book. One eighth grader created a collage for Karen Hesse's *Phoenix Rising* by including pictures of sheep ranching, nuclear power plants, people working and playing together, and people dying in the streets. She also cut out words and other symbols to enhance the story she was telling. The resulting collage was very moving and clearly demonstrated that she understood the underlying themes of the novel.

17. With increasing access to technology, students often want to create a response using **Hyperstudio** or **PowerPoint**. These software products are powerful tools that allow students to manipulate text and graphics into a plot line or character sketch. In a social studies or science class, students may bring in information about real events that parallel those in a book. These projects work well but you might need to allow more time for their completion and presentation.

GROUP PROJECTS

1. **Newspapers** are a fun way for groups to present their responses to the novel they have all read. This project allows students with different learning styles and skill levels to all participate equally. Feature articles and editorials are written about events in the novel. Cartoons are often included, as well as ads for products found in the story. Some of our students enjoy writing advice columns, which include letters in the voices of story characters soliciting advice about the conflicts they face in the story. If students have access to computers, there are good publishing programs that will make this project fun and more professional-looking. Otherwise, they can use large sheets of newspaper-size paper then cut and paste up the different parts of their newspaper page.

2. **Courtroom dramas** have been very successful for getting group members focused on a central event or theme of the novel. After reading *Words by Heart* by Ouida Sebestyen, a group of sixth graders decided to put racism on trial. They developed evidence and prepared their case using events and quotes from the story. The courtroom dramas created in this process are different from a formalized mock trial, which we discuss in more detail in chapter 4.

3. The **talk show** format allows the group to bring characters in their novel to life. The host asks questions of the characters to elicit responses that will tell the story from that character's point of view. This response requires a thorough understanding of the main characters of the story and shows each of them is integral to the outcome. One group of sixth graders read Betty Bao Lord's *In the Year of the Boar and Jackie Robinson*. Guests included Shirley Temple Wong, her parents, her baseball team friends, and Jackie Robinson. Each guest spoke about what it was like to take part in life-changing events, eventually revealing the story and theme of this modern classic.

4. A **panel discussion** can be done in several ways. The members of the panel can be fellow authors discussing the merits of the novel, or they can be characters from the novel. They can be experts on topics introduced in the story, movie producers meeting to discuss the creation of a movie based on the book, or a group of students acting as book critics. A group of seventh graders chose the latter format to discuss *So Far from the Bamboo Grove* by Yoko Kawashima Watkins. They took turns describing the character, theme, conflicts, plot, and setting of the story before opening the floor to questions from the audience. They each had a turn sharing their reactions, and the audience was treated to a lively and informative discussion about the book.

5. The **Masterpiece Theater** format allows students to script and present two or three short scenes from the book. Before each scene, the host introduces it and explains any background information the audience members may need to enhance their understanding. We have had students who wanted to script and present only one brief scene from the book, but we have found that requiring more than one or two scenes is a more comprehensive response. The scenes must represent important events in the story and, when presented together, demonstrate a thorough understanding of the characters, theme, and story line.

6. A **travel-log show** allows students to explore the setting of the novel. This project lends itself well to PowerPoint or Hyperstudio presentations. Students can include photographs, maps, written details, and music. This is a good response for groups reading novels set in locations outside their own experiences.

7. Producing a **newscast** is another way groups can present major events in the plot of their novel, make editorial comments, and describe the setting. A group reading *The Drowning of Stephen Jones* by Bette Greene may have the lead story about the citizen's group that wants to

ban "anti-Christian" books from the local library, with breaking news about the brutal death of an owner of a nearby antique store. Editorial comments could address censorship or violence against homosexuals. Advertisements about local businesses would round out the setting.

8. Students may want to use music, video, slides, and/or computers to create a **multimedia** presentation about their novel. This type of response requires some level of technical expertise and access to the technology in the classroom.

Whatever ideas you decide to try, don't forget to invite students to come up with other ideas, too. We have asked students for ideas many times, and we are repeatedly pleased and amazed with their appropriate creativity. Often their fresh perspectives give us new insights to both the books and our students.

CHAPTER 4

Using the Voices Beyond the Language Arts Class

INSIDE THE CLASSROOM

All too often, we relegate young adult literature to literary circles or book reports. In truth, this literature is well suited to science, health, and social studies classes, as well as reading clubs and counseling or support groups. The topics covered in these multicultural novels range from living in a Maasai *engang* in Kenya in the 1990s to traveling by foot across China in the 1600s. There are frank discussions about living with alcoholic or abusive parents, discovering sexuality, coping with being different, grieving the loss of a loved one, and struggling with obesity. There are countless books on traditional social studies topics like slavery, the Civil War, and the Holocaust. In this chapter, we discuss the use of these novels outside the traditional language arts class venue. We have chosen a few titles as examples in each area for you to use as a starting point, but there are many more worthwhile titles in the bibliography. These novels can be assigned as class novels, used for literary circles, read-alouds, or put on reading lists as a basis for classroom discussions. Appendix A lists books in the bibliography by topic or subject area and appendix B lists books by curriculum area.

Critical Thinking Skills

We have discovered several novels to use for teaching **comparing and contrasting** skills. Ben Mikaelsen's *Countdown* is the story of two fourteen-year-old boys. Elliot Schroeder lives with his parents on a ranch in Montana, while Vincent Ole Tome lives with his extended family in an *engang* (a small brush-enclosed village) in a remote area of Kenya. Both boys are curious about life away from their family traditions. When Elliot is selected to be the first junior astronaut to fly aboard the space shuttle Endeavor, his job is to communicate with people around the world by HAM radio. Vincent, in his curiosity about the outside world, pays nightly visits to a local Maasai doctor who has lived and trained in a more modern world.

One of the things Vincent enjoys most on these visits is listening to the doctor talk on his HAM radio. It is through this radio that Elliot and Vincent carry on sometimes heated conversations about their different ways of life. Students can do Venn Diagrams or create charts showing the differences and similarities of these two protagonists' lives. They can then tie the story to their own lives by adding a circle or section for themselves.

Problem solving involves the ability to define the problem, assess possible solutions, and create a workable plan of action. In John Marsden's *Tomorrow, When the War Began,* Ellie and her friends are faced with several situations where these skills become crucial. After returning from a camping trip, the friends discover that their homeland has been invaded, and the enemy has rounded up all the local citizens and is holding them inside the fairground in the center of town. As students read this novel, they can define each problem as it arises and name the steps the teens take to overcome it. They can also design alternative plans of action based on their own knowledge and experience.

In *Scorpions* by Walter Dean Myers, Jamal finds he has to make some hard decisions about his life. After his older brother is sent to prison, Jamal is expected to become the leader of the Scorpions, the gang his brother led until his incarceration. His decision is complicated by the worsening situation at school and by the gun his brother's friends put in his hands. Decision making is a vital skill for all students to learn and this moving novel can be used as a basis for several class discussions and projects on steps to master this skill. A good extension from this novel is to have students create a decision-making plan that will work for them when they are faced with difficult decisions.

We begin finding **patterns** in our environment from an early age and when we begin school, we use those patterns as a basis for learning math. As students get older, the search for patterns weaves its way into all subjects. *Seedfolks* by Paul Fleischman is an enjoyable vehicle to use to search for patterns in literature. Each chapter in this delightful book tells the story of a different person's life as the residents of a small apartment building prepare a garden in an abandoned lot nearby. Students can look for the patterns in each of these peoples lives that has brought them to this place. One response to the book is to have the students divide a piece of drawing paper into equal sections, one for each character, and create a "garden" filled with patterns representing each character.

Cause and effect are demonstrated clearly in Karen Hesse's moving novel, *Phoenix Rising.* When the nuclear power plant in nearby Boston has a critical accident, spreading nuclear contamination over a large area of the heavily populated eastern seaboard, Ellie and her grandmother find themselves having to change their lives to accommodate the aftermath of the catastrophe. There are plenty of effects from this disaster, and student readers can be challenged to find the causes for each of them.

From advertisements to radio talk shows to Internet research, students are constantly bombarded with information filled with biases. One of the most important skills we can pass on to these students is how to **evaluate** all this information before making choices about whether to rely on it. *Armageddon Summer* by Jane Yolen and Bruce Coville is a good place to begin teaching students about detecting bias. When the Reverend Beelson declares to his followers that he knows when the world is going to end and how to insure their place in heaven, Marina and Jed find themselves taken to a remote mountaintop to wait for the world's end. There is a great deal of discussion between Marina and Jed about what the truth might be and about who is right. This novel is a good springboard into a discussion about cults, deprogramming, and how to detect bias while rooting out the truth. This book can be paired with *Leaving Fishers* by Margaret Peterson Haddix.

Another thinking skill that is also a reading skill is determining **point of view**. One outstanding novel to use for this skill is *Out of Control* by Norma Fox Mazer. This story, told in several voices, is the story of one girl's harassment by a group of boys. Each of the people involved in the story tells his or her side of the story, and the way they saw the incidents unfold. This story is a good basis for discussions about looking at your own actions from another person's point of view and helps toward building empathy. Another interesting book to use for point of view is Walter Dean Myers's *Monster,* in which the main character writes a screenplay of his own murder trial to gain perspective on the whole set of events.

Health

Health issues are often introduced to adolescents in the science or home and family life classrooms. School districts often have adopted curriculum units that include specific printed materials, films, and lectures. We have found many young adult novels that address some of the more difficult issues in a way that our students can more directly relate to their own lives. Depression, suicide, AIDS, sexuality, alcoholism, abuse, and eating disorders are all subjects that touch too many of our young people, and they often believe they have nowhere to turn. Introducing them to literature about other young people who are dealing with the same types of problems allows our students to understand they are not alone, and that there are ways to get help.

Depression has become a serious problem for teenagers today. The suicide rate among teens has risen at an alarming rate in recent years. Unfortunately, it is difficult to get teens to talk about these issues. One way for us to help teens recognize the symptoms of depression is to put books into their hands that deal with the issue in a realistic way. In *Shizuko's Daughter* by Kyoko Mori, Yuki has to learn to live with the reality of her mother's suicide. Was she to blame? Could she have done anything to prevent it? How was she going to go on without a mother to help her grow into womanhood? As Yuki deals with her own depression, she discovers insights about herself and tools to help her deal with her crises.

Speak by Laurie Halse Anderson is a realistic story about a fourteen-year-old girl who is raped at a party just before her first day in high school. Her initial reaction is to call the police who come and break up the party where there is underage drinking going on. When her new friends get in trouble, she shrinks into the background and does not tell anyone what happened. The other students shun her, and the shame and guilt of the rape drive her into a deep depression. It is not until the rapist begins courting her former best friend that she realizes she has to speak out. The message is very clear for both young females and males.

The importance of literature and student connections became crystal clear when one of our students disclosed that her father was hitting her and her little sister. She had been reading *Don't You Dare Read This, Mrs. Dunphrey* by Margaret Haddix, which deals with **abuse**. Even with all the stories in the press and the made-for-TV-movies about this issue, she hadn't really realized she could take control of the situation and do something about it. Like Tish in the story, she believed she had to keep the secret. But she connected with Tish and decided to take a chance for a better life.

These are tough subjects to discuss with a class of young adults. Creating literary circles with titles such as *Bruises* by Anke deVries, *Chinese Handcuffs* by Chris Crutcher, *Ellen Foster* by Kaye Gibbons, *I Hadn't Meant to Tell You This* by Jacqueline Woodson, *Parrot in the Oven: Mi vida* by Victor Martinez, *Don't You Dare Read This, Mrs. Dunphrey* by Margaret Haddix, and *The Watcher* by James Howe can open dialogue during which students can discuss these sensitive issues without having to divulge all-too-personal information. At the same time, students who may be living in abusive situations will learn that they are not alone, and they can get help.

In a society where we worship thinness as beauty, being **overweight** can make a teen's life miserable. In health classes, we teach about good nutrition and in physical education classes, we teach the importance of daily exercise. But we seldom address the issues of what it is like to be overweight and think there is nothing you can do about it. In *Fat Chance* by Leslea New-man, Judi Liebowitz thinks she has a weight problem. It colors her entire life. One boy at school makes fun of her size and she believes everyone else feels the same way. She doesn't think her mother understands at all because she keeps cooking high caloric meals. Judi wants to look like Nancy Pratt, the skinniest girl in the school. Judi begins a slow descent into the world of dieting, fasting, and eventually bulimia. This story, told in diary form, is a good one to use in combination with *Slot Machine* by Chris Lynch.

In *Slot Machine*, it is the summer between eighth and ninth grade for Elvin and his friends who are going to camp. This camp is conducted by the coaches for his new high school and it is here that students are placed on the teams where they will compete during their high school careers. Elvin hates it. Elvin is overweight and he uses it as the reason he is not good at anything. Using these two books together gives students an opportunity to explore how eating disorders affect people differently. These books also present a clear picture of how people with weight problems are treated, and how that treatment profoundly affects lives.

In many school districts, **AIDS** is discussed in a very controlled environment. Politically, this is a hot topic and districts want to provide educational information about this disease without offending certain segments of the population. All too often, the emotional aspect of AIDS is not included in the conversation. Fortunately, many young adult authors have written very moving accounts of what it is like to find out you or someone you love and trust has contracted AIDS.

One particularly moving story is Lee F. Bantle's *Diving for the Moon*. Bird and Josh are best friends and they spend the summer before seventh grade hanging out at the lake. They can talk about anything with each other. Then Josh reveals that he is HIV positive and that he got it from a blood transfusion. This is a true test of their friendship and they do a lot of growing up that summer. *Earthshine* by Theresa Nelson tells a story of unflagging hope. Slim lives with her father who has AIDS. When she and Isaiah, who also lives with a PWA (person with AIDS), hear about a place where miracles take place, they make plans to take their loved ones there. Miracles do take place, but not the ones these people counted on. Much more importantly, they learn about love and caring and living each day to the fullest. Both of these stories deal with emotional issues surrounding AIDS in a clear and frank manner.

Many people think that the topic of **sexuality** should not be taught in any public school, and especially not in middle school. But this is the time when most teens are beginning to question and explore their new feelings as sexual human beings and about their relationships with members of the opposite sex. Imagine how difficult it is for adolescents who realize they don't seem to fit into the straight mold. By pretending that there are no gay or lesbian students in our schools, we only contribute to the isolation and shame felt by those who recognize their feelings as real but somehow wrong. *Am I Blue? Coming Out from the Silence* is a collection of short stories edited by Marion Bauer about young people confronting their own sexuality. The authors share stories about peer and family relationships changing, about the lack of support for gay and lesbian teens, and about the depression that often accompanies that self-discovery. In another book, *Hard Love* by Ellen Wittlinger, John finds himself in love with someone who writes zines. He figures out a way to meet this author, Marisol, and discovers she is a lesbian. The story deals with the struggles of acceptance and growing friendship between these two remarkable teens.

Alcoholism and drug abuse are issues too many of our young adults are exposed to. While use of these substances among teens has been shown to be declining in recent years, far too many young people are exposed to them and the after effects of their abuse. In *Rules of the Road,* Joan Bauer tells the story of how alcohol affected the life of sixteen-year-old Jenna and her family. Jenna's father is a drunk. He has embarrassed her most of her life. When he shows up at the shoe store where Jenna is working, she is sure she is going to lose her job. Instead, she is offered a job as a driver for the aging founder of the shoe-store chain who needs to get to Texas to save the company. Would she have taken the job, and left her family behind, if her father had been sober? This is a question the students can grapple with as they read this novel.

In another story about the debilitating effects of alcohol, Carl Deuker writes about one young boy's struggle after his father's death. *Heart of a Champion* is the story of Seth and Jimmy. Jimmy comes into Seth's life at its lowest point. Jimmy is consumed by baseball and believes he and Seth are bound for the major league. Unfortunately, family troubles, grades, and alcohol seem to be getting in Seth's way. Middle school students across the nation have increasingly easy access to alcohol and drugs and all too often see them as a way to ease the pain of adolescence. This novel paints a fairly realistic picture of the problems substance abuse can bring.

Home and Family Life

When we think of the home and family life class (what used to be called home economics), we often think only of the tempting smells of chocolate chip cookies, fresh from the oven. Or the sound of sewing machines where students are creating soft and cuddly pillows. Today's home and family life classes are much more than that. Frank discussions about nutrition, budgeting, marriage, divorce, and child rearing go on in such classes all over the country. We have found several novels to complement this curriculum, even serving as launching pads for great discussions.

A great read-aloud to accompany a unit on **parenting** is *Flour Babies* by Anne Fine. Simon and his classmates have an assignment to "adopt" a sack of flour and treat it like a real baby. Simon, whose father left when he was a baby, has not had any fathering skills modeled for him but is determined to be the best father ever. During the course of the project, he begins talking to his flour baby and to his mother, eventually figuring out several things about parenthood and about his father.

Adam and Eve and Pinch Me by Julie Johnson, *Dave at Night* by Gail Levine, *A Blessing in Disguise* by Eleanora Tate, and *Bud, Not Buddy* by Christopher Paul Curtis are all novels about young people who have lost their parents and have found themselves in new and sometimes unusual circumstances. Grouped with other books about teens who are not living with their birth parents for one reason or another, these novels make an interesting literary circle. This is real life in our cities and small towns and the insights adolescents gain by reading these works helps them to relate less fearfully with someone who is going through these experiences.

Social Studies

The social studies curriculum is filled with opportunities to use young adult literature. One teacher we work with requires her seventh graders to read two novels set in a country they know nothing about. Reading Joan Abelove's *Go and Come Back*, students learn about the Isabo people living in the Amazonian jungles and the changes created in the traditional culture and in the natural geography brought about by progress. Another student may read *A Handful of Stars* by Rafik Schami to find out about the culture of modern Syria and what it is like to be a teen there. *Adem's Cross* by Alice Mead tells the story about being a teenage Albanian living in Serbian-occupied Kosovo, while *The Voices of Silence* by Bel Mooney paints an unforgettable portrait of life in Romania under the harsh regime of Ceausescu. All of these novels have the added benefit of helping students develop empathy and understanding for other teens around the world.

U.S. history is another area where the addition of young adult literature helps the content come alive. The American Diary and My Name Is America series published by Scholastic Press are very popular with adolescents. They are well researched and filled with information and events at particular times in our history from the point of view of a teen living during the time. All the books in these series may be complemented by other works about the same time periods.

Slavery, exploration, expansion, immigration, and war are all well represented in the bibliography. Supplementing standard history textbooks with multicultural novels gives students a more well-rounded picture about the founding and building of this country. Too often, middle school students have a difficult time connecting with the people in their textbooks. Seldom are the heroes in the textbooks young teens. Having the students read novels about people more like them helps them personalize this subject and build new learning's and formulate new opinions. Additionally, several of the novels on our list develop the stories of people on opposite sides of an issue. One great example of this is Paul Fleischman's *Bull Run,* which uses sixteen points of view to discuss one battle in the War Between the States.

In presenting a unit on **wars and conflicts**, we have divided the room in half and given one half of the students *So Far from the Bamboo Grove* by Yoko Kawashima Watkins, a story about a Japanese family living in Japanese-occupied northern Korea in the 1940s, and *Year of Impossible Good-Byes* by Sook Nyul Choi, the story of a Korean family living in the same area at the same time. Both families choose to flee to the south when the Chinese military invades to drive the Japanese from the country and bring communism to its southern neighbor. After finishing the novels, both groups engaged in a debate about the issue of a third country becoming involved in struggles between countries. This debate led to a great discussion of times when the United States military forces have been involved in this kind of conflict: Vietnam, Kuwait, and Kosovo were primary to the discussion. In the end, students came away with a clear understanding that there are many sides in any conflict and that acknowledging the different points of view may help lead to dialogue, rather than violence.

In addition to the traditional subjects covered in U.S. history classes, we have included books about issues that are current and sometimes controversial. One topic we have found particularly stimulating is the question of **ethical behavior**. From the experimental historical village where a large drug manufacturing firm is exposing the residents to diptheria without their knowledge in *Running Out of Time* by Margaret Haddix, to the ethical questions raised by genetic engineering in *Star Split* by Kathryn Lasky, these issues raise important questions and stimulate exciting discussions. Steve Brown, founder of kidLAW,[1] has developed a literature-based program that takes some of these novels and creates mock trials in which the cases are based on the story. *Phoenix Rising* by Karen Hesse and *The Bomb* by

Theodore Taylor both resulted in wrongful death lawsuits against the U.S. government. Teams for both the prosecution and the defense were formed, legal documents were written, testimony prepared, and the case tried based on details from the novels. The need for expert witnesses on nuclear energy, radiation poisoning, and nuclear bombs required outside research by both teams. Jurors were selected from other classes who were not working on this project. The resulting trials were exciting, often heated, and filled with real learning. Many of the novels listed in the bibliography may be used as the basis for this project.

And not to leave the sixth graders out, we have discovered a number of books about living in the **Middle Ages**. Karen Cushman has written three charming books about life in that time from the point of view of a teenager: *The Midwife's Apprentice; Catherine, Called Birdy;* and *Matilda Bone*. Each of these delightful novels describes a different aspect of life in medieval times from the point of view of a teenage girl. *The Ramsay Scallop* and *Beduins' Gazelle* by Frances Temple describe these times from a boy's point of view. All these books are good extensions to a standard classroom unit.

Science

Environmental issues are often taught in middle school science classes. Several of the books we have read fit nicely into this curriculum. *The Ear, the Eye, and the Arm* by Nancy Farmer is set in the future in Zimbabwe. The natural environment has all but been destroyed by pollution, and people everywhere are afraid to go out at night because of all the displaced people who have banded together in violent gangs. One such group of people lives in an area of the capital city that is considered uninhabitable—a large garbage dump. These people live underground or in humps of garbage, and they look so much like the garbage that few know they are there. This is the story of three young people who venture out of their home and are kidnapped and sold to the head of this garbage-dump community.

Closer to home, *Tangerine* by Edward Bloor is the story of one family who moves into a planned community in Tangerine County, Florida. Most of the tangerine groves have been leveled to make way for these communities. This has led to vast sink holes that swallow up schools and peat bogs that burn uncontrollably for years. This novel also addresses racism and other kinds of prejudice. We have recommended it to science teachers in sixth, seventh, and eighth grade but it works well in higher grades, too.

We have included single titles that address a number of **other scientific subjects** from genetics to theories of evolution, language development to medical experiments. Often, students find a deep fascination with one particular subject in a science class but are not ready for the theoretical tomes written for experts. These books allow students to explore their interests in a fun and exciting way on their own, all the while reading about characters they can relate to. This type of reading often leads students to further research into the lives of the pioneers in their field or the newest discoveries.

OUTSIDE THE CLASSROOM

Counselor/Student Book Groups

So far, we have been talking about using literature in a classroom setting. However, there are many ways these books can also be used effectively outside of the classroom. We have often been approached by the counselors in our buildings to provide reading lists for **support groups**. We have provided lists for grief and loss groups, healthy relationship groups, children of divorce groups, and drug and alcohol abuse groups. Counselors have also found some books particularly useful with students who have family members who are living with mental illnesses.

Being an adolescent and having to cope with the physical and emotional changes that normally accompany adolescence is difficult enough. Family dynamics change, and suddenly things that didn't bother you when you were a little kid are huge. What is considered normal is heavily dictated by a closed-minded adolescent peer group. In *My Louisiana Sky* by Kimberly Holt, Tiger Ann is confronted with a previously unknown embarrassment when her mentally challenged mother shows up at school wanting to play. In *The Language of Goldfish* by Zibby Oneal, Carrie discovers that the childhood game she made up with her sister has become an obsession that is seen as very strange by her sister and her friends. *Kissing Doorknobs* by Terry Spencer Hesser is the story of a slow descent into obsessive-compulsive behavior. In each of these stories, hope is offered to the young reader that dreams do not have to be shattered and growth can come out of seemingly hopeless situations. For a school counselor to have access to these books for troubled teens can be a real boon.

Parent/Child Book Groups

When we put these books into the hands of adolescents, we often encouraged them to share the books with their families. We have shared many of them with our own children and enjoyed discussing them. The last section of appendix B lists books we believe would work well in **mother/daughter** or **father/son** book discussion groups. We selected these books for the lists because of the strong protagonists and the high-interest topics. Some of them, like *Speak* by Laurie Halse Anderson and *Make Lemonade* by Virginia Euwer Wolff, deal with difficult issues and provide a springboard for parents to begin important dialogues with their children. Some of them, like *Midwife's Apprentice* by Karen Cushman and *Sparrow Hawk Red* by Ben Mikaelsen, are just great stories that can be appreciated by all ages. We believe we should never stop reading with our children and hope that this list will provide a place to start.

NOTE

1. Steven D. Brown is a lawyer in the Seattle, Washington, area who has developed a program he takes into classrooms of all ages that ties literature to the world of the law. More information about the program may be found at www.learningspace.org/socialstudies/announcements/kidlaw.html, 2001 [accessed 28 July 2001].

CHAPTER 5

Hearing the Voices from Other Worlds

We have spent several years finding and reading books we hope will reach all our students but we still find some who just don't want to read. Both of us are avid science fiction/fantasy readers and when all else has failed, we have put some of our favorites into the hands of these reluctant readers, only to have them come back asking for more by the same author or about the same characters. We have chosen to include this genre in our book because many of the topics that we find in the multicultural novels can be found in these books as well, just in a different setting.

Science fiction/fantasy literature has often been viewed as escapist literature, without much socially redeeming value. There is always adventure and there are almost always characters that are clearly good or evil. These are the very characteristics that draw in the young reader. Science fiction literature, by definition, has a basis in scientific theory and usually takes place in a futuristic world. Starships and computer chips abound. Much of today's technology was predicted and expanded on in early science fiction novels and the novels of today continue to look to the future of technology and the psychological and physical effects of a high-tech world on the fabric of society.

In the Orson Scott Card series beginning with *Ender's Game,* the author gives us a glimpse into a world of the video game gone awry. Young people with excellent hand-eye coordination are recruited and trained in a high-tech electronic game of war. They are not told, however, that the moves they make direct a real war in a distant part of the galaxy. The series does a good job of probing the aftermath of this kind of societal manipulation, including what it does to an ordinary family, broken apart by the game.

Fantasy literature usually takes place in some past world and is filled with heroes, heroines, and magical or mystical beings. Ogres, griffins, centaurs, and dragons fill the pages of this genre. Animals talk and weapons take on human characteristics. Magic is the technology, and as in science fiction, it is often abused and misused. In many cases, the characters in these novels face moral and ethical dilemmas similar to those our students face. These characters have to solve complex problems, survive the loss of loved ones, discover the difference between right and wrong, or overcome prejudice.

The magicians and the physics students in Mercedes Lackey's *Storm Warning* have to design a complex protection system against the devastating mage storms threatening to destroy their land. Lyra loses friends and loved ones to violent deaths in Phillip Pullman's trilogy, aptly called His Dark Materials. *Mairelon the Magician* by Patricia Wrede presents us with a young heroine who is constantly facing choices between right and wrong as she attempts to aid Mairelon in the recovery of a valuable magic item. Is it okay to break into a house to recover a stolen item? In Tamora Pierce's Immortal series, a girl faces terrible acts of prejudice by her fellow villagers because she hangs out with wolves. She is eventually forced to leave all that she knows and to hide her secret to find a place where she is accepted.

Teenage angst is another well-represented subject in both science fiction and fantasy. In another series, the Circle of Magic, Tamora Pierce relates the story of four misfit teens thrown together in a college for wizards. All of them have been rescued from their own certain disasters and their rebelliousness almost leads them to complete disaster when they ignore the advise of their teachers and venture out on their own. The Xanth Chronicles by Piers Anthony is rife with the foibles of teens versus their parents. Elske, the teenage heroine of Cynthia Voight's novel of the same name, has to make her own way as she escapes certain death at the hands of her adopted clansmen. Whether these teens are human has no bearing on how our students relate to them and learn from them how to overcome some of the tougher challenges of growing up.

In addition to all the social issues this genre presents, there is the very appealing idea that ordinary teens, much like our student readers, can become heroes. And it is the very fact that the acts of heroism are so extraordinary that appeals to the teen reader, who often feels helpless in a world where they are often treated as third-class citizens. Caught in that world between being the cute and clever child without worldly responsibility and being an adult, having to make life decisions, adolescents can find some hope in the pages of the Prydain Chronicles by Lloyd Alexander or following a young girl's voyage into the realm of death to save the world in Garth Nix's *Sabriel*. Science fiction /fantasy can be a wonderful escape but it can also help the reader come to grips with real world problems.

Lois Lowry has written two novels about young people who have come into some knowledge about the cultures they belong to that bring up deep questions about the moral and ethical values of the adults who have power in the culture. *The Giver* is set in a modern world where everything is black and white. There are no surprises, no challenges, and no strong feelings. One person is the repository for all the memories of joy and pain for the entire society. Upon his twelfth birthday, Jonas is told of his future, to become the next Receiver of these memories and what he learns changes his perception of the world he has always known.

Gathering Blue is set in a more primitive world. It is a future world where everything has been destroyed by violence and pollution. Like the Receiver of Memories in *The Giver,* this society has its keeper of the stories. When Kira's mother dies, she is taken to live in the government building, where she is asked to perfect her art of dyeing thread and embroidering pictures. While there, she meets two other young people who have lost their families, and who each have a special gift, necessary to keep the story of their society alive. Both of these beautifully crafted novels engage the young reader in looking at their own cultures and asking thought-provoking questions about the morals of the broader society.

This brings us to Harry Potter. No chapter about this genre would be complete without paying homage to this phenomenon. Students who have never completed an entire novel are clamoring to get their hands on the next book in this series. Rarely has there been a series of books that have had so many families reading together or students talking in the lunchroom about reading. The J. K. Rowling series has generated a great deal of controversy but we include it in our recommended list because it fits our definition of *multicultural* in so many ways. If you have not read the first four books in this series, you may want to skip the next couple of paragraphs, lest we divulge more than you want to know.

First, there is the issue of abuse. Harry suffers abuse at the hands of his aunt and uncle, with whom he was placed after an evil wizard killed his parents. They lock him in closets, deny him food, and verbally abuse him, all because they don't like his parentage and are afraid of his presumed magical abilities. In a recent essay contest, sponsored by Scholastic Press, Ashley Marie Rhodes-Couter compared her life as an abused foster child to Harry's life with the Dursleys.[1] In her moving essay, Rhodes-Couter, a fourteen-year-old Florida resident, said she had fantasized about being rescued by someone like Hagrid. She also said that before reading *Harry Potter and the Sorcerer's Stone,* she had never liked reading.

Friendship, adjusting to change, prejudice, good versus evil, problem solving, and grief and loss are also topics addressed in this fast-paced and fun-filled series. Harry makes his first real friends when he is rescued and sent to Hogwarts School of Magic. Harry's close friends—like Harry—are a bit different and subjected to prejudice. Ron comes from a large, poor family. Hermione has Muggle parentage. They have to work hard at ignoring the insults and the pranks played at their expense by their cliquish fellow students. And always, there is Hagrid, who is treated like an outcast by many students because of his size and sometimes bumbling ways.

The death of a popular character in children's literature is not very common. When Charlotte, the spider in E. B. White's *Charlotte's Web* succumbed to death, we all wept openly. But she was only a spider. Death of human characters brings out a different response in our adolescent readers. Harry is constantly made aware of the loss of his parents because of the way they were killed. Harry bears a scar on his forehead that is a constant reminder of his mother's sacrifice to save his life. The loss of a parent is a real fear for our young readers. Loss of a friend, due to accidental death, is unexpected and difficult to deal with. In the fourth book in this series, *Harry Potter and the Goblet of Fire,* Harry and his friends have to come to grips with the death of a fellow student and friend. The grief Harry feels is compounded by his belief that he is at fault. With the high incidence of teen violence in some parts of our country, many of our readers find a way to work through their own guilt and grief by following the examples set by Harry and his friends.

While Harry Potter is hugely popular and successful, there are many great science fiction/fantasy series appropriate for our middle school readers. Some were written thirty years ago and some are being written today. Some were written specifically for our teen audience and some for the general population. We have compiled a list of the series, or single titles, we have read and given to our students with great success. Unlike the annotated bibliography, this list is not fully annotated and the books are listed by author rather than title. In our classes, we have included books from this list in our literary circles when they have fit the topic. As always, we encourage you to read any book before you place it in the hands of a young adult reader.

NOTE

1. Jacquelin Blais, "A Magical Breakfast of 'Potter' Champions," www.usatoday.com/life/enter/books/potter/hp24.htm, 2000 [accessed December 2000].

Part 2

THE VOICES SPEAK

An Annotated Bibliography of Multicultural Books for Grades Six through Nine

This annotated bibliography, in conjunction with the cultural and author indexes at the end of this book, is designed to help you find books easily for your students. We have indicated the cultural group, such as "living with abuse" or "Albanian," that we believe is most closely linked with the book. We assigned reading levels (RL) based on standard measures, adjusted by our experience with the books. We assigned interest levels (IL) based on our reading of the novels, the content, and our experience with adolescents.

3 NB of Julian Drew by **James M. Deem**   RL: 7

Houghton Mifflin, 1994   IL: 8+
Living with abuse
This is a story written from the view of a fifteen-year-old boy who starts his tale in a terse, hard-to-understand code: he is trying to come to terms with something that has clearly devastated him, and is suffering from abuse from his father and stepmother. He gradually finds more words to express himself when he meets two people he can talk to, and is able to come to terms with his past.

Absolutely Normal Chaos by **Sharon Creech**   RL: 5

HarperCollins, 1995   IL: 5–8
Grief/loss
Mary Lou Finney (whom we met in *Walk Two Moons*) keeps a journal over the summer to record her observations about her wonderful and off-beat family. As she writes, she finds she is learning about life, love, and even death.

The Acorn People by **Ron Jones**   RL: 5

Bantam, 1976   IL: 6–12
Physically/mentally challenged
The counselors at a summer camp set on a mountain lake are not well prepared for the week coming up. This is the week the physically challenged young people come for a week of camp life. This moving true story is about adjustment, friendship, and love.

Adam and Eve and Pinch Me by Julie Johnson   RL: 6

Little, Brown, 1994   IL: 6–10
Nontraditional family
Canadian
Sara has practiced blanking people out all her fifteen years: given up for adoption
at birth, she can't wait to leave foster homes behind the minute she turns sixteen.
But her new foster family is different, and so are the people who start to fill her
life. As she pours her story onto a computer, a woman who might be her birth
mother suddenly appears.

Adam Zigzag by Barbara Barrie   RL: 6

Delacorte, 1994   IL: 7–10
Mentally challenged: dyslexia
Adam cannot read: the lines break up and dance on the page, so reading and writing are too hard. His parents' frantic attempts to help seem to compound the trouble. Charming and personable, Adam has a great social life, which his sister, who
also struggles, resents. Told in alternating viewpoints between Adam and his sister, this is a fast-paced story of how severe dyslexia affects an entire family.

Adem's Cross by Alice Mead   RL: 5

Farrar, Straus, Giroux, 1996   IL: 5–9
Albanian
Adem is a fourteen-year-old Albanian boy in 1993 when the Serbs are occupying
his homeland. He wonders how his family can accept the terror and oppression:
can't they do something? But when his beloved older sister tries to read a poem
during a peaceful protest, everything changes for Adem and his family, and the
nightmare intensifies.

The Adventures of Blue Avenger by Norma Howe   RL: 7

Holt, 1999   IL: 8+
Grief/loss
Nontraditional family
David becomes Blue Avenger and performs amazing tasks. Omaha Nebraska
Brown searches for answers and finds some. Lemon meringue pie becomes
weepless—finally! Life is questioned, determinism is examined, and this book is
nothing if not whimsical.

After the Dancing Days by Margaret Rostkowski   RL: 6

Harper & Row, 1986   IL: 6–10
Physically challenged

Thirteen-year-old Annie is glad when her physician father returns from World War
I. When he continues to work with veterans at a nearby hospital, Annie strikes up
a friendship with a terribly disfigured soldier. Annie's mother forbids her to continue visiting, but Annie defies her mother, and begins to realize there are many
definitions of the word *hero*.

AK by Peter Dickinson   RL: 6.1

Delacorte, 1992   IL: 7–10
African

Paul Kagomi is an orphaned child guerrilla: his only mother is the war, and his only
schooling is in warfare. He places his trust in his AK and in the man he first calls
"Uncle" then "Father," Michael Kagomi, leader of the command unit who trained
him to fight as a proud, fierce warrior. With the promise of peace, Paul buries his
beloved AK, but peace is short-lived, and Paul's country is torn asunder once
again. This time Michael cannot guide him—can his AK?

Alias by Mary Elizabeth Ryan   RL: 6

Simon and Schuster Books for Young Readers, 1997   IL: 7–10
Nontraditional family

At fifteen, Toby is used to it by now: his mom breezes in and grabs big garbage bags
to stuff their few possessions into, and they are off to another new place. But on
this move to Idaho, Toby stumbles onto information that causes him to start asking his mother questions.

Am I Blue? edited by Marion Dane Bauer   RL: 7

HarperCollins, 1994   IL: 8+
Gay/lesbian

This is a strong collection of stories from some of today's best authors for teens, including Bruce Coville and Jane Yolen, that deal with gay and lesbian teens. The
collection is thought-provoking and opens with an equally thoughtful introduction including facts about teens and their sexual identities.

The Amah by Laurence Yep   RL: 5

Putnam, 1999   IL: 5–8
Chinese American

Amy's mother finally found work after her father's death. She was going to be a
Chinese nanny, or Amah. To Amy, this meant having to give up her ballet lessons
to watch her younger siblings, and she also thought it meant losing her mother to
the new "daughter."

Amazing Gracie by A. E. Cannon   RL: 5

Delacorte, 1991   IL: 7–10
Mentally challenged: depression

Gracie tries hard to keep things together, keep things going smoothly. Otherwise, her
mom might get depressed and ill again. When her mom remarries and her new family moves to Salt Lake City, everything seems to fall apart. Gracie isn't sure she can
hold things together this time—especially after her mom tries to kill herself.

Amazon Papers by Beverly Keller   RL: 6

Browndeer Press, Harcourt Brace, 1996   IL: 7–10
Nontraditional family

A delightful, quirky cast of characters walk and run through this enjoyable story.
Fifteen-year-old Iris has many talents in her 5-foot, 10-inch frame, although most
don't seem to be talents her mom appreciates. When her mom goes out of town
and leaves Iris in charge of her two little cousins, things get unexpectedly complicated, then downright crazy: bowling, love, a hearse, garlic, spiked heels, and
pizza are involved, and it takes a great deal of sorting out to get things straight
before Mom returns.

American Dragons edited by Laurence Yep   RL: 7

HarperCollins, 1995   IL: 7+
Asian American

Emma Wu is a math whiz who is faced with a dilemma when her chief competitor
in math competitions says he will take her to the prom if she promises to drop out
of the state competition. This and other works in this collection deal with many
of the challenges of adolescents, especially with the cultural differences and gen-
erational differences faced by these Asian American teens.

Among Friends by Caroline Cooney   RL: 6

Bantam Books, 1987   IL: 7+
Gifted

Told in diary format from a group of high school juniors, this is a story of the struggles of a young gifted woman who, because of her talents, finds herself struggling
with the resentment and rejection of her closest friends.

Among the Hidden by Margaret Peterson Haddix   RL: 5.5

Simon and Schuster Books for Young Readers, 1998   IL: 4–7
Grief/loss

Luke has never been to school. He has met only four people in his life: his mom,
dad, and two brothers. Luke is an illegal third child, forbidden by the Population

Police. Pacing in the attic and peering out the vents at the world one day, he sees another face in a home where a family of four have already left for the day: is this another Shadow Child? When he does finally meet Jen, another illegal, she suggests plans that seem risky and terrifying.

Among the Volcanoes by **Omar S. Castaneda**   RL: 5

Lodestar Books, 1991   IL: 5–9
Latino: Central America

Isabel is a young Mayan woman of fourteen in Guatemala who wants something different. She wants to stay in school and become a teacher herself. But she is faced with many problems: her mother is very ill, and the local healer's potions and bloodletting don't help. Her boyfriend, Lucas, seems to be growing distant, and someone is leaving threats in the form of evil spells in front of their door.

Amos Fortune, Free Man by **Elizabeth Yates**   RL: 5

Aladdin Books, 1950   IL: 5–8
African American

Told in a simple, straightforward style, this is the story of Amos Fortune, who is captured in Africa at age fifteen and brought by slavers to Massachusetts. He retains his dignity even as a slave and is finally able to buy his own freedom and that of others.

Angus, Thongs, and Full-Frontal Snogging by **Louise Rennison**   RL: 7

HarperCollins, 2000   IL: 7+
English

In the pages of her journal, fourteen-year-old Georgia frets about her huge nose, her three-year-old sister's overflowing nappies, her crazed cat Angus, and how to kiss properly. She writes an introduction to her "American chums" to point out that she created a glossary to explain the British terms she uses, since ". . . apparently American people are not English." The journal is an enjoyable, irreverent, and hilarious look at a year in a teenage girl's life.

Anna Is Still Here by **Ida Vos**   RL: 5

Houghton Mifflin, 1993   IL: 6–8
Dutch
Jewish

Anna is a thirteen-year-old Jewish girl who has just emerged from hiding by herself for three years during the Nazi occupation in Holland. Even though the Nazis left, Anna's nightmares remain, as do too many anti-Semitic taunts. Anna's life becomes entangled with that of another survivor, Mrs. Neumann, whose daughter was lost during the war. Can both Anna and Mrs. Neumann find what they have lost?

Anne of Green Gables by L. M. Montgomery   RL: 6

L.C. Page & Company, 1908   IL: 6+
Canadian
Nontraditional family

Orphaned Anne Shirley lives mainly in a dream world until she is adopted by an elderly couple and comes to the glorious world of Green Gables where she laughs and cries through adventures and misadventures.

Another Kind of Monday by William E. Coles Jr.   RL: 6

Atheneum Books for Young Readers, 1996   IL: 8+
Nontraditional family

When he picks up a copy of *Great Expectations* from the school library, Mark finds three one-hundred dollar bills and a cryptic note inside challenging him to a "quest" for some great expectations of his own. His quest takes him on a study of Pittsburgh that makes Mark see himself, his city, and others in a new light.

Another Way to Dance by Martha Southgate   RL: 5.5

Delacorte, 1996   IL: 7–9
African American

Vicki has loved ballet ever since seeing *The Nutcracker* at age eight, and now finally she has the summer she has dreamed of and worked for: six weeks in New York City at the School of American Ballet. But here she runs into prejudice and other problems which shake her dreams.

Appointment with a Stranger by Jean Thesman   RL: 6

Houghton Mifflin, 1989   IL: 7+
Physically challenged: asthma

Keller is deeply self-conscious about her asthma. She's new to Cascade High School, where she is living with her grandma until her parents can join her. Keller finds solace in the company of an attractive young man at a nearby pond, but why is he unknown to everyone else? Can Keller be falling in love with a ghost?

April and the Dragon Lady by Lensey Namioka   RL: 6

Browndeer Press, 1994   IL: 7–12
Chinese-American

April is happy with her life, except for living with her grandmother who seems to disapprove of everything she does. She treats April's boyfriend as a "foreign devil" and will not share family treasures with April. And why, wonders Grandmother, would a girl need to go to college?

Armageddon Summer by Jane Yolen and Bruce Coville   RL: 6

Harcourt Brace, 1998   IL: 7–10
Religious cults

"This time, the world will end in fire." So preaches Reverend Beelson who has the date of Armageddon and a mountaintop reserved for 144 Believers. Marina and Jed are from very different backgrounds, and their alternating viewpoints weave a thought-provoking story of beliefs, questions, peace, and violence—all in the name of religion.

Asylum for Nightface by Bruce Brooks   RL: 6

Laura Geringer Books, 1996   IL: 7+
Religious cults

Fourteen-year-old Zimmerman has found his own peace with God and spirituality. He lets his parents' craziness bounce off him as they urge him to be less perfect. But after a trip to Jamaica where they find a quirky new brand of religion, Zim starts worrying about his parents' plans to make him a poster child and model of goodness—for their new religion.

Athletic Shorts by Chris Crutcher   RL: 7

Greenwillow Books, 1991   IL: 7–12
Gay/lesbian
Nontraditional family

Athletics is the common thread of this collection of six short stories, which address a host of other significant themes as well. Angus can't dance but is elected as Winter Ball King as a joke by classmates who make fun of him because both his parents are gay. Louie overcomes his prejudices to befriend a stranger with AIDS. Five of these stories feature characters from other Crutcher novels.

Babcock by Joe Cottonwood   RL: 5.6

Scholastic, 1996   IL: 6–8
African American

Babcock has only one name, carries a briefcase, loves animals, and can call dragonflies. On the day that he runs into a blonde girl named Kirsten, then is almost run over by his Uncle Earl, many things begin to change for Babcock in this poignant, funny, thoughtful tale.

Baby Alicia Is Dying by Lurlene McDaniel   RL: 5

Bantam Starfire, 1993   IL: 6–9
Physically challenged: AIDS

Childcare is a home for sick babies—specifically for babies who are HIV positive.
Desi starts to volunteer there as she begins ninth grade with a lot of things on her
mind: she's not as pretty or as talented as her older sister; she's serious about
school, and she's serious about helping baby Alicia, who is HIV positive and has
been given up by her teenage mother.

Backwater by Joan Bauer   RL: 7

Putnam, 1999   IL: 7+
Nontraditional family

Sixteen-year-old Ivy Breedlove is an historian in a family of lawyers: but she's determined to have her voice heard as she digs through records and climbs a mountain in the dead of winter to find the rest of the story about her family.

Bad News Travels Fast by Gar Anthony Haywood   RL: 7

G.P. Putnam, 1995   IL: 8+
African American

Joe and Dottie Laudermilk are off to Washington, D.C., in their Airstream trailer to
see the sights: but instead they find themselves trying to get one of their sons, Eddie, off a charge of murder. Is this what retirement is about? The Laudermilks'
story is a funny, clever, and interesting mystery.

The Ballad of Lucy Whipple by Karen Cushman   RL: 5

Clarion, 1996   IL: 5–9
Nontraditional family

Lucky Diggins, California, is nothing more than a cluster of tents of hardworking,
rough-living miners when Lucy Whipple and her mother, sisters, and brother arrive. Lucy can think of only one thing: she wants to go back to Massachusetts. As
Lucky Diggins grows, facing good times and bad, so does Lucy.

The Bamboo Flute by Garry Disher   RL: 5

Ticknor & Fields, 1992   IL: 5–8
Australia

In 1932, Australia was deep in an economic depression. Paul felt it most when the
family no longer had time or energy for music. Against his parents' instructions,
Paul befriends a homeless man who teaches him to play the flute, and slowly music and peace come back to his family.

Baseball in April: And other stories by Gary Soto   RL: 5

Harcourt, 1991   IL: 5+
Latino American
In this collection of short stories about Latino teens in Central California, read about
how these youngsters cope with trying out for a baseball team, falling in love, or
auditioning for the local ballet.

Beardance by Will Hobbs   RL: 5

Maxwell Macmillan International, 1993   IL: 5–9
Native American
Cloyd thought he'd seen the last grizzly in the Colorado Rockies killed, but now
there is talk of a mother grizzly and her three cubs on the mountain. Cloyd is determined to find them and help them survive, no matter what.

Bearstone by Will Hobbs   RL: 5

Atheneum, 1989   IL: 5–8
Native American
Orphaned as a young boy, fourteen-year-old Cloyd was always in trouble. He is sent
by his tribe to live with an old rancher, Walter. While hiking in the high Colorado
mountains, Cloyd finds a small, carved, turquoise bear. This small fetish leads
him on a journey of self-discovery and healing.

Beduins' Gazelle by Frances Temple   RL: 7

Orchard Books, 1996   IL: 7+
African: Beduin
Atiyah and Halima are cousins in the Beduin tribe of Beni Khalid: their lives are
full and complementary. But, then Atiyah is sent to Fez to study, away from his
beloved desert and Halima. There he meets Etienne (a young Frenchman from
Temple's earlier novel, *Ramsay Scallop*) who becomes his friend—and when
they learn Halima is lost, the two set out to find her.

Beggar's Ride by Theresa Nelson   RL: 5.6

Orchard Books, 1992   IL: 7–10
Nontraditional family
Running away from an abusive situation to her favorite of her mother's ex-
boyfriends (Joey) seemed like a good idea to Claire. Tennessee to Atlantic City
is a long way, though, and when she finds Joey is gone, she is uncertain where to
turn. So she joins a gang of homeless kids with whom she may stay if she can
prove her worth.

Belle Prater's Boy by **Ruth White**   RL: 5

Farrar, Straus, Giroux, 1996   IL: 5–9
Nontraditional family
Grief/loss

Set in mining country in Virginia, this story starts when Woodrow's mom Belle walks away from home one morning and vanishes. When his father takes to drink, Woodrow moves to town with his grandparents and next door to his cousin Gypsy. The two of them form a wonderful friendship and learn to deal with hard secrets in their lives.

The Best Little Girl in the World by **Steven Levenkron**   RL: 7

Contemporary Books, 1978   IL: 7+
Physically challenged: weight issues

When she looks in the mirror, what does she see? Her body is disgusting, and she wants to change it. This is a powerful true story of one girl's battle with anorexia nervosa.

Between a Rock and a Hard Place by **Alden Carter**   RL: 6

Scholastic, 1995   IL: 7–10
Physically challenged: diabetes

Family tradition says it's time for Mark and his diabetic cousin Randy to fish and canoe their way through the Boundary Waters on a coming-of-age trip. Mark's not thrilled, but wants to prove he doesn't always mess up. But when disaster strikes, Mark wonders if they will survive at all.

Between Two Worlds by **Candice F. Ransom**   RL: 5

Scholastic, 1994   IL: 5–8
Native American

This is a fictionalized account of the life of Sarah Winnemucca, a young Piute woman, who in real life worked hard to help her people.

Beyond the Burning Time by **Kathryn Lasky**   RL: 6

Blue Sky Press, 1994   IL: 7+
Puritan

The story of the Salem witch trials is told in this well-researched novel through the eyes of twelve-year-old Mary Chase. The madness that springs up around her in 1691 is frightening, yet compelling. Then, when her mother is accused of witchcraft, the whole incident becomes a nightmare. This works as a great follow-up for *Witch of Blackbird Pond*.

Beyond the Mango Tree by Amy Bronwen Zemser   RL: 6

Greenwillow Books, 1998   IL: 6–8
African

Sarina's new life in Liberia is not that different from her old one in Boston. Her mother is still crazy and ties her to trees to keep her nearby. While tied to the mango tree in the front yard, Sarina is rescued by a young Liberian boy. Sarina begins to learn about his culture, and they become fast friends until tragedy separates them.

The Big Wander by Will Hobbs   RL: 5

Maxwell Macmillan International, 1992   IL: 5–9
Native American

Clay is fourteen-years-old and on a "big wander" with his older brother in the summer of '62. On the trail of a favorite uncle in the Southwest, Clay is delighted with the country around him, but his brother wants to go home. So Clay finds a job that allows him to stay alone and continue the pursuit of his uncle.

Bill by Chap Reaver   RL: 5

Delacorte, 1994   IL: 5–7
Nontraditional family
Physically challenged: alcoholism

Thirteen-year-old Jessie lives with her dad in the hills of Kentucky: he is a bootlegger and a drunk, but Jessie has her dog, Bill, for a friend. When Wrong Man, the Alcohol Beverage Control agent, comes looking for Jessie's father, a number of things happen, and Jessie must make some important decisions about her life.

The Black Pearl by Scott O'Dell   RL: 5

Houghton Mifflin, 1967   IL: 6–9
Latino

Ramon's father deals in precious pearls. Ramon can't wait until he is old enough to go out in the boats and dive for these pearls. One day, he takes a boat out to a neighboring cove and finds an enormous black pearl. This discovery leads to many changes in his small fishing village.

Black Star, Bright Dawn by Scott O'Dell   RL: 5.5

Houghton Mifflin, 1988   IL: 6+
Eskimo

Bright Star does many things with her father, things Eskimo girls don't traditionally do. She goes hunting with him and helps him train for sled racing, particularly for the Iiterod. When her father is injured and cannot compete, Bright Star finds herself challenged as she never has been: a seventeen-year-old girl racing 1,179 perilous miles in the Iditerod.

A Blessing in Disguise by Eleanora E. Tate   RL: 5

Delacorte, 1995   IL: 5–8
African American

Twelve-year-old Zambia Brown lives with her aunt and uncle in tiny Deacon's Neck. Life is pretty unexciting until Zambia's father opens a nightclub down the road. Zambia has visions of reuniting with her father and living the good life until the realities of that life come crashing in.

Blood Red Ochre by Kevin Major   RL: 5

Delacorte, 1989   IL: 7+
Native American

Two young people decide to do their history assignment on the Beothuk Indians who lived near their home. After some initial research, the two decide to travel to the island that was the burial ground for the Beothuk. When they arrive, the past and the present begin to merge.

Bloomability by Sharon Creech   RL: 5.5

HarperCollins, 1998   IL: 5–8
Swiss

In her thirteen years, Dinnie has always been on the move with her eccentric family, never more than a year in one place. So when Aunt Sandy and Uncle Max offer her a year in Switzerland, she's uncertain, but also a little pleased, and finds a year full of new people and opportunities.

Blue Willow by Doris Gates   RL: 5

Viking Press, 1940   IL: 5+
Migrant workers

Janey sits on the step of a one room shack in San Joaquin Valley and wonders how long they'll stay this time. She is the daughter of a migrant worker who has arrived on Mr. Anderson's ranch to pick cotton, constantly on the move since her family has lost everything in the Dust Bowl.

A Boat to Nowhere by Maureen Wartski   RL: 5

Westminster Press, 1980   IL: 5–8
Vietnamese

This story gives a human angle to the idea of boat people. When the new regime comes to "settle" a small village in South Vietnam, two young people, their grandfather, and another boy use their quick wits to escape. After surviving harrowing odds on the open sea, they learn that they are not welcome anywhere they try to land.

The Bomb by Theodore Taylor   RL: 6

Harcourt Brace & Co, 1995   IL: 6–10
Pacific Islanders

In 1944 Sorry and his family live simple lives on the Bikini Atoll: the Japanese have been taken care of by the Americans, who left only a U.S. flag behind. But then more Americans appear and announce that Bikini will be a test site for an atomic bomb. Does this mean the end of the existence they know?

Bone Dance by Martha Brooks   RL: 6

Orchard, 1997   IL: 7+
Canadian

This is the story of two teens, each troubled by vivid dreams that are tied to their Native heritage. A piece of land that one feels tied to is inherited by the other, and the lives of Lonnie and Alexandra become entwined.

A Bone from a Dry Sea by Peter Dickinson   RL: 6.1

Delacorte, 1993   IL: 7+
Nontraditional family
African

Dealing with a far-from-mainstream theory of evolution, this novel traces events in the twentieth century, as Vinny joins her father on an archeological dig, while in a parallel story, a young female member of a prehistoric tribe tries to help advance her people. The evolution-laden plot line is apt to meet some parental resistance.

Boomer's Journal by R. E. Kelly   RL: 4.5

PAGES Publishing Group, 1995   IL: 5–7
Nontraditional family
Living with abuse

Boomer can't always spell correctly, but his words are straightforward and from the heart; his dad and stepmom leave early, come home late, and fight. And when his dad has been drinking, he's mean. But there are positives in Boomer's life, too: friends, his English teacher, and good, caring neighbors.

Briar Rose by Jane Yolen   RL: 8

T. Doherty Associates, 1992   IL: 8+
Jewish

The old German tale of Briar Rose, the Sleeping Beauty, is told afresh, set in a time when the forests are patrolled by the German army during World War II. As a granddaughter searches for the story of her grandmother, she is lead through the mists and thorns of time in a haunting, exquisite tale of the Holocaust.

The Bridge to Terabithia by **Katherine Paterson**   RL: 5

Crowell, 1977   IL: 5–8
Grief/loss

Jess plans on being the fastest runner in fifth grade. When he is beaten by a new girl named Leslie on the first day of school, Jess is amazed. The two become fast friends, because Jess is in awe of Leslie's vivid imagination. Together they create Terabithia, a magical kingdom, where they reign as king and queen until a tragedy occurs.

The Brightest Light by **Colleen McKenna**   RL: 7

Scholastic, 1992   IL: 7–9
Nontraditional family

Kitty Sue is enjoying summer in West Virginia: next year is her senior year, and she's working at Dairy Queen to save money for a car. Then a white Mercedes pulls in, and the most handsome man she's ever seen steps out. This man and his company have a profound effect on Kitty, her best friend, and Kitty's realizations about her mother.

Broken Bridge by **Lynne Reid Banks**   RL: 6

Morrow Junior Books, 1994   IL: 7–9
Israeli

The sequel to *One More River* opens in Israel in 1992. Lesley is married with two children. Lesley's family and her parents are still in the kibbutz, and now the conflict between the Israelis and Arabs strike the family personally. The complex passions of the struggles in Israel are examined in this riveting sequel which could stand on its own.

The Broken Bridge by **Philip Pullman**   RL: 6

Knopf: Distributed by Random House, 1992   IL: 7+
Welsh/Haitian

A variety of mature themes from sexuality to child abuse to racism are all explored in this story of sixteen-year-old Ginny who is a talented young artist of mixed heritage. Her British father has told her stories about her Haitian mother, also an artist. Ginny and her father have a good life in their Welsh village until pieces of stories about her father's past begin to unravel what Ginny believed was her family history.

The Bronze Bow by **Elizabeth George Speare**   RL: 6

Houghton Mifflin, 1961   IL: 6–9
Israeli/ Palestinian

A young man is tormented by his all-consuming hatred for the Romans in his country, desiring nothing but revenge on them for the deaths of his father and mother. But then he finds the voice of a man named Jesus who helps him toward love and understanding.

Bruises by Anke deVries   RL: 6

Front Street/Lemniscaat, 1995   IL: 8–10
Dutch
Living with abuse

Judith lives in fear of doing anything wrong: even being at the wrong place when her mother walks in might mean another beating. The abuse from her mother is both physical and mental. If only, Judith thinks, she could stop making her mom so angry. Then she is befriended by Michael, a boy who has come to live away from his father who heaped a different kind of abuse on Michael. Can Michael figure out Judith's problems and help her find solutions?

Bud, Not Buddy by Christopher Paul Curtis   RL: 5

Delacorte, 1999   IL: 4–7
African American

Bud has a lot of things figured out about life at the age of ten. When his newest foster home includes a boy who beats him up, Bud decides it's time to find his father. His only clues are some fliers about "Herman E. Calloway and the Dusky Devastators of the Depression!!!!!" So he decides to go find Herman himself. Be sure to read the afterword.

Bull Catcher by Alden Carter   RL: 6

Scholastic, 1996   IL: 8+
Nontraditional family

In his senior year, Bull, who lives with his grandfather, is doing his senior project by writing his personal history of baseball. Pulling together all his notes and journals to write his story, he's waiting to see how the last part comes together. In his story Bull contemplates love, family, friendship, death, and most of all, baseball.

Bull Run by Paul Fleischman   RL: 6

HarperCollins, 1993   IL: 5–9
Multiethnic

Sixteen participants in the Civil War—individuals from the South and the North, black and white, male and female—each give their perspective on, during, and after the first major battle of the Civil War. The story provides excellent discussion on point of view and voice.

Buried Onions by Gary Soto   RL: 7

Harcourt Brace, 1997   IL: 6–10
Latino American

Eddie has just dropped out of community college and is trying to make a living
painting numbers on the curbs of homes on the richer side of Fresno. But the violence and unrest of the barrio life continue to surround him, making his escape
to a better life terribly hard.

The Burning Time by Carol Matas   RL: 5.5

Delacorte, 1994   IL: 6–9
French

Rose is fifteen years old when her father dies, and suddenly sixteenth-century
France becomes a dangerous place for her and her mother, who is a gifted healer
and midwife. Talk of witchcraft is in the air, and the threat of being persecuted
for witchcraft becomes real for Rose and her mother.

Burning Up by Caroline Cooney   RL: 6

Delacorte, 1999   IL: 7–10
African American

Macey is assigned to do a local history project, but when she tries to learn the story of
a burned-out barn across the road from her grandparents' home in a well-to-do Con-
necticut town, she meets resistance at every turn. Finally the story of a night in 1959
begins to emerge: arson had been aimed at the town's first African American teacher.
Macey's quest to understand what happened goes further than she ever imagined.

The Bus People by Rachel Anderson   RL: 6

Holt, 1992   IL: 7+
Physically/mentally challenged

Who rides on Bertram's bus for special kids every day? Some can't walk; some
can't talk, but each has a story to tell: from Rebecca who has an extra chromo-
some, to Mick who is trapped in a body that doesn't do what he wants it to do, to
Fleur who was locked in a closet for much too long. These and other passengers
have their stories to tell.

The Cage by Ruth Minsky Sender   RL: 6

Macmillan, 1986   IL: 8+
Polish

From the German invasion of Poland in 1939 to the liberation of its concentration
camp in 1945, the author tells of her true adolescent experiences through the horrors of the Holocaust where she survives because of her faith and fortitude.

Cages by Peg Kehret   RL: 5

Cobblehill Books/Dutton, 1991   IL: 5–8
Physically challenged: alcoholism

Kit is already upset about not getting a part in a play, so when she runs home to find
   her stepfather drunk and her mother making excuses, she makes a bad decision
   to shoplift. Her community service sentence has her working at the Humane Society where she learns many things about herself.

California Blue by David Klass   RL: 7

Scholastic, 1994   IL: 8+
Physically challenged

John is wandering on land owned by a local lumber company when he discovers a
   new species of butterfly. His discovery immediately polarizes the town into the
   faction that supports the environment versus the faction that supports the town's
   industry of logging. A strange subplot has John infatuated with one of his teachers.

Call Me Ruth by Marilyn Sachs   RL: 6

Doubleday, 1982   IL: 6–10
Russian American

A young Jewish girl and her mother live in Russia in the time of pogroms. When
   they are finally able to cross to the United States to join her father, they find a different, hard life awaiting them. While young Ruth embraces the new American
   ways enthusiastically, her mother struggles until she finds the cause of the union,
   which she embraces wholeheartedly, much to the embarrassment of her daughter.

Canyons by Gary Paulsen   RL: 5

Delacorte, 1990   IL: 6+
Native American: Apache

Fifteen-year-old Brennan Cole isn't thrilled when he finds himself having to go on
   a camping trip up Dog Canyon near El Paso, Texas. Coyote Run, an Apache boy,
   is thrilled when he takes part in a raid near the same area a hundred years earlier.
   Somehow the two boys become mystically connected as both face challenges by
   which they become men.

The Captive by Joyce Hansen   RL: 6

Scholastic, 1994   IL: 6–10
African

This is an interesting, thoughtful account of Kofi, the son of an Ashauti chieftain be-
   trayed by his father's servant, sold into slavery and taken across the sea on a
   slave-trader ship and smuggled into New England. The shock of the cold, alien

landscape, a language he does not understand, and completely foreign culture are all beautifully and clearly related by Kofi, whose only goal is to find family until he meets Paul Cuffe. This story was inspired by the autobiography of an African man kidnapped and sold into slavery.

Catherine, Called Birdy by **Karen Cushman**   RL: 6

Clarion Books, 1994   IL: 7+
English: medieval

Catherine is the daughter of a medieval lord. Her older brother has taught her how to read and write and has commanded her to keep a journal. This look at the Middle Ages is more realistic than most stories set in this time period. The insight into the roles of people is well done: women, villagers, and noblemen all come under scrutiny in Catherine's journal.

The Cay by **Theodore Taylor**   RL: 5

Doubleday, 1969   IL: 5–8
Caribbean

Phillip is excited to see boats and submarines near his home near Curacao, South America: World War II seems more exciting than frightening. But then Phillip and his mother are on a boat that is attacked, and Phillip finds himself on a raft in the ocean with an old West Indian man named Timothy. Through trials and attempts for survival, Phillip loses his prejudice and learns a new way to see what is important.

Chain of Fire by **Beverley Naidoo**   RL: 6

Lippincott, 1990   IL: 6–10
African

In this sequel to *Journey to Jo'burg*, Naledi and her friends join to fight the new government policy of removal of tribal people to a "homeland." The schoolmates organize an anti-removal march which is met with terrible violence by the police.

Changes in Latitude by **Will Hobbs***   RL: 6.1

Atheneum, 1988   IL: 7+
Grief/loss

Travis is busy acting cool: it's a family trip to Mexico, and he wants to check out the females. His nine-year-old brother wants to check out all the shops. His mother just wants to check out. What starts as a vacation without dad turns into a life-changing trip for Travis and the rest of his family.

Charlie Pippin by **Candy Dawson Boyd**   RL: 5.3

Macmillan, 1987   IL: 5–7
African American

Eleven-year-old Charlie is an energetic entrepreneur by day at school, but she also devotes time to trying to understand the Vietnam War. Her veteran father has survived physically but seems to have lost his spirit, and Charlie wants to understand why.

Chasing Redbird by Sharon Creech   RL: 5

> HarperCollins, 1997   IL: 5–8
> Grief/loss

As she works to clear a strange trail that she finds behind her family's Kentucky farm, thirteen-year-old Zinnia finds more than she bargained for. Her discoveries include family secrets and much about herself.

The Chemo Kid by Robert Lipsyte   RL: 6

> HarperCollins, 1992   IL: 6–10
> Physically challenged: cancer

Fred's a low-profile kind of guy, until Mora finds a lump on his neck as they are dancing: Fred has cancer. In a blitz of treatments including chemotherapy, Fred's doctor gives him an experimental drug that turns Fred's skin slightly green, makes him tingle when something is not right, and gives him superhuman powers! Finally, can Fred make a difference?

Child of the Owl by Laurence Yep   RL: 6

> Harper & Row, 1977   IL: 6–10
> Chinese American

Casey is twelve years old when her gambling-addicted father's lifestyle ends him up in the hospital. She gets shuffled from one relative to another, ending up with her grandmother in Chinatown, where a whole new cultural world opens for her, creating conflicts and decisions for her to make.

Children of the River by Linda Crew   RL: 7

> Delcorte, 1989   IL: 7–12
> Cambodian American

Sundara is a seventeen-year-old Cambodian girl who has escaped the Khmer Rouge and found a new home in Oregon with her family. This is a story about assimilation and acculturation. Sundara is caught between wanting to fit in and her family's need to retain its own culture.

Chinese Handcuffs by Chris Crutcher   RL: 7

> Greenwillow Books, 1989   IL: 8+
> Nontraditional family
> Grief/loss

Dillon Hemingway watched his brother commit suicide. He's not having much success getting over it. He starts writing long letters to his brother to help sort things out. Jen Lawless is the top girl's basketball player who seems to have it all. Unknown to everybody else, she's sexually abused by her stepfather. Dillon is her best friend. The lives of these two are intertwined, unraveled, and torn apart before the conclusion of this powerful novel which includes very mature themes.

Choosing Up Sides by John Ritter   RL: 6

Philomel Books, 1998   IL: 6–9
Living with abuse

In 1921 Luke moves to a new town along the Ohio River with his fundamentalist preacher father, his mother, and sister. Although Luke is a natural lefty, his father has forbidden him to use the "Devil's arm." When he sees a baseball game, a forbidden pastime, and pitches an errant ball powerfully in with his left hand, he is mobbed by the town boys to join their team. But to play baseball and throw left-handed would be to disobey his father.

A Circle Unbroken by Sollace Hotze   RL: 6

Clarion Books, 1988   IL: 6–10
Native American

Rachel Porter was captured by Indians in 1838. Now, seven years later, she is more Dakota Sioux than white when she is taken by a band of men back to her family. Her father will not tolerate any remarks or reminders of her Sioux ways, and Rachel is horribly torn between her two worlds.

The Circuit by Francisco Jimenez   RL: 6

Houghton Mifflin, 1999   IL: 5+
Migrant workers
Latino American

Through the eyes of a young boy we see the travels of a migrant family that has come to California to try to leave poverty behind. In this series of intertwined stories, we follow the family's struggles as they move constantly but continue to carry hope in their hearts.

The Clay Marble by Minfong Ho   RL: 7

Farrar, Straus, Giroux, 1991   IL: 5–9
Cambodian

Dara's family must flee their war-torn village in Cambodia. They establish a makeshift camp with other refugees on the Thai–Cambodia border. Dara is separated from her family and must learn self-reliance. Her candid observations on the warring factions, and on her brother's change from farmer to soldier are part of a moving story of Cambodian refugees in the 1980s.

Coal Miner's Bride: The Diary of Anetka Kaminska by Susan Campbell Bartoletti   RL: 5

    Scholastic, 2000   IL: 5–8
    Polish American
It is 1896 in a small village in Poland, and thirteen-year-old Anetka has just received a letter from her father who is working the coal mines in the United States. He has arranged a marriage for her to a fellow miner in exchange for passage to the United States for Anetka and her younger brother Josf. Anetka is devastated, but circumstances compel her to leave her village and marry this stranger in Pennsylvania. She arrives at a crucial time in the history of coal mining, and her life is deeply affected by the events of the time.

Color Me Dark: The Diary of Nellie Lee Love by Patricia McKissack   RL: 5

    Scholastic, 2000   IL: 5–8
    African American
The year is 1919 and Nellie Lee Love is very happy the war in Europe is over because her uncle and brother can come home. Home is Bradford Corners, Tennessee, and life in the Love household is pretty good until Uncle Pace is murdered on his way home. Pace's death begins a series of circumstances that take Nellie Lee, her sister, and parents to Chicago, becoming part of the Great Migration.

Come a Stranger by Cynthia Voigt   RL: 7

    Atheneum, 1986   IL: 6+
    African American
You first met Mina in *Dicey's Song* as she became one of Dicey Tillerman's first friends in her new school. Now you will get to know Mina as a young girl who loves the ballet but is thwarted in her ambition through the thoughtlessness and prejudice of a predominately white world of dance.

Confess-O-Rama by Ron Koertge   RL: 5.8

    Orchard Books, 1996   IL: 7–9
    Nontraditional family
    Grief/loss
As the new kid in school, Tony vows to blend in with the crowd and avoid personal attachments which he sees, from his mother, seem to always end disastrously. But the next thing he knows, he's spending time with an intriguing, flamboyant young woman.

Confessions of a Teenage Drama Queen by **Dyan Sheldon**   RL: 7

Candlewick Press, 2000   IL: 7–9
Nontraditional family

Lola is nothing if not dramatic: life is her stage, and she flings herself into every role with passion—if not always truthfulness. When she is forced to move from her beloved Manhattan to the boring 'burbs of New Jersey with her potter mother and bonkers twin sisters, she is determined to make her mark: but Carla Santini rules this school with power and flair, and tries to shut down the irrepressible Lola in this humorous story.

The Cookcamp by **Gary Paulsen**   RL: 4.5

Orchard Books, 1991   IL: 5–7
Nontraditional family

World War II means huge changes for many people, including one little boy who is sent by his mother from the city to a road-building camp in northern Minnesota where his grandmother cooks for the road builders.

Countdown by **Ben Mikaelsen**   RL: 6

Hyperion Books for Children, 1996   IL: 6–9
African: Maasai

In parallel stories, fourteen-year-old Elliot is selected by NASA to be the first junior astronaut while a fourteen-year-old Maasai herder is facing initiation into manhood and the world of a warrior. Both boys have many questions about family traditions and their places in the world—and when they are connected by radio when Elliot is in space, they also get to question each other.

Cousins by **Virginia Hamilton**   RL: 5

Philomel Books, 1990   IL: 5–7
African American

Cammy loves most of her family, especially her Gram who is now in a nursing home. The relatives she doesn't like are her perfect cousin Patty Ann and her family. But a day-camp incident causes Cammy to reevaluate her perceptions about Patty Ann and about life.

Crash by **Jerry Spinelli**   RL: 6

Knopf: Distributed by Random House, 1996   IL: 6–8
Quaker

Crash: that's his nickname, and that's the way he lives, running over people on and off the football field. Webb, the Quaker who lives down the street, is just someone else to tease and annoy, until something happens that makes Crash reexamine the meaning of friendship.

Crazy Jack by **Donna Jo Napoli**   RL: 6

> Delacorte, 1999   IL: 7+
> Grief/loss
> British

Why *did* Jack sell the family cow for a handful of beans? Napoli weaves the story of "Jack and the Beanstalk" from when he is a happy child who loves to help his parents to when he loses his father and becomes crazy with grief, earning himself the moniker of "Crazy Jack." Set in the English countryside where magic mixes with reality, this is a fascinating and well-woven tale.

Crazy Lady by **Jane Conley**   RL: 6

> HarperCollins, 1993   IL: 5–9
> Mentally challenged
> Grief/loss

Vernon has a lot of problems. He misses his mom, who has died. He has trouble in school, and despite the fact that he practices for hours on end, he doesn't make the baseball team. So when Maxine, the crazy lady, and her special-needs son, Ronald, walk into his life, his first impulse is to shut them out. But instead he gets involved in their lives, and then many things change for Vernon.

Crazy Weekend by **Gary Soto**   RL: 6

> Scholastic, 1994   IL: 6–10
> Latino American

Hector and Mando take the train from Los Angeles to Fresno to spend the weekend with Hector's Uncle Julio. Julio is a photographer who takes the boys up in a small plane to photograph one of the local farms. During the flight, they photograph a Brink's truck robbery in progress. After their pictures and names get published in the local paper, the boys' vacation becomes more exciting than anyone could have predicted.

The Crossing by **Gary Paulsen**   RL: 7

> Orchard Books, 1987   IL: 5–10
> Latino: Mexican

Juarez, Mexico, is where streetwise orphan Manny Bustos is scrambling for survival, trying to hold on to the coins American tourists toss to him before older boys beat him up to take them away. Maybe he should try to escape across the border to the United States. Sergeant Robert S. Locke is a Vietnam veteran who has stayed in the army: he tries to forget the shadows and faces of the dead from the war, so he comes to Juarez to drink and escape his haunted past. Can the two of them help each other?

Dakota Dream by James Bennett   RL: 7

Scholastic, 1994   IL: 7–10
Native American

Floyd is a fifteen-year-old Native American who has been shuttled among white foster homes and mental institutions most of his life. He finally decides the only way to find himself is to move to the reservation. The state fights this decision, but Floyd prevails.

Dancing on the Edge by Han Nolan   RL: 7

Harcourt Brace, 1997   IL: 8+
Mentally challenged

Miracle: she was given the name because her mother was dead when she was born. Raised by her brilliant father and his mother who lived more in the mystical world than anywhere else, Miracle finds no friends or stability in her life, and ends up setting herself on fire as she dances frantically among lit candles. Then she meets a young psychologist who offers her hope.

Danger Zone by David Klass   RL: 6

Scholastic, 1996   IL: 7+
African American
Nontraditional family

Jimmy Doyle knows he's a good basketball player in his hometown of Granham, Minnesota—but is he really good enough to play on an All American Teen "Dream Team"? Jimmy's trip to Los Angeles, then Rome, with his fellow team-mates shows Jimmy many sides of life, including ugly racism and violence, but also the power of respect.

Dangerous Skies by Suzane Fisher Staples   RL: 5.5

Farrar, Straus, Giroux, 1996   IL: 6–8
African American

Hypocrisy and prejudice twist the events of a murder to implicate two children who are friends: one from a prominent white family, the other from an African American family.

Danny Ain't by Joe Cottonwood   RL: 6

Scholastic, 1992   IL: 7+
Latino American
Nontraditional family

Danny's dad still has a war wound from Vietnam, but it's in his head, and sometimes his dad gets really bad. When Danny calls a friend for help, his dad is taken to a VA hospital, which leaves Danny on his own with no food and no money, but a strong sense of self-reliance. This novel deals with the same characters as *Babcock*.

Dark Light by Mette Newth   RL: 7

    Farrar, Straus, Giroux, 1995   IL: 7+
    Norwegian

Set in the 1800s during the Napoleonic Wars in Bergen, Norway, this story is a haunting look at a hospital for lepers. The story revolves around thirteen-year-old Tora who is moved from her home in the mountains to the hospital where she is first robbed of her precious money and food, then is befriended by a very angry rich woman who is close to death. Tora receives her greatest gift from this woman: the gift of reading.

Darnell Rock Reporting by Walter Dean Myers   RL: 5

    Delacorte, 1994   IL: 5–8
    African American

There's not a lot that excites Darnell about school: he replays cartoons in his head during math and falls asleep over homework. But two things begin to change that: Darnell joins the school newspaper, and he meets a homeless man named Sweeby Jones.

Dave at Night by Gail Levine   RL: 6.5

    HarperCollins, 1999   IL: 6–9
    Grief/loss
    Jewish

Dave is eleven when his father dies and his stepmom delivers him to the Hebrew Home for Boys, which is a mixture of good and bad. The bad is the food, the lack of heat, and a director who loses control and beats boys senseless when they are brought to him for discipline. The good is the close camaraderie of the eleven-year-old boys there, and the friends Dave finds when he sneaks out at night into the rich world of the Harlem Renaissance.

A Day No Pigs Would Die by Robert Newton Peck   RL: 7

    Knopf, 1972   IL: 6–9
    Shaker

This autobiographical story takes an interesting look at life in the Shaker community in Vermont. Robert makes a painful journey into adulthood as he struggles with school problems, his father's illness, and the mixed blessing of a pet pig.

The Dead of Night by John Marsden   RL: 6

Houghton Mifflin Co., 1997   IL: 7–10
Australian

Ellie continues to tell the tale of the six teens hiding out in the bush after the invasion of Australia in this sequel to *Tomorrow, When the War Began*. The stakes have gotten higher as Ellie and her friends try to rescue two friends and wreak more havoc on the enemy.

Dean Duffy by Randy Powell   RL: 6

Farrar, Straus, Giroux, 1995   IL: 7+
Physically challenged

Dean Duffy's brilliant baseball career is over by the time he's eighteen because of injuries to his arm. So what comes next? A summer and fall of contemplation and an offer from an unexpected quarter give him much food for thought as people from his past and present try to influence his future.

Deep Dream of the Rain Forest by Malcolm Bosse   RL: 7

Farrar, Straus, Giroux, 1993   IL: 7–10
Borneo

Harry and Bayang come from very different worlds. In 1920, in the jungles of Borneo, fifteen-year-old Harry is captured by Bayang, a young Iban tribesman. Bayang doesn't want to harm Harry but he believes Harry has the key to a mysterious dream prophecy. Through the ordeal, a friendship is formed that changes both lives.

Deliver Us from Evie by M. E. Kerr   RL: 7

HarperCollins, 1994   IL: 8+
Gay/lesbian

Evie comes to terms with the fact that she is a lesbian. As she reveals this fact to her friends and family, she is met with a variety of reactions in her Missouri farming community, including a sister who wishes it would all go away.

The Devil's Arithmetic by Jane Yolen   RL: 6

Viking Kestrel, 1988   IL: 5–9
Jewish

Hannah would rather go hunt Easter eggs with her Christian friend than suffer through another Passover dinner with her family. But during the Seder dinner she opens the door for Elijah and suddenly is swept back to a Polish village in 1942 where she is captured by Nazi soldiers and relives the terrors of the Holocaust.

The Diary of a Young Girl by Anne Frank

RL: 8

Constellation Books, 1952

IL: 6–9

Jewish

Anne's diary of her seemingly endless days in hiding during the Nazi occupation is amazing in its ability to draw us in to her life and the lives of those in hiding with her. Her struggles to be Anne and to understand the horrors of war are beautifully told.

Dicey's Song by Cynthia Voigt

RL: 5

Fawcett, 1982

IL: 6–8

Nontraditional family

Once she and her siblings have settled in with Gran, Dicey still continues to struggle with issues of family and responsibility. She agonizes as her sister struggles to read and despite Gran's presence feels something like parental responsibility for her siblings in the absence of her mother. This sequel to Voigt's *The Homecoming* can stand alone.

A Different Beat by Candy Dawson Boyd

RL: 5

Puffin, 1996

IL: 5–7

African American

Jessie loves attending Oakland Performing Arts Middle School, but it's also stressful, and while her sister seems to do everything perfectly, Jessie finds herself lacking in comparison. When one of Jessie's teachers badly hurts her feelings, Jessie must learn to grow to discover who she is, and that to be different from her sister is okay.

Dissidents by Neal Shusterman

RL: 6

Little, Brown, 1989

IL: 7–9

Russian

Set in 1989, this is a story of fifteen-year-old Derek who has just moved from Chicago to Moscow where his mother is the U.S. ambassador. Derek is dealing with dragon-size anger about many things, and finds only one thing in his life to be interesting and good: Anna Shafiroff, daughter of an expelled Russian dissident.

Dive by Adele Griffin

RL: 6

Hyperion Books for Children, 1999

IL: 6–8

Grief/loss

Nontraditional family

Eleven-year-old Ben and his mother have moved from place to place as long as he can remember. When they meet and move in with Lyle and his son Dustin, Ben finally feels at home. When Mom and Dustin say that it is time to move on, Ben decides he is going to stay with Lyle. It is only a diving accident that brings them face-to-face again.

Diving for the Moon by Lee F. Bantle   RL: 5.5

> Macmillan Books for Young Readers, 1995   IL: 5–7
> Physically challenged: AIDS

Bird loves summers at the lake with her best friend Josh. They can talk about anything: growing up, being in seventh grade next year, Bird's mom having a baby. Then Josh tells Bird he is HIV positive from a blood transfusion he received. How will they deal with that?

Do Angels Sing the Blues? by A. C. LeMieux   RL: 6

> Tambourine Books, 1995   IL: 7–10
> Physically challenged: alcoholism

Boog and Theo are best friends, and life is good, until Casey walks in on the first day of twelfth grade. When Theo falls for Casey, whose father is an alcoholic and loads of trouble, everything seems to change, and Boog struggles to control his resentment.

Dog Years by Sally Warner   RL: 4

> Knopf: Distributed by Random House, 1995   IL: 4–6
> Nontraditional family

Case Hill wants sixth grade to be okay, so he doesn't want anyone to know his dad is in prison, but he does want to work on the class newspaper for his English teacher. He creates an off-beat cartoon, "Dog Years," which brings many lessons, some good and some bad.

Dogsong by Gary Paulsen   RL: 5

> Bradbury Press, 1985   IL: 7–10
> Eskimo

Russel senses something is missing in his life, so he turns to the only old Eskimo in his village, Oogruk, who can tell him of the old ways. Through dream-trances, Russel learns of the old ways, and sets out to the north on a dogsled to experience the old ways. Through his travels he learns of life, death, and hunting, and hears his song: "Dogsong."

Dogwolf by Alden Carter   RL: 7

> Scholastic, 1994   IL: 7–10
> Native American

Pete is having a strange summer: it's so hot that the Northern Wisconsin woods are trying to burn up, and the dogwolf living nearby is driving Pete crazy with his continual howling. Pete is struggling to understand his mixed heritage (Chippewa, Metis, and Swedish), the death of his father, and his best friend's drinking problem in this summer of changes.

Doing Time by **Rob Thomas** RL: 7

Simon and Schuster Books for Young Readers, 1997 IL: 8+
Multiethnic

Ten stories of students tell the tales of Lee High School seniors who must do two hundred hours of community service to graduate. From a food bank job, to a convalescent hospital, to an adoption service, to a play with at-risk junior high students, each senior's story is told in a unique, true-to-life voice. Mature themes are addressed.

Don't You Dare Read This, Mrs. Dunphrey
by **Margaret Haddix** RL: 6

Simon and Schuster Books for Young Readers, 1996 IL: 7+
Nontraditional family
Living with abuse

School is definitely not a top priority for sixteen-year-old Tish: she's too busy trying to work to put food on the table for her little brother and herself, since her abusive father has walked out, and her mother first mentally, then physically, has checked out, too. Her journal entries required by her English teacher all give explicit "Don't Read" warnings, but who can Tish turn to for help?

Dove and Sword by **Nancy Garden** RL: 7

Farrar, Straus, Giroux, 1995 IL: 7+
French

This is the story of Joan of Arc told from the viewpoint of Gabrielle, a childhood friend, who longs to learn to read and be a healer. She disguises herself as a page to be near her amazing friend Jeanne who leads the fight for Charles and France.

Dovey Coe by **Francis O'Roark Dowell** RL: 6

Atheneum Books for Young Readers, 2000 IL: 6+
Physically challenged: deaf

Dovey Coe is a feisty twelve-year-old living in rural North Carolina in 1928 and has been accused of murder because of circumstantial evidence. In her own distinct voice Dovey tells the story of her family and their connection to Parnell Caraway which leads to her accusation of murder. Character portraits are strong and Dovey's voice is true as she tells her story.

Downriver by Will Hobbs   RL: 6

Maxwell Macmillan International Publishing Group, 1991   IL: 7+
Nontraditional family

Jessie and seven other teens have been in enough trouble that they get sent to an out-
door camp for "Wilderness Therapy." They call themselves "Hoods in the
Woods" and decide they should dump their leader to go white-water rafting: all
by themselves, illegally, without a river guide or a whole lot of experience. Can
they survive the Grand Canyon as well as each other?

Dragon's Gate by Laurence Yep   RL: 7

HarperCollins, 1993   IL: 7+
Chinese-American

Young Otter dreams of joining his father and uncle in the United States. One day,
Otter insults one of the Mandarin leaders in his village and is forced to flee. He
gets a boat to San Francisco and is reunited with his father who is working on
building the railroad. Otter then begins his career on the rail crew in nightmarish
conditions.

Dragonwings by Laurence Yep   RL: 6

Harper & Row, 1975   IL: 6–10
Chinese American

Set in the years 1903–1910, this is the story of Moonshadow, a young Chinese boy
who comes to live with his father in the land of demons—America. His father,
Windrider, is a builder of magnificent kites and gliders, and even corresponds
with the Wright Brothers about building a flying machine. Set in a time of discoveries, prejudice, and the San Francisco earthquake, Moonshadow shows us
much about the world around him.

Dreams in the Golden Country: The Diary of Zipporah
Feldman by Kathryn Lasky   RL: 5

Scholastic, 1998   IL: 5–8
Jewish
Russian-American

Zipporah Feldman is not sure how she likes New York City in 1903. Newly arrived from Russia, Zipporah and her two sisters have to share a small apartment
in the Lower East Side with their parents and an aged Jewish scholar. Anxious
to find her place in this new world, Zippy hurries to learn English and the ways
of her new neighbors. Sometimes this puts her at odds with her very traditional
mother.

Drive-By by **Lynne Ewing**   RL: 5

HarperCollins, 1996   IL: 5–8
Grief/loss

This is a short but powerful tale of gang life told through the eyes of a young boy. When
his older brother Jimmy is killed in a drive-by shooting, Tito is shocked to learn not
only that his brother was in a gang, but that the gang is coming after him next.

Driving Lessons by **Catherine Dexter**   RL: 6

Candlewick Press, 2000   IL: 7–10
Nontraditional family

Mattie is unhappy that her mom has sent her to a friend of the family in South
Dakota for the summer of her fourteenth year. Mattie's mom says it is so she can
finish her master's thesis, but Mattie thinks it's so she can spend more time with
Harry, a potential new husband whom Mattie doesn't like. In South Dakota, Mattie meets Lester, who has also been sent away from home for the summer. But
while Lester's goal is to stay out of trouble, Mattie seems determined to find it as
she struggles with many different issues.

The Drowning of Stephen Jones by **Bette Greene**   RL: 6

Bantam Books, 1991   IL: 7+
Gay/lesbian

As her librarian mother battles a citizen's group that wants to ban "anti-Christian"
literature from the library, Carla faces her own battle of torn loyalties when her
boyfriend starts persecuting the gay owners of an antique store.

The Eagle Kite by **Paula Fox**   RL: 6

Orchard Books, 1995   IL: 7+
Physically challenged: AIDS
Gay/lesbian

Liam's father has AIDS, and no one in the family wants to talk about it. But Liam
has a memory from three years before, a memory he shared with no one, and now
as his father is living apart from the family, Liam is seized with a desire to talk
to his father about his memory.

The Ear, the Eye, and the Arm by **Nancy Farmer**   RL: 7

Orchard Books, 1994   IL: 7+
African

This science fiction story is set in Zimbabwe in 2194. The story is inspired by Shona
mythology and follows the lives of three children who are kidnapped and made

to work in the toxic waste dump mining plastic while three detectives with unique mutations and abilities try to catch up with them.

Earthshine by Theresa Nelson   RL: 6

Orchard Books, 1995   IL: 6–9
Physically challenged: AIDS
Nontraditional family

When you need a miracle, it's best to get an early start. That's what Isaiah tells Slim, and they both need miracles to save the PWAs (persons with AIDS) in their lives. Slim lives in Los Angeles with her charming father, an actor, who is dying of AIDS: can the Miracle Man truly hold an answer for their problems?

Echoes of the White Giraffe by Sook Nyul Choi   RL: 6

Houghton Mifflin, 1993   IL: 6–10
Korean

In this sequel to *The Year of Impossible Goodbyes,* Sookan and her mother struggle through their lives as refugees in South Korea after they have fled for their lives from the North at the end of World War II.

The Eclipse of Moonbeam Dawson by Jean Davies Okimoto   RL: 6

TOR, 1997   IL: 7–10
Canadian

Moonbeam Dawson has lived with his mom for most of his life on communes, so when the latest one—The Happy Children of the Good Earth—falls apart, Moonbeam decides to try for a more "normal" life. But Moonbeam learns that his resort job has pitfalls as well.

Edith Jackson by Rosa Guy   RL: 5

Viking Press, 1978   IL: 6–12
Nontraditional family

This is a powerful story of a young woman with more than her share of life challenges. Edith longs to get a job and make a home for her three sisters, but that is not easy to do when you're only seventeen years old.

The Education of Little Tree by Forrest Carter   RL: 7

Delacorte/ E. Friede, 1971   IL: 7+
Native American

Little Tree's parents die when he is only five, so he goes to live in the hills of Tennessee with his grandparents during the Depression, and learns the way of the

Cherokee as well as how to make moonshine. Little Tree's five-year-old voice candidly reports all he sees in times of joy and pain.

Ellen Foster by Kaye Gibbons   RL: 8

Taylor Publishing Co., 1987   IL: 8+
Living with abuse
Ellen Foster tells her own story in an honest, straightforward, unsympathetic voice: at eleven, Ellen has been through too much, but she doggedly goes on, looking for a way to make things better. In her story is embedded, too, the story of "her little black friend" Starletta.

The Endless Steppe by Esther Hautzig   RL: 6

T. Y. Crowell Co., 1968   IL: 7–10
Polish
Esther is ten when her good life in Vilna, Poland, is shattered by Russian soldiers who place her and her parents under arrest for being capitalists. A six-week nightmarish train journey ends, and they find themselves in Siberia. For the next five years, their sheer determination, absolute courage, and occasional luck pull them through. This true account is very well-written.

Escape from Warsaw by Ian Serraillier   RL: 6

Scholastic, 1985   IL: 7+
Polish
During World War II, many Polish people were removed from their homes and sent to labor in Nazi camps or on German farms. Ruthk's parents were taken in the middle of the night leaving Ruthk to care for her little sister and brother. They get word that their father may have escaped and is waiting for them in Switzerland. Ruthk and the smaller children decide to travel to Switzerland to find their father.

Esperanza Rising by Pam Muñoz Ryan   RL: 6

Scholastic, 2000   IL: 6+
Latino American: Mexico
Esperanza lives a life of leisure, with her loving parents to provide her with anything she wants, her grandmother who teaches her to crochet, and servants who dote on her. On the eve of her thirteenth birthday, tragedy strikes, and she must leave her beautiful Rancho de las Rosas in Mexico, along with her mother and the servants. In the middle of the night they begin their trek to the United States, where they all find work on a large company farm in California's Central Valley. Esperanza is overwhelmed by the changes in her circumstances but learns what she needs to do for her and her family to survive.

Everywhere by Bruce Brooks

RL: 4.5

Harper & Row, 1990
African American
Grief/loss

IL: 4–7

Meet Lucy, the nurse, who really isn't even a nurse. Her amazing nephew Dooley claims to know the secret of "soul-searching." Both come to the home of a grandfather, who may be dying, and his grandson, who is not quite sure what is going on, knows he really needs his grandfather. This is a short, lovely tale.

The Examination by Malcolm Bosse

RL: 8

Farrar, Straus, Giroux, 1994
Chinese: Ancient

IL: 7–12

In sixteenth-century China, older brother Chen is determined to become a revered scholar. He is allowed to take the local examination and passes to the district level. On his return from a successful regional examination, younger brother Hong announces he will accompany his older brother to Peking to take the national examination. Practical Hong does not think scholarly Chen can make the journey across China on his own. Their adventures are beautifully described in this well-written novel.

The Facts Speak for Themselves by Brock Cole

RL: 7

Front Street, 1997
Living with abuse

IL: 8+

Linda is thirteen when she witnesses a murder. As she begins to explain what she saw, her own story of neglect and abuse come to light. This is a haunting, disturbing tale of Linda recounting the facts in her own way and addressing mature themes.

The Fall of the Red Star by Helen Szablya and Peggy Anderson

RL: 5.5

Boyds Mills Press, 1996
Hungarian

IL: 6–9

The autumn of 1956 is the setting of this novel which tells the story of fourteen-year-old Stephen and his family as the revolution in Hungary begins to stir. Can the Hungarians drive out the communists and restore the freedom to learn, have scouts again, and be with one's whole family?

Fall-Out by Gudrun Pausewang

RL: 7

Viking, 1994
German

IL: 7+

Janna is at school when the alarm rings, and suddenly everyone is told to run home. There has been an accident at a nuclear plant ninety kilometers away. As Janna tries to decide what is best for herself and her brother, a nightmare begins.

Fallen Angels by Walter Dean Myers   RL: 6.5

Scholastic, 1988   IL: 8+
African American
This is a critically acclaimed story of one young man's tour of duty in Vietnam as he watches the chaos of war around him in confusion and fear. Because this is a war story, some sections are graphic.

Far North by Will Hobbs   RL: 6

Morrow Junior Books, 1996   IL: 6–10
Canadian
Gabe Rogers is fifteen when he flies to the Northwest Territories to go to school in Yellowknife while his father mines for diamonds. A trip to take his Dene roommate back to his village turns into a nightmare, and Gabe, Raymond, and his Dene uncle, Johnny, are suddenly left in the wilderness and stunning cold of the far north to try to survive. What results is a thrilling tale of suspense, adventure, and friendship.

Farewell to Manzanar by Jeanne W. Houston   RL: 6

Houghton Mifflin, 1973   IL: 7+
Japanese American
This is the story of one family's ordeal in a Japanese relocation camp in the interior of California. We follow the family from their comfortable lifestyle on the California coast to the loss of everything they own. We also follow their years of adjustment in the camp until their release several years later.

Farm Team by Will Weaver   RL: 5.5

HarperCollins, 1995   IL: 7+
Grief/loss
Billy Baggs is fourteen and loves to play baseball, but he realizes farm duties come first. When his father is jailed for trashing a used car lot in anger, Billy's whole summer becomes consumed by the heavy responsibilities of farm work, until his mother suggests having Friday evening baseball games for anyone who wants to come play or watch.

Fat Chance by Leslea Newman   RL: 6

Putnam, 1994   IL: 7–10
Physically challenged: weight issues

Judi's English teacher, Mrs. Roth, gives her class an assignment to keep a journal, and from September to December, we follow Judi, who is obsessed with losing weight. When the "thinnest girl" in eighth grade shares her secret of how to purge, Judi thinks this might be her ticket to wonderful thinness. The story is an interesting look at a real problem with a believable heroine.

Fever 1793 by Laurie Halse Anderson   RL: 6

Simon and Schuster Books for Young Readers, 2000   IL: 6–10
Physically challenged: epidemic
Nontraditonal family

During a horrendously hot summer in Philadelphia in 1793, Matilda is living with her mother and grandfather, helping to run a coffeehouse. But a terrible fever has the denizens of Philadelphia fleeing the city in droves. Mattie's mother becomes ill, so she and her grandfather head to the country but are thrown out of the wagon when Grandfather falls ill. Mattie's nightmare grows, and she wonders how she will survive. This novel includes a glimpse of George Washington, and an account of the Free African Society.

Fiddle Fever by Sharon Arms Doucet   RL: 5

Clarion Books, 2000   IL: 6–8
Cajun/Creole

Inspired by the life story of Canray Fontenot, a well-known Cajun fiddler, this is the story of music, perseverance, Cajun living, and love. Felix LeBlanc lives with his parents and younger brother on the family farm in Louisiana. Felix, more than anything, wants to learn to play the fiddle. After his parents forbid him, Felix creates a fiddle from an old cigar box, scrap wood, window screen wire, and thread. Felix discovers that he has the gift of music, and this gift causes him much suffering until he and his family come to terms with it.

Find a Stranger, Say Goodbye by Lois Lowry   RL: 5

Houghton Mifflin, 1978   IL: 7–10
Nontraditional family

Natalie is graduating from high school and has decided on her path. She's determined to be a doctor just like her adopted father, and equally determined to find her birth mother who gave her up when Natalie was five days old.

Finding My Voice by Marie G. Lee   RL: 6

Houghton, 1992   IL: 7–10
Korean American

Ellen Sung is in her senior year in a small town in Minnesota. She has a lot on her mind: trying to letter in gymnastics, trying to get accepted to Harvard, and trying to decide what to do about hateful racial slurs she must endure at times. Amid all of this, she must find her own voice.

Flour Babies by Anne Fine   RL: 5.8

Little, Brown, 1994   IL: 6–9
Nontraditional family

Room 8 is for underachievers, troublemakers: the ones who have to do dorky stuff for the science fair like "flour babies." But Simon, whose own father walked out on him when he was only six weeks old, starts getting attached to his flour baby: he talks to it, to his mother, and to himself. In the process, Simon begins to figure out several things about parenthood and his own father.

Flowers for Algernon by Daniel Keyes   RL: 7

Harcourt, Brace & World, 1966   IL: 6–10
Physically/mentally challenged

Charlie Gordon is a thirty-year-old mentally challenged man. Scientists have performed daring experiments on mice to raise their intellectual ability, and now they perform them on Charlie, too, changing him into a genius: but for how long?

For the Life of Laetitia by Merle Hodge   RL: 6

Farrar, Straus, Giroux, 1993   IL: 6+
Caribbean

Laetitia is the first of her family to attend a secondary school. But to do so, she must move away from her extended family and move in with her father, whom she barely knows. The changes brought by school, by a new friend, and by the distance of her former life all change how she views things, and bring her hard choices and discoveries.

For the Love of Venice by Donna Jo Napoli   RL: 6

Delacorte, 1998   IL: 7–9
Italian

Percy feels like a real outsider when his family goes to Venice, Italy, for a summer. His father is working on a project to help keep Venice from flooding during storms. When he meets Graziella, who is fiercely determined to keep Venice the way it is, Percy finds himself in conflict over old and new ways in the city of canals.

Forbidden City: A Novel of Modern China by William Bell   RL: 6

Bantam, 1990   IL: 7–12
Chinese

Teenager Alex Jackson accompanies his photojournalist father to Beijing to cover the arrival of a Russian leader's visit to China. Just before that event, the students of the Beijing universities stage demonstrations in Tiananmen Square. Alex is separated from his father and finds himself videotaping the events as they occur. Now Alex must find a way to smuggle his tape out of China to let the rest of the world see what was taking place.

Forest of the Clouded Leopard by **Christopher and Lynne Myers**   RL: 5.5

Houghton Mifflin, 1994   IL: 6–9
Iban

The death of his grandfather forces a fifteen-year-old Iban boy to face the conflicts between traditional beliefs of his Iban tribe and the modern ways he is learning at a boarding school. This story paints an interesting picture of Borneo as well as the beliefs and cultures of the Iban people.

The Forestwife by **Theresa Tomlinson**   RL: 6

Orchard Books, 1995   IL: 6+
English: Medieval

Fifteen-year-old Mary cannot believe she has to marry an elderly widower who has black stumps for teeth and smells of sour ale, so she grabs her warmest cloak and flees to the forest. There she finds the Forestwife and another world of people trying to survive cruelty and loss of land. This is an interesting retelling of the Robin Hood legend.

The Forty-Third War by **Louise Moeri**   RL: 6

Houghton Mifflin, 1989   IL: 6–9
Latino: Central American

Uno is only twelve years old when he and his best friend are conscripted into the army of the revolutionary forces in their Central American country. More questions than answers seem to present themselves to Uno as he battles for hope and a better life for his people.

Freak the Mighty by **Rodman Philbrick**   RL: 6

Blue Sky Press, 1993   IL: 6+
Physically challenged
Gifted

This is a story about a slow learner who is very large for his age and is the image of his father who is in prison for murdering his mother. It is also the story of a very small boy who is a genius with a disabling and fatal disease. They become inseparable and unstoppable in this very moving story.

The Friends by **Rosa Guy**   RL: 7

Holt, Rinehart and Winston, 1973   IL: 6+
Caribbean American

This is the story of a teenage girl who is uprooted from her home in Jamaica to live
in New York City. She is continually teased by her new classmates because of her
way of dressing and speaking. She is involved in many fights and has no friends
until the day one of her classmates takes her under her wing.

From the Notebooks of Melanin Sun by **Jacqueline Woodson**   RL: 6

Blue Sky Press, 1995   IL: 7+
Gay/lesbian
African American

The summer he turns thirteen is a tough one for Mel: he is trying to start his first relationship with a girl, but also must deal with his mother falling in love—with another
woman, a woman who is white—causing Mel to face his own prejudice, anger, and
fear.

Frozen Stiff by **Sherry Shahan**   RL: 5.3

Delacorte, 1998   IL: 4–7
Nontraditional family

Cody and her cousin Derek decide to sneak out for a two-day kayaking trip while
their mothers are in Juneau. But the trip quickly takes an unexpected turn, plung-
ing Cody and Derek into a nightmarish situation. Each must call upon hidden
strengths to survive the wilderness and their own doubts.

Gathering Blue by **Lois Lowry**   RL: 5

Houghton Mifflin, 2000   IL: 5–10
Physically challenged
Grief/loss

When her mother dies, Kira finds herself alone in a primitive future society where
only the fittest survive. She is deemed useless because of her lame leg, which
means she cannot work as others do, and she fears she is doomed. But the
Council of Guardians unexpectedly take charge of her, giving her housing in
the grand Council Edifice because of her talent with threads and sewing. Kira
begins to wonder about the attention paid to her and others who have artistic
talents.

Gathering of Pearls by **Sook Nyul Choi**   RL: 6

Houghton Mifflin, 1994   IL: 8+
Korean

This is the conclusion to the story begun in *The Year of Impossible Goodbyes* and *Echoes of the White Giraffe*. Sookan Bak travels to the United States to attend college and struggles with the language, customs, and fitting in the new world while part of her misses her home, especially her mother. But she remembers her mother's wise advice: turn the pain or hard times into pearls and use them to make your life richer and stronger.

Gentlehands by M. E. Kerr   RL: 6

Harper & Row, 1978   IL: 8+
German American

Buddy is in love and wants to impress the wealthy girl he is so attracted to. He turns from his disapproving family to his cultured, sophisticated grandfather, whom he has never known well. He loves his time with him, until rumors start to circulate: surely his grandfather cannot be the notorious Nazi war criminal, Gentlehands.

The Gentleman Outlaw and Me–Eli by Mary Downing Hahn   RL: 5

Clarion Books, 1996   IL: 5–8
Nontraditional family

In 1887, Eliza decides to leave the abuse of her aunt and uncle in Kansas to go look for her father whose last letter had come from Tinville, Colorado. Disguising herself as a boy, she falls in with young Calvin Feathervone, or as he calls himself, the Gentleman Outlaw, for a series of adventures and misadventures.

Getting Near to Baby by Audrey Couloumbis   RL: 5.5

Putnam, 1999   IL: 5–8
Grief/loss

Willa Jo and Little Sister are up on the roof of Aunt Patty's house, and Willa Jo is quite determined to stay there; three weeks of Aunt Patty's bossiness has made her more stubborn than usual. Aunt Patty has brought the girls to stay with her to allow their mother some time alone with her grief after her youngest daughter, Baby, dies. But none of them seems to know how to help each other through this time of grief.

Ghost Canoe by Will Hobbs   RL: 6

Morrow Junior Books, 1997   IL: 5–8
Native American

In 1874 Nathan and his parents are lighthouse keepers on Tatoosh Island off the tip of Cape Flattery in Washington. But the weather is hard on Nathan's mother, so the two of them move into the Makah village a few miles away. There Nathan learns of Makah life and is involved in a mystery.

The Ghosts of Stony Clove by **Eileen Charbonneau**   RL: 5.5

Orchard Books, 1988   IL: 6–9
Native American

Combining history, a ghost story, and a romance set in the early 1800s in a Dutch settlement in the Catskill Mountains, this story of Asher and Ginny weaves many strands. Asher, the indentured servant, frequently is accused of doing the Devil's work, and Ginny, a ghostly figure, one night unleashes a whole chain of events.

A Girl Named Disaster by **Nancy Farmer**   RL: 5

Orchard Books, 1996   IL: 5–10
African

"The paths of the body are long, but the paths of the spirit are short." Nhamo remembers these words as she goes on a journey of both body and spirit while fleeing an arranged marriage to a cruel man with three wives. Nhamo searches for the family of the father she's never known in Zimbabwe.

The Girl with the White Flag by **Tomiko Higa**   RL: 6

Farrar, Straus, Giroux, 1991   IL: 6–9
Japanese

Tomiko is six years old when she, two of her sisters, and one of her brothers realize they must flee from their home on Okinawa, Japan. Her brother is killed by a stray bullet as she sleeps on his shoulder, then she is separated from her sisters and must use her six-year-old wiles to stay alive. This autobiographical account was inspired by the photograph taken of Tomiko by a U.S. soldier.

The Giver by **Lois Lowry**   RL: 6

Houghton Mifflin, 1993   IL: 6–9
Grief/loss

This is a powerful story set in a perfect world where there are no worries, no disease, and no choice. The story focuses on Jonas as he reaches the time when his future job is announced for him. He learns he is to be the Receiver of Memories, but those memories hold ideas that Jonas cannot accept.

The Glory Field by **Walter Dean Myers**   RL: 6

Scholastic, 1994   IL: 6–10
African American

This is the story of the Lewis family through generations: from Muhammad, brought in chains to be a slave in America, through 1994 when one young Lewis man fights a crack addiction while his cousin contemplates the beauty and intricacies of music. The power and hope of one family and the land that holds them is the story of the Glory Field.

Go and Come Back by Joan Abelove   RL: 6

DK InK, 1998   IL: 6+
South American: Peruvian

The Isabos live in the Amazonian jungle along the eastern slopes of the Andes Mountains; they live as they always have—or (as they would say) whatever. When two old white ladies (American anthropologists in their late 20s) come to live in their village for a year, Alicia, one of the young Isabos, is uncertain about them, but forms a bond with them as the year progresses.

Goodbye, Vietnam by Gloria Whelan   RL: 5

Knopf, 1992   IL: 5–7
Vietnamese

Mai and her family are struggling to live in Vietnam. When they learn the authorities want to arrest her grandmother, they must flee at night, taking only what they can carry. They travel to a port city, then get aboard a horribly overcrowded boat to try to get to Hong Kong. This simply told tale clearly paints the hard lives of the "boat people."

Grab Hands and Run by Frances Temple   RL: 5

Orchard Books, 1993   IL: 6–9
Latino: Central America

Felipe is twelve when he overhears his father tell his mother, "If they come for me, you and the children grab hands and run. Go north, all the way to Canada. If I ever get free, I'll come there." Life in El Salvador is full for Felipe, and although there is danger all around him, it is home; and then one day, his father does not come home.

Green Thumb by Rob Thomas   RL: 6

Simon and Shuster Books for Young Readers, 1999   IL: 6–9
South American

Thirteen-year-old Grady Jacobs is amazed but pleased when Dr. Phillip Carter asks him to spend the summer helping him on his project to re-forest the depleted Amazon rain forest: maybe those National Science Fair awards he'd won were really paying off. But once he meets Carter, he realizes he's up to his neck in trouble, and must go to a local tribe for help.

Habibi by Naomi Shihab Nye   RL: 7

Simon and Shuster Books for Young Readers, 1997   IL: 7+
Palestinian

Liyana is half Palestinian on her father's side. She hasn't really paid too much attention to her heritage until her family moves to Jerusalem. Liyana's adjustment is difficult because she does not know the language or the customs, and the friend she makes, Omar, is Jewish. Liyana and Omar build their friendship and try to help their families.

A Handful of Stars by Rafik Schami, translated by
Rika Lesser   RL: 7

Dutton Children's Books, 1990   IL: 7+
Syrian

A teenage boy who wants to leave his father's bakery behind to pursue journalism keeps a diary in Damascus, Syria. In it he tells of the love of his life, of his friendships, of his dreams, and of the suppression of his people. When he and two friends start an underground newspaper, he finds out just how seriously writing can be taken.

Hang a Thousand Trees with Ribbons by Ann Rinaldi   RL: 7

Harcourt Brace & Co, 1996   IL: 8+
African American

This is a fictionalized biography of an eighteenth-century African woman, Phillis Wheatly, who is brought to New England to be a slave. After publishing her first poem as a teenager, she gains fame, but she also struggles to find her role and identity in the colonies.

Hannah in Between by Colby Rodowsky   RL: 5

Farrar, Straus, Giroux, 1994   IL: 5–8
Physically challenged: alcoholism

Hannah feels her life is comfortable, even predictable, until her photographer mom starts drinking way too much. Doesn't anyone but Hannah notice? Hannah suffers her mother's drinking and bad behavior in silence, unable to decide who to turn to, until it all comes apart when her mother is in an accident.

Hard Ball by Will Weaver   RL: 6

HarperCollins, 1998   IL: 7+
Grief/loss

In the third of the Billy Baggs novels, Billy has a hard time controlling his anger, as does his arch rival King Kenwood. Their coach decides they need to spend a week together as a consequence, and both find unexpected common grounds. This novel explores issues of anger and families as well as the game of baseball.

Hard Love by Ellen Wittlinger   RL: 8

> Simon and Schuster Book for Young Readers, 1999   IL: 8+
> Gay/lesbian

John feels like he's isolated from the world. His mother doesn't touch him since his father left six years ago, and his father is busy flirting with women whenever he has John up to the city for the weekend. So John creates a zine (magazine) where he tries to be cool and funny. But when he meets Marisol, whose zine intrigues him, he feels a strong connection even though Marisol makes it clear from the start that she is a lesbian.

Harris and Me by Gary Paulsen   RL: 4.5

> Harcourt Brace & Co., 1993   IL: 5+
> Nontraditional family

A city boy whose parents are alcoholics gets sent to his cousin Harris's for the summer. There the two of them wrestle pigs, leap out of barn lofts, and live a life of pure country in a story that is howlingly funny.

Hatchet by Gary Paulsen   RL: 5

> Viking Penguin, 1988   IL: 4–8
> Nontraditional family

Brian is headed for the Canadian wilderness in a single-engine plane so he can visit his father for the first time since his parents' divorce. But the plane crashes and Brian must use his wits and the hatchet his mother gave him as a parting gift to survive in the wilds of northern Canada.

Haveli by Suzanne Fisher Staples   RL: 7

> Knopf: distributed by Random House, 1993   IL: 7–10
> Pakistani

In this sequel to *Shabanu: Daughter of the Wind,* our heroine is the youngest of Rahim's four wives. She continues to yearn for her independent life in the desert, but finds solace with Rahim's mother at their *haveli* (home) in the city. However, there she also faces new and different dangers.

Hawk Moon by Rob MacGregor   RL: 6

> Simon and Schuster Books for Young Readers, 1996   IL: 7–10
> Native American

Will Lansa is back in Aspen after spending the summer on a Hopi reservation with his father. His time with the Hopis has changed him, so he tells his girlfriend that they need to go their separate ways. Immediately afterward, she disappears, and evidence points to Will as the guilty party.

Heart of a Champion by **Carl Deuker**   RL: 5.6

> Joy Street Books, 1993   IL: 7–9
> Nontraditional family
> Alcoholism

Seth is looking for something to fill the gap that his father's death has left when it is filled by Jimmy and baseball. Jimmy is consumed by the game, knowing he is bound for the majors, and he decides Seth should come with him. But stumbling blocks appear in the form of family troubles, grades, and alcohol: is baseball enough to pull them through?

Heaven by **Angela Johnson**   RL: 5

> Simon and Schuster Books for Young Readers, 1998   IL: 6+
> African American
> Adoption

Fourteen-year-old Marley lives in Heaven, and every day she walks to the Superette to wire money to her Uncle Jack, who writes letters to her faithfully. But one day, Momma and Pops sit down to tell Marley something that changes the way Marley sees everything.

Hero by **S. L. Rottman**   RL: 6

> Peachtree Publishers, 1997   IL: 6–8
> Nontraditional family

Fifteen-year-old Sean is bitter and angry. He never sees his father and is abused by his mother. His constant brushes with the police land him on a farm doing community service. It is here that he finds a strong role model and begins to grow up, becoming strong enough to face an unexpected tragedy.

Hero of Lesser Causes by **Julie Johnston**   RL: 6

> Lester Pub., 1992   IL: 6–9
> Physically challenged: polio

Set in the 1940s when polio was still very much a threat to life, this is the heart-wrenching and hilarious story of a young girl who faces the challenge of keeping her brother interested in living after he is crippled by polio.

Heroes by **Robert Cormier**   RL: 6

> Delacorte, 1998   IL: 8+
> Physically challenged

A grim, dark novel about Francis Cassavart who returns home to Frenchtown in New England after World War II with no face. It was blown off when he threw himself onto a grenade, earning him a Silver Star. But he has only one thought on his return, and that is to find his boyhood hero, Larry La Salle, so he can kill him.

Hiroshima by John Hersey   RL: 7

  Knopf: Distributed by Random House, 1985   IL: 8+
  Japanese

John Hersey interviewed survivors of Hiroshima's bomb while the ashes were still warm. Told in segments are stories of the survivors just before the bomb fell, after the bomb fell, and life changes to each as a result of their near encounters with the deadly blast. Hersey has written a memorable account here that vividly depicts the horror of the atomic bomb.

Holes by Louis Sacher   RL: 5.5

  Farrar, Straus, Giroux, 1998   IL: 5–8
  Multiethnic

Stanley Yelnats's family has a history of bad luck, so Stanley is not surprised when he's accused of a crime he didn't commit. He is surprised by Camp Green Lake, the detention camp he is sent to, where there is no water, just a giant dried up lake where he and the other boys must dig one 5-by-5-foot hole every day. Stanley starts to believe there's a reason for digging, and sets out to dig up the true story.

Home Boy by Joyce Hansen   RL: 5

  Clarion Books, 1982   IL: 7–10
  Caribbean American

Marcus moves with his family from his Caribbean island home to the Bronx. He doesn't fit in, so he gets into several fights. During one, a fellow student is stabbed. Marcus runs and tries to figure out where things went wrong.

Home for a Stranger by Joan T. Weiss   RL: 5

  Harcourt Brace Jovanovich, 1980   IL: 5–7
  Latino American

Juana lives in an orphanage in Mexico when doctors from the United States come to visit. One of them notices her deformed mouth and arranges for her to come to America for an operation. That's when Juana's story begins to unfold, and Juana discovers who she really is.

Homecoming by Cynthia Voigt   RL: 5

Fawcett, 1981   IL: 6–10
Nontraditional family

When their mentally ill mother abandons them at a shopping mall, four children decide to set out in search of relatives to take them in. Led by the stubborn oldest
sister, Dicey, the children struggle to survive as they look for a place to call home.

Homeless Bird by Gloria Whelan   RL: 6.5

HarperCollins, 2000   IL: 5–8
Indian

Koly's parents think it's time their daughter has a husband, even though it means
selling their only cow to raise money for her dowry. Koly leaves the security of
her village home to marry a sickly boy whose parents are interested only in the
dowry money to help cure their boy. But he dies and Koly is a thirteen-year-
old-widow in a culture that has no use for widows. Here is a fascinating look at
a part of India's culture through the eyes of a teen.

Homesick: My Own Story by Jean Fritz   RL: 5

Putnam, 1982   IL: 5–9
Chinese

This is an autobiography about the author's life in China as she was growing up and
her yearning to see the United States. This is also a story about troubled times in
China when foreigners were unpopular.

Honus and Me by Dan Gutman   RL: 4.8

Avon Books, 1997   IL: 4–7
Nontraditional family

This is a story not only about baseball, but also about the importance of believing
in oneself. When Joe cleans out his neighbor's attic, he finds a Honus Wagner
card worth a half million dollars. But the tingling sensation he gets when he holds
it has nothing to do with its value, and everything to do with life and love.

Hoops by Walter Dean Myers   RL: 6

Delacorte, 1981   IL: 6–10
African American

Lonnie Jackson plays basketball. As he is struggling with growing up and finishing
school, he meets Cal and joins a team for the citywide basketball Tournament of
Champions. Lonnie may be good enough to make the pros but there are some
people who are offering him other options that could ruin his future. Lonnie and
Cal have to make the right choice.

The House of Dies Drear by **Virginia Hamilton**   RL: 5

Macmillan, 1968   IL: 5–10
African American

Dies Drear was a conductor on the Underground Railway in a small Ohio town.
When he died, his house was the center of much attention. Most of the people in
the town believed the house to be haunted. A young black family moves into the
home and tries to unravel the mysteries of this very interesting house.

House of Sixty Fathers by **Meindert DeJong**   RL: 5

Harper, 1956   IL: 6–8
Chinese

Alone in a sampan with his pig and three ducklings, a little Chinese boy is whirled
down a raging river, back to the town from which he and his parents had just escaped a Japanese invasion during World War II. He spends long and frightening
days trying to find his family and a new home.

The House on Mango Street by **Sandra Cisneros**   RL: 7

Arte Publico Press, 1983   IL: 7+
Latino American

This is the story of a young girl growing up in the Hispanic quarter of Chicago. Esperanza Cordero's story is told in a series of short vignettes. My seventh graders
really enjoyed this book, which does deal with some mature themes.

The House You Pass on the Way by **Jacqueline Woodson**   RL: 5.5

Delacorte, 1997   IL: 7+
African American
Gay/lesbian

Staggerlee is fourteen and feels cut off from many things because she's different:
her parents represent the only interracial marriage in town, her grandparents'
tragic death made them famous, and Staggerlee finds love in her heart for other
girls. When her cousin Tyler comes to visit, she helps Staggerlee feel better about
herself, giving her both hope and sorrow.

Humming Whispers by **Angela Johnson**   RL: 6

Orchard Books, 1995   IL: 7+
African American
Mentally challenged: schizophrenia

Sophy remembers when her sister Nicole first heard the humming whispers—the
voices of the schizophrenia—at fourteen. Now Sophy is also fourteen, and she is

fearful something will happen to her, too. Her worries stack up: about Nikki, about storms on Lake Erie, about low-flying airplanes, and about the box under her bed she fills with things she's "found" or, rather, shoplifted.

I Am an Artichoke by Lucy Frank   RL: 5.5

Holiday House, 1995   IL: 7–9
Physically challenged: weight issues

Sarah is fifteen and anxious to be away from her parents and perfect sister for the summer. So the job as a "mother's helper" in New York City sounds great, even though the mom and daughter she'll be with seem a little strange. The two seem to fight continually, especially about Emily eating—or more precisely, not eating. What exactly can Sarah do?

I Am the Clay by Chaim Potok   RL: 8

Knopf: Distributed by Random House, 1992   IL: 8+
Korean

An elderly couple are fleeing North Korea and the Chinese when they find a seriously injured boy in a ditch at the side of the road. Despite the pleadings of the old man to leave the boy be, the woman puts him in their cart and nurses him back to health as they continue their flight southward. This is a book for higher level readers.

I Am the Ice Worm by Mary Ann Easley   RL: 5

Boyd Mills Press, 1996   IL: 5–8
Eskimo

Fourteen-year-old Allison Atwood is going up to visit her mother who's teaching north of the Arctic Circle in Alaska. But the plane she's in crashes and kills the pilot. She and her duffle bag and bedroll are rescued by an Inupiat trapper, and Allison enters a very different world as she waits to reach her mother. Life in Southern California has nothing in common with life in an Inupiat village–or does it?

I Can Hear the Mourning Dove by James Bennett   RL: 6

Houghton Mifflin, 1990   IL: 8+
Mentally challenged

Her father has died, and Grace has fallen into despair. In the aftermath of having tried to kill herself, she fights mental illness which comes in the form of voices from the sky, fear of others, and getting "scrambled." She struggles to live, but finally makes unexpected connections with two people who might be people she can call friends.

I Hadn't Meant to Tell You This by Jacqueline Woodson   RL: 5

Delacorte, 1994   IL: 6+
African American
Living with abuse

"I hadn't meant to tell you this. I swore to Lena I wouldn't. Even crossed my heart."
But Marie decides it is time to tell Lena's story, so other girls won't have to be
afraid. Both girls have lost their mothers, but now Lena's terrible secret presses
on both of them, as Lena desperately tries to protect herself and her younger sister from their father's abuse.

I Hate Being Gifted by Patricia Hermes   RL: 5+

Putnam, 1990   IL: 4–7
Gifted

Starting sixth grade with her two very best friends in the same class with a teacher
they love is great. Except for one thing: KT is in LEAP, the gifted program. KT
worries that being away from her class and friends will make things too hard. As
the year progresses, everything changes, including KT.

I Have Lived a Thousand Years by Livia Bitton Jackson   RL: 6

Simon and Schuster Books for Young Readers, 1997   IL: 8+
Czechoslovakian

This is the true story of Elli L. Friedmann, born in Czechoslovakia, who is thirteen
when she, her mother, and brother are taken to Auschwitz. She tells of the
roundups, transports, selections, and camps. Although her experiences are horrifying, she focuses on the humanity and hope, which keep her alive.

I Heard the Owl Call My Name by Margarite Craven   RL: 8

Doubleday, 1973   IL: 8+
Native American

Mark is a young priest sent to a remote Kwakuitle village where he discovers the
simplicity and beauty of this way of life is being systematically destroyed by the
influence of whites. Not aware that he has only three years to live, Mark embraces the old culture and becomes a part of the village.

I Rode a Horse of Milk White Jade by Diane Lee Wilson   RL: 6

Orchard Books, 1998   IL: 6+
Mongolian

Oyuna lives on the Mongolian steppes at the end of the thirteenth century. She is
crippled as a young girl and is kept sheltered by her parents. All she wants to do
is ride a horse. One day, after the death of her mother, she gets her wish. Dis-

guised as a boy, she rides off with Kublai Khan's soldiers. Her adventures take her all over Khan's kingdom and eventually to the palace in the royal city.

I Was There by Hans Peter Richter; translated from German by Edite Kroll   RL: 6

Holt, Rinehart and Winston, 1972   IL: 6–10
German
This first-person account of daily life in the Third Reich provides an intimate glimpse into the lives of German young people. The story is told in a direct, understated style.

Ice by Phyllis Reynolds Naylor   RL: 5.5

Atheneum Books for Young Readers, 1995   IL: 6–9
Nontraditional family
Thirteen-year-old Chrissa has been confused, silent, and angry with her mother for three years. Where is her father? Why isn't he around? Chrissa's mother finally sends her to the country to spend a year with her father's mother, and there Chrissa learns more about her father, herself, and the meaning of family.

If I Should Die Before I Wake by Han Nolan   RL: 6

Harcourt Brace, 1994   IL: 8+
Jewish
Polish
An unhappy young woman who thinks she has found a place to belong with a Neo-Nazi group lies horribly injured in a Jewish hospital after a motorcycle accident. There, she relives the life of a Polish girl whose family is sent to first the ghetto then the concentration camps during World War II. A disturbing and compelling story.

If It Hadn't Been for Yoon Jun by Marie G. Lee   RL: 4

Houghton Mifflin, 1993   IL: 4–8
Korean-American
Alice has adjusted to being the only Korean-American in school, but the appearance of a new Korean boy causes her to reexamine her feelings about her heritage, and about people's reactions to one another.

If You Come Softly by Jacqueline Woodson   RL: 6

Putnam, 1998   IL: 7–10
African American
Told from alternating points of view, Ellie is a fifteen-year-old Jewish girl struggling with the issue of trust: her mother has walked out on the family twice and

come back. Miah is a black fifteen-year-old boy whose famous parents are split and live across the street from one another. Ellie and Miah meet at the private school they both attend and feel an attraction that leads to a wonderful relationship; but not everyone accepts their relationship.

Imani All Mine by Connie Porter   RL: 7

Houghton Mifflin, 1999   IL: 8+
African American

Tasha tells her story in her way, with her words, at her pace, in a strong, unforgettable voice. Tasha is a single mom at fifteen who lives in the projects with her mom who is on welfare. They hear gunshots all too often in their neighborhood, but Tasha goes regularly to school with her baby to keep up her grades and to try and figure out about the deep places inside of herself and others. This lyrically written story has mature themes.

In the Time of Wolves by Eileen Charbonneau   RL: 6

Forge, 1994   IL: 7+
Native American
French Canadian

Set in upstate New York in the 1840s this is the story of a fourteen-year-old boy whose mixed heritage and the prejudices of the time create inner and outer struggles for him and his twin sister. Included in this coming-of-age story are some mature themes.

In the Year of the Boar and Jackie Robinson by Betty Bao Lord   RL: 5

Harper & Row, 1984   IL: 5–8
Chinese American

A young girl moves from China to New York City where she encounters prejudice for the first time. She spends a lot of time trying to fit in. She discovers baseball and becomes a fan of Jackie Robinson. From him, she learns to not give up.

Ironman by Chris Crutcher   RL: 7

Greenwillow Books, 1995   IL: 8+
Nontraditional family

When no one else seems to care, Beauregard Brewster turns to someone he thinks really listens: Larry King. In letters to Larry, Bo describes the conflicts he has with his father, his "anger problem," and his progress in training for a triathlon.

Is Kissing a Girl Who Smokes Like Licking an Ashtray? by Randy Powell RL: 7

Farrar, Straus, Giroux, 1992 IL: 7+
Nontraditional family

Shy and quirky Biff is trying to work up the nerve to ask out the girl he's been interested in for almost two years when he crosses paths with an irrepressible, spontaneous girl named Heidi who shows him a different side of life.

An Island Like You: Stories of the Barrio by Judith Ortiz Cofer RL: 7

Orchard Books, 1995 IL: 8–12
Puerto Rican American

Twelve short stories set in a New Jersey barrio illustrate the worlds of different Puerto Rican-American teens. Their problems range from family troubles to macho classmates, to running away from home, to sex and drugs, and AIDS. The collection brims with life and with real people.

Island of the Blue Dolphins by Scott O'Dell RL: 5

Houghton Mifflin, 1960 IL: 5–8
Native American

This is a story of survival of a young Native American girl who unwittingly becomes stranded on an island off the California coast. The story is based on a true account of this young woman who survived alone for 18 years.

The Islander by Cynthia Rylant RL: 5

DK InK, 1998 IL: 6+
Canadian
Grief/loss

This short, lyrical story is about an extraordinary set of events in the quiet childhood of Daniel Jennings. Living with his grandfather on a small island off the coast of British Columbia, Daniel is terribly lonely until one day he hears his name called as he sits by the ocean.

It Happened to Nancy by Anonymous, ed. by Beatrice Sparks RL: 7

Avon Books, 1994 IL: 8+
Physically challenged: AIDS

This is the true diary of a young woman whose life is shattered as she first is date-raped, then learns she has AIDS. Her diary traces the rapid course of the deadly disease and the reactions of those around her.

It's A Matter of Trust by Marcia Byalick   RL: 6

> Browndeer Press, 1995   IL: 7–10
> Jewish

Erika is sixteen and her life seems pretty good, until her father receives a call in the car over the speaker phone with Uncle Ray saying "It's all over . . . they know everything." "Everything" turns out to be bribery and corruption in a government office that centers on Erika's father and uncle. Erika's life plunges into a crazed media circus, and Erika's love for her father turns to hatred.

Izzy, Willy-Nilly by Cynthia Voigt   RL: 6

> Atheneum, 1986   IL: 6–10
> Physically challenged

Izzy is pleased when a senior asks her out, but when he drinks too much at a party, Izzy's life is changed forever. Losing part of her leg and being a "cripple" rearranges everything from her friendships to her family relationships to her values and views.

Jack by A. M. Homes   RL: 7

> Macmillan, 1989   IL: 7+
> Gay/lesbian
> Nontraditional family

Jack is confused when his father moves out of the house without any explanation. Jack's mother is furious and gets terribly angry whenever his father tries to see Jack. It is years later that Jack's father takes him out in a rowboat in the middle of a lake to tell Jack that he is gay and living with another man. Jack struggles first with revulsion, then anger, and then confusion at this news from his father.

Jason's Gold by Will Hobbs   RL: 6

> Morrow Junior Books, 1999   IL: 6–9
> Nontraditional family

Jason has been away from his two brothers for almost a year, riding the rails and discovering life in 1897. When word of the Yukon gold rush reaches him, he returns home, intent on being a part of it. But his brothers have already taken their inheritance and his to head for the gold, and Jason must struggle through gold rush craziness and harsh conditions to try to catch up with them. One of the people whose path he crosses more than once is Jack London.

Jesse by Gary Soto   RL: 6

> Harcourt Brace, 1994   IL: 8+
> Latino-American

Jesse is seventeen. He's moved out of his home, which isn't a good place because of his stepfather who drinks too much. He has dropped out of high school and is trying a junior college where he wants to pursue art—but so many things get in the way.

Jip: His Story by **Katherine Paterson**   RL: 5

> Lodestar Books, 1991   IL: 6–9
> African American

Jip fell off the back of a wagon as a child, so is taken to the town's poor farm where he works well with both the people and animals on the farm. When a stranger comes to town to start asking questions about Jip, the true story of his past begins to emerge. Jip's story also continues the story of Lyddie, who is a teacher in town.

John Riley's Daughter by **Kezi Matthews**   RL: 6

> Front Street/ Cricket Books, 2000   IL: 6–9
> Nontraditional family
> Mentally challenged: mental illness

After her mother's death, twelve-year-old Memphis Riley is left to live with her grandmother and her mentally handicapped aunt, Clover. After a fight between Memphis and Clover, Clover takes off and cannot be found. Memphis, as usual, is blamed. In this bittersweet story, Matthews explores the world of the adolescent who is living in the shadow of a mentally challenged family member, and how this affects the entire family.

Join In: Multiethnic Short Stories by Outstanding Writers for Young Adults edited by **Donald Gallo**   RL: 6

> Dell, 1995   IL: 7+
> Multiethnic

In this collection of short stories, we hear from strong young adult authors such as Linda Crew, Lensey Namioka, and Julius Lester. The stories include tales of friendship, problems, connections, confrontations, and expectations.

The Journal of Joshua Loper: A Black Cowboy by **Walter Dean Myers**   RL: 5

> Scholastic Press, 1999   IL: 5–8
> African American

Sixteen-year-old Joshua Loper finally feels like a man when his boss tells him he is old enough to help take the cattle to market in Abilene, Kansas. In 1871, the Chisholm Trail was the direct route from the vast cattle ranches in Texas to the cattle trains in Kansas. Joshua rides many miles of the trail bringing up the rear of the drive, and his journal entries recount tales of life on the trail.

The Journal of Wong Ming-Chung: A Chinese Miner by Laurence Yep   RL: 5

> Scholastic, 2000   IL: 5–8
> Chinese American

As the youngest son in a poor family, Ming-Chung does not think he will be fortunate enough to follow his uncle to the Gold Mountain. But when his uncle sends money home to China and says there could be more if he had help, Ming-Chung gets his chance. His daily journal entries tell the story of life in the gold fields of California in 1852.

Journey Home by Yoshiko Uchida   RL: 5

> Atheneum, 1978   IL: 5–8
> Japanese American

Yuki and her parents are released from the internment camp they have been in during World War II, and Yuki feels intense relief. However, when they return to San Francisco, she finds more challenges in the face of violence and prejudice, as well as with her brother who was wounded in the war. Despite the challenges, she and her family and friends remain determined to rebuild their lives.

Journey of the Sparrows by Fran Leeper Buss   RL: 6

> Lodestar Books, 1991   IL: 6+
> Latino: Central American

How long could you be stuffed with three other people in a crate? And how would you feel when you finally got out of the crate to stand on shaky legs and find yourself in a land where you are an illegal alien, where people speak a language you barely know, where your next meal is uncertain? This story relates the plight of a family trying to escape the horrors of the political unrest of El Salvador.

Journey to Jo'burg by Beverley Naidoo   RL: 6

> J.B. Lippincott, 1985   IL: 6–10
> African: South African

Naledi and Tiro leave their aunt's home to walk to Johannesburg to find their working mother. The three-day trip is overwhelming and takes the children into the world of apartheid.

Journey to Topaz by Yoshiko Uchida   RL: 6

Creative Arts Book, 1985   IL: 6–10
Japanese American

Eleven-year-old Yuki and her family are taken from her home, made to stay in horse
barns and then shipped to Topaz, an internment camp in Idaho. The hardships endured are exacerbated by a difficult decision her brother has to make.

Jubilee Journey by Carolyn Meyer   RL: 5

Harcourt Brace, 1997   IL: 5–9
African American

Thirteen-year-old Emily Rose loves her "double" heritage, with an African American mother and a French American father. But when she, her mother, and her
brother travel down to Dillon, Texas, to join her great-grandmother Rose Lee for
the seventy-fifth anniversary of the end of Freedomtown, she acquires a new view
of her life and her history. This sequel to *White Lilacs* can also stand on its own.

Julie by Jean Craighead George   RL: 7

HarperCollins, 1994   IL: 6–9
Eskimo

This sequel to *Julie of the Wolves* directly continues Julie's story as she returns to
the home of her father and continues to struggle with conflicts between modern
and Eskimo cultures.

Julie of the Wolves by Jean Craighead George   RL: 5

G. K. Hall, 1973   IL: 6–10
Eskimo

Miyax is a thirteen-year-old Eskimo girl with a pen pal in San Francisco who calls
her Julie and urges her to visit. So when Miyax finds herself in a horrible situation, she heads out across the Arctic tundra to walk hundreds of miles to a boat
and San Francisco. But she becomes lost and turns to the only companions she
can find: a pack of wolves. Miyax's struggles are to survive and to understand her
goals. Is it the life of an Eskimo she wants where one's wealth is based on intelligence, fearlessness, and love, or is it the modern world of airplanes and pink
bedrooms?

Julie's Wolf Pack by Jean Craighead George   RL: 5

HarperCollins, 1997   IL: 5–9
Eskimo

This is the third book dealing with Julie (Miyax) and her wolf pack, and this story
is told from the viewpoint of the wolves. The story continues the tale of Kapu the
wolf and his pack as they struggle to survive in their changing world.

Jump Ship to Freedom by James L. Collier and Christopher Collier
RL: 6

Delacorte, 1981   IL: 6–10
African American
Daniel's father earned enough soldier's notes during the Revolution to buy his
family's freedom. When Daniel's father died, Mrs. Ivers took the notes and re-
fused to free Daniel and his mother. After being caught stealing the notes back,
Daniel is forced on a ship bound for the West Indies. Yearning for freedom and
facing an uncertain future, Daniel jumps the ship in New York and his adventures begin.

Karen by Marie Killilea
RL: 6

Prentice-Hall, 1952   IL: 6–9
Physically challenged: cerebral palsy
This is an inspiring story of Karen and her struggles to learn to walk, read, and talk
despite the challenge of cerebral palsy.

The King's Swift Rider: A Novel on Robert the Bruce by Mollie Hunter
RL: 6

HarperCollins, 1998   IL: 6–10
Scottish: Medieval
Near the end of the thirteenth century, Scotland is in upheaval as clans quarrel and
England attempts a stronger hold on the country. This is the story of sixteen-year-
old Martin who becomes a messenger and spy for Robert the Bruce, who seems
to be Scotland's strongest hope for freedom from the English. Hunter has researched well for this historical fiction.

Kiss the Dust by Elizabeth Laird
RL: 6

Dutton Children's Books, 1992   IL : 7+
Iraqi
Thirteen-year-old Tara must flee with her family from Iraq across the border into
Iran because of her father's involvement with the Kurdish resistance movement.
In Iran, they must endure a brutal refugee camp. When will they ever find a place
to call home again?

Kissing Doorknobs by Terry Spencer Hesser
RL: 6

Delacorte, 1998   IL: 6–10
Physically challenged: obsessive-compulsive
Tara says she'd been happy most of her life till she heard the chant: "Step on a
crack, break your mother's back." From that day on, she develops multiple

quirks—like having to count the cracks uninterrupted, from home to school, and having to pray aloud when anyone swears. She and her family struggle until finally Tara learns she is obsessive-compulsive.

Kokopelli's Flute by Will Hobbs   RL: 6

Atheneum Books for the Young Reader, 1995   IL: 5–9
Native American

Tepary Jones's parents don't mind if he spends the night up in the Picture House cave dwelling on the night of the eclipse. But pot hunters are disturbing the ancient place, and in the aftermath of what they disturb, Tep blows an ancient flute and changes into a packrat: but only at night! His dog Dusty still knows him in packrat form, but somehow he must unravel this mystery, catch the pothunters, help his parents, and find out more about an old man named Cricket.

The Language of Goldfish by Zibby Oneal   RL: 6

Viking Press, 1980   IL: 6–9
Mentally challenged

Thirteen-year-old Carrie is talented in math and art. But growing up is a change that is too big and too frightening for her. Things start slipping for Carrie until one night she tries to kill herself.

Lasso the Moon by Dennis Covington   RL: 7

Delacorte, 1995   IL: 7+
Latino: Central American

April Hunt is living in Georgia with her recovering alcoholic father who is a cardiologist known as "Mad Jack Hunter." Many of his patients are now illegal aliens, and April gets to know Fernando, an illegal alien from El Salvador, who piques her curiosity. As Fernando's horrifying stories emerge, April begins to see things much differently.

Last Safe Place on Earth by Richard Peck   RL: 6

Delacorte, 1995   IL: 7–10
Nontraditional family

Walden Woods is the suburbs: with safe schools, and neighborhoods, this is a safe place to be, and Todd and his family are happy and secure. Then suddenly things change when Laurel Kellerman, who looks like the perfect girl, starts to baby-sit Todd's little sister. The forces of fundamentalism and censorship hit Todd and his family amid the celebration of Halloween. Meanwhile Todd's class is musing over Bradbury's *Fahrenheit 451*. What does it all mean?

Later, Gator by Laurence Yep   RL: 4

Hyperion Books for Children, 1995   IL: 4–7
Chinese American

Teddy's last birthday present to his younger brother had been socks: plain, white
socks, which Bobby said he *loved!* So, this year, when his mom tells him to get
something cool and different, he decides to get his brother an alligator!

Leaving Fishers by Margaret Peterson Haddix   RL: 5

Simon and Schuster Books for Young Readers, 1997   IL: 7–10
Religious cults

When she is uncertain and lonely at her new school, Dorry is amazed to find herself being drawn in by dynamic students who then introduce her to Pastor Jim and
the Fishers of Men. Little by little, Dorry finds her life overtaken by the Fishers,
then amid a spiritual awakening, finds herself wanting to escape their entrapment.

Leaving Home edited by Hazel Rochman and Darlene
Z. McCampbell   RL: 7

HarperCollins, 1997   IL: 8+
Multiethnic

This is a collection of stories and excerpts from novels that deal with the journey of
leaving home and taking journeys of various types. Distinguished writers in the
collection include Sandra Cisneros, Toni Morrison, Amy Tan, and Gary Soto.

Let the Circle Be Unbroken by Mildred D. Taylor   RL: 6

Dial Press, 1981   IL: 6+
African American

This is a moving sequel to *Roll of Thunder, Hear My Cry*. The family faces more
difficulties as the Depression worsens and the children begin to grow. This is the
story of how one close-knit family survives the horrors of poverty and prejudice.

Letters from Rifka by Karen Hesse   RL: 4

Holt, 1992   IL: 5–9
Russian
Jewish

In a series of letters to her cousin, written in tiny script in the margins of her vol-
ume of Pushkin, Rifka tells of her escape from Russia with her Jewish family in
1919. Her kindness to a fellow train passenger has disastrous results, and Rifka
is left behind as her family sails to America. She surmounts many obstacles to finally reach Ellis Island, and again she is detained. Will she ever be reunited with
her family?

Letters from the Inside by **John Marsden**   RL: 7

Pan Macmillan, 1992   IL : 7+
Australian

What starts as a seemingly innocent correspondence between two girls turns into an intense, haunting story as we learn one girl fears the violence of her brother, while the other girl is writing from a juvenile prison.

Letters to Julia by **Barbara Ware Holmes**   RL: 6

HarperCollins, 1997   IL: 7+
Nontraditional family

One of her best outlets to offset the craziness of her divorced parents, Liz finds, is her writing. When she submits some of her writing to an editor named Julia, the two begin an interesting correspondence that addresses not only writing, but also issues of life and death.

The Library Card by **Jerry Spinelli**   RL: 4

Scholastic, 1997   IL: 5–9
Multiethnic

Four short stories each feature the power of libraries and how they affect the lives of four different young adults: one whose friend wants him to drop out of school; one who lives in the country; one who is addicted to television; and one who lives in a car because of his sociopathic tendencies.

Life in the Fat Lane by **Cherie Bennett**   RL: 6

Delacorte, 1998   IL: 7+
Physically challenged: weight issues

Lara Ardeche has it all: beauty, popularity, a great boyfriend, and great parents. But suddenly, despite rigorous workouts and strict dieting, Lara is gaining weight—a lot of weight—and suddenly Lara's self-perception and wonderful world fall to pieces.

Life's a Funny Proposition, Horatio by **Barbara G. Polikoff**   RL: 5.8

Holt, 1992   IL: 6–8
Grief/loss

Horatio Tuckerman is having a tough time: his father has died of cancer, his grandfather has moved in and taken Horatio's room, he hates his name, and everything seems to make him angry. What will it take to get him back on track?

The Light in the Forest by **Conrad Richter**   RL: 5

Knopf, 1953   IL: 6+
Native American

A young white boy who was kidnapped and raised by the Indians is suddenly forced to leave the only home he knows and move into the white world with his original family. He is angry and has a great deal of trouble accepting this change.

Lisa, Bright and Dark by John Neufeld   RL: 6

S.G. Phillips, 1969   IL: 7+
Mentally challenged

Three teenage friends help Lisa cope with the mental illness that her parents and her teachers refuse to acknowledge.

Little Brother by Allan Baillie   RL: 5

Viking, 1992   IL: 6–9
Cambodian

Vithy and his brother Mang escape into the jungle while being pursued by their Khmer Rouge captors. After Mang runs away from Vithy to protect him from the gunfire, Vithy finds himself alone on the long journey across Cambodia to the refugee camps in Thailand.

Living Up the Street by Gary Soto   RL: 6

Strawberry Hill Press, 1985   IL: 6+
Latino American

In this collection of prose recollections, the reader follows the life of a young Latino boy growing up in Fresno, California, in the industrial part of town. The stories ring true, as they are based on the author's life.

Lizard by Dennis Covington   RL: 5.8

Delacorte, 1991   IL: 9+
Physically challenged

He gets the nickname "Lizard" because his eyes are almost at the sides of his head, and his nose is a bit flat and sideways. He got the nickname at a school for retarded boys, even though Lizard isn't retarded. Then a man shows up claiming he's Lizard's father and asks to take Lizard. So Lizard goes, even though he's sure his father is dead. Sexually descriptive terms of male and female anatomy, and sexual insults, target this book for mature readers.

The Long Season of Rain by Helen Kim   RL: 6

Holt, 1996   IL: 7+
Korean

Junchee is not fond of the gray rainy season, nor with being cooped up with her three sisters, mother, and grandmother. This year, an orphaned boy comes to their home and many deep family concerns are stirred up by his presence.

A Long Way from Home by **Maureen Wartski**   RL: 6

Westminster Press, 1980   IL: 7–10
Vietnamese American

In this sequel to *A Boat to Nowhere*, Kien, Mai and Loc finally arrive in the United States, hosted by the family of the man who helped rescue them. But will this truly be home? As Mai and Loc settle in to this new life, Kien encounters strong prejudice, hatred, and violence, and his promise to Grandfather Van Chi becomes very hard to keep.

The Lost Years of Merlin by **T. A. Barron**   RL: 5

Philomel Books, 1996   IL: 6–10
English: Medieval

Young Emrys goes on a journey to find himself and the answers to the many questions he has about his past, his identity, and his mysterious powers in this story of the childhood of Arthur's wizard, Merlin.

Lostman's River by **Cynthia De Felice**   RL: 5.5

Maxwell Macmillan International, 1994   IL: 5–8
Native Americans: Seminoles

In 1906 Lostman's River in the Florida Everglades is a place for people to hide or do illegal acts. Ty McCauley and his family are hiding so his father won't be charged with murder. But danger comes to the swamp in the form of greed, and Ty and his family are caught in a series of frightening events for themselves and the birds of the Everglades.

Love Among the Walnuts by **Jean Ferris**   RL: 6.5

Harcourt Brace, 1998   IL: 7+
Physically/mentally challenged

In a tale that harkens back to a kinder, gentler style of storytelling, this is the story of Sandy, who has been surrounded by a quiet Utopia all his life. So when his mother and father are poisoned by his two jealous uncles, he's introduced to a different side of life—and love—among the unique and interesting residents of Walnut Manor.

Low Tide by **William Mayne**   RL: 5

Delacorte, 1993   IL: 5–7
Maori: New Zealand

When Charlie, Elizabeth, and Wiremu go out fishing one morning, they are astounded at how low the tide is. Where has the ocean gone? In a rush, their question is answered and in a once sunken ship, they ride a tsunami up to the mountains.

The Luckiest Girl in the World by Steven Levenkron   RL: 5

Scribner, 1997   IL: 7+

Mentally challenged: self-abuse

Fifteen-year-old Katie is pushed by her mother to be the best ice skater, an Olympic competitor. Her schedule is rigorous, and the pressure intense, but sometimes she finds herself spacing out, almost losing consciousness, so to focus herself, she secretly cuts herself with a pair of scissors she keeps for that purpose. When she's finally caught, will she allow therapy to help?

Lupita Mañana by Patricia Beatty   RL: 6

Morrow, 1981   IL: 6–10

Latino: Mexican

Thirteen-year-old Lupita hopes it will all be better mañana. She and her brother cross the Mexican border illegally, hoping to be able share the wealth their aunt has written about. But dodging "la migra" while working desperately hard for low wages that they must send back to their poverty-stricken family in Mexico is a grim business.

Lyddie by Katherine Paterson   RL: 6

Lodestar Books, 1991   IL: 7+

Nontraditional family

During the 1840s, Lyddie Worthen decides to leave her impoverished farm in Vermont to become a factory worker so that she may be independent. Working conditions, however, are harsh and the hours long. But Lyddie remains determined to succeed, even when factory conditions threaten the health of her and her co-workers.

M. C. Higgins, the Great by Virginia Hamilton   RL: 6

Macmillan, 1974   IL: 6–9

African American

M. C. is the oldest child in the family and is responsible for his younger brothers and sisters when his mom and dad leave the mountainside home to work in a hamlet in the valley. M. C.'s best friend is the son of a local "witch," and he has to hide his friendship from everyone. M. C. is torn between wanting to have a better life away from the hills and staying there where his roots are so deep.

The Magical Adventures of Pretty Pearl by Virginia Hamilton   RL: 6

Harper & Row, 1983   IL: 6+

African

This is a fantasy about Pretty Pearl, a god-child who lived high on a mountaintop in Africa with all the other gods. When she comes to America and sees the suffer-

ing of the black people, Pearl knows it is time to act. Here is a good story that re-
lies heavily on African legend, myth, and folklore.

Make Lemonade by Virginia E. Wolff   RL: 7

> Thorndike Press, 1993   IL: 7–10
> African American

Written in compelling blank verse, this novel is an eloquent and realistic portrayal
of an unwed teenage mother who struggles endlessly to make ends meet and get
ahead. Her champion, baby-sitter, and sometimes friend is a fourteen-year-old
girl who has very definite goals set for herself, but who also is lured by the needs
of the young mother.

Mama, I Want to Sing by Vy Higginsen with Tonya Bolden   RL: 7

> Scholastic, 1992   IL: 7–10
> African American

Set in Harlem in 1946, this is the story of Doris who loves music and singing: she
learns her love of both in her father's church, but the love grows beyond gospel
music to more worldly music, which creates a conflict between Doris and her
mother.

The Man Who Loved Clowns by J. R. Wood   RL: 5

> G.P. Putnam's Sons, 1992   IL: 5+
> Physically/mentally challenged

Punky has Down syndrome. He lives with his sister and her family. Delrita loves
her Uncle Punky but is sometimes embarrassed by his behavior and the way he
looks. This is a moving story about how Delrita comes to terms with her mixed
feelings.

The Man Who Was Poe by Avi   RL: 5.6

> Orchard Books, 1989   IL: 6–10
> Nontraditional family

A mystery set in the time of Poe, the story opens in a cold, dark garret where Edmund and his sister are nearly starving. They are waiting for their aunt, who may
have disappeared. Edmund goes out for bread and his sister, too, vanishes. Only
a strange reluctant man can help: a man named Poe.

Maniac Magee by Jerry Spinelli   RL: 6

> Little, Brown, 1990   IL: 5–10
> Nontraditional family
> Grief/loss

When Jeffrey Magee's parents die in a trolley accident, Jeffrey is sent to live with
his aunt and uncle who stop speaking to each other. Jeffrey runs away and runs
into the lives of many others in a town divided by color. Jeffrey crosses those
lines and helps to break them down in a wonderful story.

Mara, Daughter of the Nile by **Eloise Jarvis McGraw**   RL: 7

Puffin Books, 1985   IL: 6–9
African

Mara is a seventeen-year-old slave girl who grows up during the reign of Hatshep-
sut about 1550 B.C. Mara gets caught in a web of intrigue surrounding the
pharaoh and those who would be pharaoh.

Marisol and Magdalena: The Sound of Our Sisterhood
by **Veronica Chamber**   RL: 6.7

Jump at the Sun, 1998   IL: 7–9
Panamanian-American

Best friends Marisol and Magdalena are both American-born, but their families and
community are rich in Panamanian culture and want the two girls to understand
their heritage better. The summer before eighth grade, Marisol's mother decides
to send her to Panama for a year to live with her grandmother. What will the year
mean for Marisol?

Marked by Fire by **Joyce Carol Thomas**   RL: 6.5

Avon Books, 1982   IL: 7+
African American

This novel traces the first twenty years of the life of Absynnia Jackson who is born
in the cotton fields of Oklahoma in 1951. Her friend and teacher, Mother Barker,
tells her, "Daughter, you're destined to unbearable pain and unspeakable joy," and
we are shown times of both for Abby in this moving and lyrically written story.

The Master Puppeteer by **Katherine Paterson**   RL: 6

Crowell, 1975   IL: 6–9
Japanese

This short novel is set in ancient Japan when the land was ruled by warlords. During a time of terrible drought, many villagers are going hungry. One young boy
apprentices himself to the local puppeteering troop so that he won't be a burden
to his family. There he learns some difficult lessons about life.

Matilda Bone by **Karen Cushman**   RL: 5

Clarion Books, 2000   IL: 6–8
English: Medieval

Fourteen-year-old Matilda has always lived in the manor house. After her mother runs off and her father dies, she is raised by the manor priest, a pious, closed-minded man. When he is called to London, Matilda is left to serve the bone-setter in a nearby village. Matilda is horrified at the prospect, as she has always thought she would be better suited to life in a convent or martyrdom. As we follow Matilda's adjustment to her new life, we learn a great deal about medicine in the Middle Ages.

May I Cross Your Golden River? by Paige Dixon   RL: 7

    Atheneum, 1975   IL: 7+
    Grief/loss
    Physically challenged: Lou Gehrig's disease
Eighteen-year-old Jordan has a busy, wonderful life with plans for law school, a lovely girlfriend, and a wonderful family. Everything crashes around him when he is diagnosed with Lou Gehrig's disease, and there is much he has to cope with. What's harder—watching the people you love trying to cope with the fact that you are dying, or coping with the fact yourself?

The Maze by Will Hobbs   RL: 5.5

    Morrow Junior Books, 1998   IL: 6–9
    Nontraditional family
Rich Walker is fourteen when he lands in a tough juvenile center. When the opportunity comes, he runs away and ends up in a remote part of Utah where he meets Lon, who is working on a project to help endangered condors in the area. Here Rich finds good and bad experiences that help him learn who he really is.

Melitte by Fatima Shaik   RL: 6

    Dial Books for Young Readers, 1997   IL: 5–8
    African American
    French American
It is 1772 in the Louisiana Territory, and the French King has just given the territory to his Spanish cousin. Melitte is barely tall enough to reach the top of the table in the mean cabin she shares with Monsieur and Madame, but she is beginning to understand what it means to be a slave and not know any kind of love. This story is filled with historical information about this time period; it is revealed through the growth and change that takes place in Melitte's life.

Memoirs of a Bookbat by Katherine Lasky   RL: 6

    Harcourt Brace, 1994   IL: 7+
    Nontraditional family

Fourteen-year-old Harper is an avid reader of fantasy. But she must hide what she
reads from her ardently fundamentalist parents. They begin to travel around the
country to combat "bad books," and Harper realizes their promotion of censorship threatens her freedom and her choices.

Mick Harte Was Here! by **Barbara Park**   RL: 4

> Knopf: Distributed by Random House, 1995   IL: 5–8
> Grief/loss

How can someone as lively as Mick be dead? Thirteen-year-old Phoebe tries to
make sense of her brother's death by telling the story of his life after he dies in a
bicycle accident.

The Midwife's Apprentice by **Karen Cushman**   RL: 5

> Clarion Books, 1995   IL: 7+
> English: Medieval

In medieval England, a girl without a name or home is taken out of a dungheap into
the home of a sharp-tempered midwife. In spite of obstacles, the girl finds a name
and three things she wants most in life: a full belly, a contented heart, and a place
in the world.

Mind's Eye by **Paul Fleischman**   RL: 7

> Henry Holt, 1999   IL: 7+
> Physically challenged

This short novel is written in play form and tells the story of Courtney who has
been placed in a care facility in North Dakota after an accident on her horse
has left her paralyzed. Her roommate is an older blind woman, a former English teacher, who requests that Courtney take them on a journey to Italy with
a 1910 travel guide and her imagination. But the journey takes unexpected
turns for both.

Miracle's Boys by **Jacqueline Woodson**   RL: 5.5

> G.P. Putnam's Sons, 2000   IL: 5+
> Grief/loss
> Puerto Rican American

Brother to brother: that's how it is now that Lafayette's parents are both dead. His
older brother has had to set aside college plans to be the breadwinner, while his
middle brother Charlie has anger and hatred swirling in and around him. What
can Lafayette do to deal with his terrible grief for his mother, and to help his
brothers so that the three will be a loving family again?

Missing May by **Cynthia Rylant**   RL: 6

Orchard Books, 1992   IL: 5–9
Grief/loss

When May dies, her husband Ob is lost, so he and Summer spend time and energy trying to find a sign or word from May. Summer's friend, Cletus, is the one who directs them to a "Small Medium at Large" to help them on their quest.

Missing Pieces by **Norma Fox Mazer**   RL: 6

Morrow Junior Books, 1995   IL: 7–9
Nontraditional family

Jessie is fourteen when she starts wondering a lot about her father who walked out one day, never to return. Why did he leave? What was he like? Why didn't he care about her?

Monster by **Walter Dean Myers**   RL: 7

HarperCollins, 1999   IL : 7+
African American

As he goes on trial for murder, sixteen-year-old Steve decides to try to look at what's going on from a moviemaker's point of view. In his notebook he records his observations by writing a script of the trial, trying to understand what has happened, and trying to get some perspective on how people look at him—especially the prosecutor who points at him and calls him "Monster."

The Moon Bridge by **Marcia Savin**   RL: 5

Scholastic, 1992   IL: 5–7
Japanese American

Set during World War II, this is the story of Ruthie and her new best friend, Mitzi, who is Japanese American and suffers abuse at school from students and even one teacher. When Mitzi and her family are relocated, Ruthie is sad and confused. A letter she sends to Mitzi is returned to her, but she continues to write, saving the letters for Mitzi's return.

Moon Dancer by **Margaret Rostkowski**   RL: 6

Browndeer Press/ Harcourt Brace & Co., 1995   IL: 7–9
Nontraditional family
Native American

Miranda sets out on a backpacking trip with her sister, her cousin Emily, and Emily's friend Max. Emily wants to find pictographs recorded by a woman who visited Anasazi or Hisatsinon settlements many years before. Miranda finds strong connections to the place and to the women who had been there before her on this journey of self discovery.

Morning Girl by Michael Dorris   RL: 5

Hyperion Books for Children, 1992   IL: 5–8
Caribbean

A short, simple story set in 1492, this depicts the lives of Taino islanders in the Bahamas. In alternate chapters we see the lives of these people from the perspective of Morning Girl and her brother Star Boy. Their island lives are simple until one day Morning Girl sees a canoe full of strangers approaching.

Morning Is a Long Time Coming by Bette Greene   RL: 6

Dial Press, 1978   IL: 7+
Jewish

In this sequel to *Summer of My German Soldier,* Patty Bergen is graduating from high school and still dreaming of going to find Anton's mother in Germany. She takes her trip abroad despite threats from her family, and finds many things she had not anticipated, including love.

Motown and Didi by Walter Dean Myers   RL: 6

Viking Kestrel, 1984   IL: 7+
African American

Didi is trying to work hard enough to get into a college far away from Harlem. Motown is working to end his homeless status. They are shoved together when Didi tries to save her brother from the drug pushers who have him hooked. Their friendship has to overcome differences in values and troubles with the drug lords in the neighborhood.

The Moved-Outers by Florence Crannell Means   RL: 6

Houghton Mifflin, 1945   IL: 6–10
Japanese American

After the Japanese bomb Pearl Harbor in 1941, life changes drastically for eighteen-year-old Sumiko Ohara and her family as they are sent from their comfortable home in California to a series of relocation camps.

The Moves Make the Man by Bruce Brooks   RL: 6

HarperCollins, 1984   IL: 6–8
African American

It is the early '60s, and Jerome is more concerned about playing basketball than with being the only black kid at an all-white school. Jerome is smart and observant, and when he notices a white kid named Bix who is a flawless baseball short-stop, he becomes curious as to why he acts so strangely. As he tells Bix's story, Jerome tells his own as well.

Music from a Place Called Half Moon by **Jerrie Oughton**   RL: 6

Houghton Mifflin, 1995   IL: 6–9
Native American

Edie Jo is thirteen in the spring of 1956 in the town of Half Moon, North Carolina. Edie Jo tells of that spring and summer, when her grandmother's home is de-stroyed by arson, when her father creates mayhem by proposing that *all* children, including Indians, be included in church camp, and when she learns that the boy Cherokee Fish can make beautiful music.

Music of Dolphins by **Karen Hesse**   RL: 5

Scholastic, 1996   IL: 5–9
Physically/mentally challenged

Mila, who has been raised by dolphins from the age of four, is "rescued" off the coast of Florida and taken to a place for scientific study. Becoming human again is aston-ishing for Mila, but becomes too hard when so many boundaries are imposed on her.

My Brother Has AIDS by **Deborah Davis**   RL: 6

Maxwell Macmillan International, 1994   IL: 6–9
Physically challenged: AIDS
Gay/lesbian

Lacy is a swimmer, and her goals for this season are high. Then she learns her older brother, who is gay, has full-blown AIDS and is coming home to die. Friends, family, teachers, and her coach all react very differently, and when Lacy has to do a report in her health class, she decides to do it on AIDS. This well-told story has a believable protagonist and is realistically written.

My Brother, My Sister, and I by **Yoko Kawashima Watkins**   RL: 6

Maxwell Macmillan International, 1994   IL: 6–10
Japanese

In this sequel to *So Far from the Bamboo Grove,* Yoko continues to tell of the strug-gle of her much diminished family at the end of World War II. Through harsh, horrible circumstances, Yoko and her brother and sister try to locate their father and keep faith that things will get better.

My Louisiana Sky by **Kimberly Holt**   RL: 5

Holt, 1998   IL: 5–7
Mentally challenged

Tiger Ann is a smart twelve-year-old, but her parents are both mentally slow. Growing up in the 1950s in a small town in Louisiana, Tiger struggles with many problems, including her parents, the teasing of school mates, her best friend, Jesse, and her taciturn grandmother in this beautifully written coming-of-age story.

My Posse Don't Do Homework by Lou Anne Johnson   RL: 7

St. Martin's Press, 1992   IL: 7+
Multiethnic

Coming to the screen as *Dangerous Minds,* this is the inspiring, true story of a Marine-turned-teacher who struggles with the troubled students she comes to care for deeply in an inner-city school.

Name Me Nobody by Lois-Ann Yamanaka   RL: 7

Hyperion Books, 1999   IL: 8+
Gay/lesbian
Physically challenged: eating disorders

Emi-Lou is thirteen. She lives with her grandmother and resents her mother who left her to live in California. She's not sure who her father is, and she often feels like a nobody because she's overweight. But she can always depend on her very best friend, Von, and follows her even into situations that make her uncomfortable, like the women's softball team they join. When Von seems to be having a relationship with another woman on the team, Emi-Lou is hurt and confused.

Necessary Roughness by Marie G. Lee   RL: 7

HarperCollins, 1996   IL: 7–10
Korean American

Chan Kim was always popular, and now he was a soccer star. He was looking forward to the upcoming season with his team until his father's brother gets into some business trouble and the family has to move to a small town in Minnesota where there is no soccer team and where they are the only Korean family in the area. Chan has to learn how to fit in to this new environment and it is not always easy.

Net Bandits by Michael Coleman   RL: 4

Bantam Skylark, 1997   IL: 4–7
Physically challenged

Tamsyn Smith isn't sure about computers: all she knows is that her friend Josh spends too much time on them. But when the school's computers are hooked to the Internet, she and Josh volunteer to study the pros and cons of the Internet and end up in contact with someone who sends them a strange call for help.

Never Trust a Dead Man by Vivian Vande Velde   RL: 6

Harcourt Brace, 1999   IL: 7+
English: Medieval

Selwyn has little time to do anything when the people in his village come after him
for the murder of Farold; his protests of innocence are ignored, and his sentence
is to be sealed in the burial cave with his victim. Elswyth, the witch, who is looking for ingredients for a powerful charm stumbles upon him there and, in exchange for years of service, agrees to help him try to discover the real murderer.

Night by Elie Wiesel   RL: 7

Hill and Wang, 1960   IL: 8+
Jewish

This is a powerful true account of Wiesel's experiences between 1943 and 1945, beginning when he and his family are sure they will not be bothered, and Elie's life
is centered around his faith. But soon they, too, are herded into a ghetto, then onto
cattle cars, and on to concentration camps where Wiesel watches the destruction
of life and his own faith.

Night Hoops by Carl Deuker   RL: 6

Houghton Mifflin, 2000   IL: 7–10
Grief/loss
Nontraditional family

Nick wants to focus on basketball instead of the troubles around him. Troubles include his father leaving his mother, his neighbor Trent who has criminal tendencies, and his grades, which seem to be slipping. When his coach asks him to keep
an eye on Trent, Nick is hesitant to get involved in Trent's life, but also wants to
do what's best for the team.

Night Journeys by Avi   RL: 5

Pantheon Books, 1979   IL: 5–8
Quaker
Nontraditional family

Peter York is twelve when he goes to live with the Shinns, a Quaker family in Pennsylvania. Mr. Shinn is a Justice of the Peace. When Peter and Mr. Shinn join a
party to hunt for two runaway indentured servants, both learn something about
life and values.

The Night the White Deer Died by Gary Paulsen   RL: 6

T. Nelson, 1978   IL: 6+
Native American

Janet and her mother move to a small New Mexico town where she is one of the few Anglo teens. Janet befriends an older alcoholic man she meets in the town plaza. This encounter changes Janet's life forever.

Nightfather by Carl Friedman   RL: 5.5

> Persea Books, 1994   IL: 8+
> Dutch

In this compelling tale translated from Dutch, a young daughter of a Holocaust survivor listens in fascination and fear as her father recounts endless stories about his nightmarish experiences in camp. Her father paces the floor at night and feels compelled to talk more and more as his three children struggle to understand his past and his pain.

Nightjohn by Gary Paulsen   RL: 6

> Delacorte, 1993   IL: 5–10
> African American

Told in a deceptively calm, simple style, this is a story of slaves on a plantation. The storyteller is a young girl who matter-of-factly relates the horrors and inhumane treatment of those around her as well as the arrival of John, a slave who wants to teach other slaves to read. The story is short, graphic, compelling, yet hopeful.

No Big Deal by Ellen Jaffe-Gill   RL: 6

> Lodestar Books, 1994   IL: 7- 10
> Gay/lesbian

Janice's favorite ninth-grade teacher is Mr. P. He's a great social studies teacher, and she looks forward to his class every day. She also struggles with being teased about her size (large), and argues with her overprotective mother. When Mr. P. is attacked for being gay, she doesn't hesitate for a minute to defend him and his right to teach.

No Easy Answers: Short Stories About Teenagers Making Tough Choices edited by Donald Gallo   RL: 6.5

> Delacorte, 1997   IL: 7+
> Multiethnic

When two boys find out that one of their favorite teachers has been spotted skinny dipping at a lake late at night, they decide to sneak out to snap her picture. The picture reveals her jumping into the arms of another woman: so now what do they do with the photo? This is just one of sixteen short stories dealing with teens making choices about doing the right thing by some of the best of today's young adult writers including Walter Dean Myers, M. E. Kerr, and Rita Williams-Garcia.

Number the Stars by **Lois Lowry**   RL: 5

Houghton Mifflin, 1989   IL: 5–8
Dutch

What does it mean to be brave? Annemarie is well aware of the Nazi soldiers who
stand on every street corner in Denmark. To her they are frightening, but to her
Jewish friend Ellen, they hold a much deeper threat. How far is Annemarie willing to go to help her friend?

One Bird by **Kyoko Mori**   RL: 6

Henry Holt, 1995   IL: 7+
Japanese

Megumi is fifteen when her mother leaves: she says she must leave to survive.
Megumi's father says she may not see her mother for seven years, and Megumi
searches for a source of hope, which she finds in the person of Dr. Mizutani, a
young vet who teaches Meg much about birds, life, and hope.

One Fat Summer by **Robert Lipsyte**   RL: 6

Harper & Row, 1977   IL: 7–9
Physically challenged: weight issues

It is summer in 1952: an enjoyable time of year unless you weigh more than 200
pounds and are fourteen years old. It was a time for shorts and swimsuits for other
people, but not for Robert Marks. But when his father hounds him into getting a
job, he begins working at a tough job for low wages, then runs into trouble when
another boy thinks the job should be his instead. The summer turns into one of
lessons about people, appearances, and life.

One More River by **Lynne Reid Banks**   RL: 6

Morrow Junior Books, 1992   IL: 6–10
Israeli

Lesley has it all—she's rich, she's popular, she's beautiful, and she loves her life in
Canada. Suddenly her parents announce they're moving to Israel, and Lesley's
life is turned upside-down. A new language and a new way of life are only part
of what she faces: she is also witness to the Six Day War and learns about new
cultures and life in a kibbutz.

Only Twice I've Wished for Heaven by **Dawn Turner Trice**   RL: 7

Crown, 1996   IL: 6–9
African American

Tempest and her parents are chosen to move into well-manicured Lakeland, a planned
community carved out of the center of a Chicago ghetto. Tempest, desperate to get

away from the snooty kids in her new school, finds a way through the fence into the colorful neighborhood of 35th Street. There she makes new friends, and learns that life is not always the way it's planned to be.

The Other Shepards by Adele Griffin   RL: 6

Hyperion Books for Children, 1998   IL: 6–9
Grief/ loss
Holland and Geneva have grown up with stories about the "other Shepards," their two brothers and sister who died in an accident before they were born. The memories of the others seems to overshadow the living sisters until one day, Annie comes into their lives.

Out of Control by Norma Fox Mazer   RL: 6

Morrow Junior Books, 1993   IL: 7+
Nontraditional family
Sexual harassment
This is a realistic story told from the viewpoints of several people, including the victim of harassment, and those who harassed her. It starts with unkind remarks and jostling in the high school halls, but then escalates into an incident that is truly out of control. A timely look at a topic that needs to be addressed in our schools.

Out of Nowhere by Ouida Sebestyen   RL: 6

Orchard Books, 1994   IL: 6–9
Nontraditional family
On the same evening, in the middle of the Arizona desert, two beings get cast off. One is a dog, who tries racing after the truck that left him. The other is a boy named Harley, whose mom rides off with yet another new man in his BMW. Harley and the dog find each other, and maybe a new place to belong to as well with May, who is feeling abandoned; with Bill, a collector of everything; and with a girl named Singer. What can this group of misfits offer each other?

Out of the Dust by Karen Hesse   RL: 7

Scholastic, 1997   IL: 7+
Grief/loss
Billie Jo is fourteen, and life in Oklahoma in the Dust Bowl years are hard at any rate, but when tragedy strikes her family, life seems too hard to bear. Told in a series of free-verse poems, Billie Jo's story brings life in the Dust Bowl into such sharp focus that readers will feel the dust.

Over the Water by Maude Casey

RL: 6

Holt, 1994   IL: 7–9
Irish

This is a story of three generations of Irish women, told through the eyes of
fourteen-year-old Mary as she and her family go to visit her grandmother for the
summer. There is tension between Mary and her mother, and all are missing her
beloved grandfather in this summer of growth and understanding.

P.S. Longer Letter Later by Paula Danziger and Ann M. Martin

RL: 5

Scholastic, 1998   IL: 5–7
Nontraditional family

Elizabeth and Tara*Starr can't believe they now live states away from each other,
but are determined to continue being best friends through letters. During their
seventh-grade year as they correspond, each faces new challenges as Elizabeth's
stable family skids and Tara*Starr's young parents become more stable.

Pacific Crossing by Gary Soto

RL: 5

Harcourt Brace Jovanovich, 1992   IL: 6–9
Latino American
Japanese

The protagonists of *Taking Sides,* Lincoln and Tony, continue their adventures, this
time as exchange students for the summer to Japan. As they spend the summer
with two families, both boys learn about themselves as well about life in Japan.

Painting the Black by Carl Deuker

RL: 6

Houghton Mifflin, 1997   IL: 7+
Sexual harassment

Ryan watches with interest when a family moves in across the street from his own home
in Seattle. Seventeen-year-old Josh is a serious pitcher who decides Ryan needs to be
his catcher, even though Ryan has been away from baseball for years. The duo works
well together, but tensions creep in when Josh harasses a girl at school.

Parrot in the Oven: Mi Vida by Victor Martinez

RL: 6

HarperCollins, 1996   IL: 7+
Latino American
Living with abuse

Manny Hernandez lives in a hard world: while his mother scrubs their house in the
projects in California, his father drinks at the pool hall. This lyrically told tale
takes us through a year of challenges, discoveries, sadness, and tension.

Peeling the Onion by **Wendy Orr**   RL: 6

Holiday House, 1997   IL: 7+
Physically challenged
Australian

The day Anna wins a karate championship is one of the best and worst days of her
life. On the way home with the young man she likes, her neck is broken in a car
crash. Told in first person, this is a powerful narrative of despair, hope, devasta-
tion, recovery, and love.

Petey by **Ben Mikaelsen**   RL: 6

Hyperion Books for Children, 1998   IL: 6+
Physically challenged: cerebral palsy

Petey was born in 1920 with cerebral palsy, but that condition was not understood
then, so at age two he is put into Warm Springs Insane Asylum where he spends
the next fifty-six years lonely and misunderstood. When he is transferred to a
nursing home in Bozeman, his path crosses a teenage boy's, and a unique and
wonderful friendship is born.

Philip Hall Likes Me, I Reckon, Maybe by **Bette Greene**   RL: 5

Dial Press, 1974   IL: 5–7
African American

Beth Lambert is the smartest student in her school, but nobody knows it. Beth is
in love with the second smartest student and always lets him win. This is
a funny story about a year in the lives of two eleven-year-olds in the rural
South.

Phoenix Rising by **Karen Hesse**   RL: 6

Holt, 1994   IL: 5–9
Nontraditional family
Grief/loss

Nyle Sumner is in the eighth grade. She's an orphan living with her grandmother on
a Vermont sheep farm. It's a life she's happy with, except she doesn't want to
watch anyone else die after losing her mom, then her grandfather. But a nuclear
plant explosion nearby changes many things in Nyle's life. Although the radiation is drifting away from her farm, two victims from the accident have come to
live with them—or will it be to die with them?

Picking Up the Pieces by **Patricia Calvert**   RL: 6

Maxwell Macmillan International, 1993   IL: 6–10
Physically challenged

Megan's life has been terribly changed—she'll never be able to score the winning basket again for her team. In fact, she will be in a wheelchair for the rest of her life. Accepting this is hard for Megan: almost as hard as realizing that there are others who face difficult situations, too, like her new friend, Harris.

Pickle Song by Barthe DeClements   RL: 6

Viking, 1993   IL: 6–9
Nontraditional family

Sukey and her mom have hit some hard luck and now they are living out of their car in a small town in the Pacific Northwest. Paula, a local girl, tries to befriend Sukey when she sees her at school. Sukey does not want to reveal how she is living. Paula perseveres and the girls learn a lot about life from each other.

A Picture of Freedom: The Diary of Clotee, a Slave Girl by Patricia C. McKissack   RL: 5

Scholastic, 1997   IL: 5–8
African American

The year is 1859 and the country is on the verge of great changes. Twelve-year-old Clotee is a house slave who has secretly taught herself to read and write. On any scrap of paper she can find, she records in her journal the daily life of the plantation. One day, she discovers the word *freedom* and her life takes on new meaning.

Pinballs by Betsy Byars   RL: 4.5

Harper & Row, 1977   IL: 4–7
Grief/loss
Nontraditional families: foster children

Carlie says what she thinks—and she thinks that she and two boys in a new foster home are like pinballs that are bounced from place to place but have no control of their own. Learning to care for others, however, changes the way Carlie, Harvey, and Thomas T. see things.

The Pirate's Son by Geraldine McCaughrean   RL: 6.5

Scholastic, 1998   IL: 7–10
Nontraditional family

The year is 1717 and Nathan Gull is at a boarding school—along with Tamo White, who is the son of a real pirate—when his father dies penniless. Summarily tossed out of the school, he is rescued by Tamo who takes him and his sister on the boat of one of his guardians to Madagascar, where the three find the unexpected and a totally new life.

The Place of Lions by Eric Campbell   RL: 6

Harcourt Brace Jovanovich, 1991   IL: 6–9
African: Tanzanian

The Serengeti Plain comes alive with sights, sounds, and struggles in this story of
Chris, who with his father, is setting out for a new life in Tanzania. When the
small plane they are in crashes, Chris faces a life-and-death struggle among a
pride of lions, some poachers, and a hunter.

Places I Never Meant to Be edited by Judy Blume   RL: 7

Simon and Schuster Books for Young Readers, 1999   IL: 7+
Multiethnic

This is a strong collection of short stories by some of the top writers of young adult
literature, including Jacqueline Woodson, Walter Dean Myers, and Katherine Paterson. They have all also had encounters with censorship. While the stories
themselves are an interesting collection, the afterwords they write about censorship are more powerful.

Plain City by Virginia Hamilton   RL: 7

Blue Sky Press, 1993   IL: 7–10
African American

Buhlaire Sims comes alive as she tells her story of life in Plain City. Where is the
father she'd thought for so long was dead? Why are the other members of her
family so reluctant to talk about him?

Prank by Kathryn Lasky   RL: 6

Macmillan, 1984   IL: 8+
Living with abuse

Birdie would like to get away from her family: the yelling, hitting, and troubles
are too much. Her brother is arrested for defacing a synagogue, and her sister's
husband beats her. Where are the answers to Birdie's questions about life and
happiness?

Probably Still Nick Swansen by Virginia Euwer Wolff   RL: 6

Holt, 1988   IL: 6–10
Mentally challenged

The most important aspect of this novel is the strong voice in which it is told: the
voice of high school junior Nick Swansen, a special education student who describes what he sees, feels, and hears. This is a moving story that we all need to
listen to.

Prophecy Rock by Rob MacGregor   RL: 6

Simon and Schuster Books for Young Readers, 1995   IL: 7+
Native American: Hopi

Will Lansa is visiting his father for the summer on the Hopi reservation where his
father is a tribal police officer. Will works at a hospital, where he meets Ellie, is
involved in a mystery, and learns much of his Hopi heritage.

A Proud Taste for Scarlet and Miniver by E. L. Konigsburg   RL: 6.7

Atheneum, 1973   IL: 6–10
English: Medieval

This story opens in heaven, as Eleanor of Aquitaine waits impatiently to see if her
husband Henry II will be joining her. As she waits, Eleanor and her companions
remember stories of their outrageous days on earth. This is a delightful, joyous,
and well-researched romp through history.

Radiance Descending by Paula Fox   RL: 4

DK InK, 1997   IL: 5–8
Physically/mentally challenged: Down syndrome

Twelve-year-old Paul has worked hard for the past seven years to ignore his
younger brother, Jacob. Jacob has Down syndrome, and while others find him be-
guiling, Paul finds him embarrassing and annoying. What would it take to make
Paul think otherwise? This is a beautifully written story.

The Rain Catchers by Jean Thesman   RL: 5

Houghton Mifflin, 1991   IL: 6–9
Nontraditional family
Grief/loss

Every story has a beginning, a middle, and an end. At least that's how the stories are
that are served with tea and lemonade at 4 p.m. each day at grandmother's house.
An extended family of women and friends, they wait for the honeysuckle rain, for
love, for the death of a loved one, and for an ending of a story of Grayling's childhood, a story that has always puzzled her.

Rainy Season by Adele Griffin   RL: 5

Houghton Mifflin, 1996   IL: 7–9
Panamanian

Lane worries. She worries when someone comes home late, when her brother Charlie acts weird—which is often—and just worries. Living on a base in Panama
near the canal in 1977 is worrisome, too, as talk is rampant about giving the canal
back to the Panamanians.

The Ramsay Scallop by Frances Temple   RL: 5.6

Orchard Books, 1994   IL: 6-10
English: Medieval

Elenor is fourteen, and her betrothed, Thomas, is returning from the Crusades a dis-
illusioned man. Father Gregory sends the two on a long pilgrimage to Spain. The
sights, sounds, people, and stories are a rich backdrop to the story of Elenor and
Thomas.

Rats Saw God by Rob Thomas   RL: 6

Simon and Schuster Books for Young Readers, 1996   IL: 8+
Nontraditional family

Steve is eighteen and living in San Diego. He won't graduate, despite being a National Merit Finalist, because he's one credit short in English: unless he does
what his counselor asks and writes a one-hundred-page paper. So Steve decides
to write about what he knows best, himself, telling of his journey from a promis-
ing student to a troubled teen.

Red Sails to Capri by Ann Weil   RL: 5

Puffin Books, 1988   IL: 5–9
Italian

Michele works for his parents in their inn on the Isle of Capri. Three visitors come
to stay at the inn and go in search of adventure. The adventure they decide on
could cause much trouble for Michele's family. In the end, the search leads them
to a discovery that changes Capri forever.

Red Scarf Girl: A Memoir of the Cultural Revolution by Ji-Li Jiang   RL: 5

HarperCollins, 1997   IL: 6+
Chinese

This is a true account of one family's struggle to survive China's Cultural Revolution. As a twelve-year-old, Ji-Li is faced with challenges, persecution, and many
hard choices including having to decide whether to renounce her family or sacrifice a future with the Party.

Rescue Josh McGuire by Ben Mikaelsen   RL: 5.5

Hyperion, 1993   IL: 6–8
Living with abuse

Since the death of Josh's older brother, Josh's dad has been a different man: he
drinks too much, seems angry all the time, and has even hit Josh. When Josh and
his dad go hunting, Josh's dad kills a mother bear, orphaning her cub. Josh de-

cides it's up to him to rescue the cub, but doing so unleashes a chain of events that spiral into danger for Josh, the cub, and many others.

The Return by Sonia Levitin   RL: 6

Atheneum, 1987   IL: 6+
African: Ethiopian

During the terrible drought in Ethiopia, tens of thousands of Ethiopians left their country to live in refugee camps where they could get food from relief agencies. The Ethiopian Jews were not welcomed in these camps. This is the story about two young Ethiopian Jews who leave their homes to go to Israel.

Ribbons by Laurence Yep   RL: 5

G. P. Putnam's Sons, 1996   IL: 5–7
Chinese American

Ballet means everything to Robin, but no one seems to care—everyone is so involved with bringing Robin's grandmother over from Hong Kong to the United States! Money is tight, and even when grandmother arrives, things seem to get only harder. Who cares about Robin's ballet except Robin?

Rice without Rain by Minfong Ho   RL: 6

Lothrop, Lee & Shepard Books, 1990   IL: 7–10
Thai

In the highlands of Thailand, the drought has been long. The landlords have demanded high rents. And the university students have been fighting for the rights of the peasants. Some of these students come to Jinda's village to spend the summer and learn how Jinda's people live. The strangers bring both positive and tragic changes to the village and change Jinda's life forever.

Righteous Revenge of Artemis Bonner by Walter Dean Myers   RL: 5

HarperCollins, 1992   IL: 5–8
African American

In May 1880, fifteen-year-old Artemis Bonner is living in New York City when he and his mother receive a letter from his aunt Mary in Tombstone, Arizona, saying that her husband Ned has been gunned down in the streets. Aunt Mary names a "no-good card cheat rat . . . named Catfish Grimes" as the killer and asks that Artemis come to avenge his uncle's death. This is Artemis's account of the Wild West chase that ensues.

Rio Grande Stories by Carolyn Meyer   RL: 6

Harcourt Brace, 1994   IL: 6–8
Multiethnic

At Rio Grande Middle School in Albuquerque, New Mexico, a unique group of students come up with an idea for a fund-raiser: each will tell a story about something important from their heritage, and those stories will be a book. From recipes to heroes, tradition to family tales, each is unique, and the project is a learning experience for the entire class.

River Thunder by Will Hobbs   RL: 6

> Delacorte, 1997   IL: 7+
> Nontraditional family

In this taut sequel to *Downriver,* Jessie and Star go back to the Colorado River to reunite with their "Hoods in the Woods" rafting companions and float legally down the river. But the river is running at an all-time high, and Troy has ulterior motives for bringing them all together again.

The Road Home by Ellen Emerson White   RL: 7

> Scholastic, 1995   IL: 9+
> Physically/mentally challenged

Rebecca Phillips goes to Vietnam for a lot of wrong reasons. As a nurse she is assigned to triage and sees the worst of the war from all angles. The only positive is Michael, but when he is wounded and loses both his legs, he seems to lose interest in Rebecca, too. Returning home, she is desperately at a loss, and finally decides she needs to find Michael. There are mature themes running throughout the story.

Roll of Thunder, Hear My Cry by Mildred Taylor   RL: 8

> Dial Press, 1976   IL: 7–10
> African American

Set in the South in the 1930s, this is the story of Cassie and her family who struggle to maintain their pride and their independence against hard times and racial inequalities. Why do only the white children get to ride the bus? Why must they use only cast-off books at school? Must Cassie endure being knocked to the ground for not letting a white girl pass her? And will the family escape the terrors of the Nightriders?

Ruby in the Smoke by Philip Pullman   RL: 6.7

> Knopf: Distributed by Random House, 1985   IL: 7+
> English: Victorian

Sally Lockhart finds herself in the middle of an intrigue that deals with the death of her father and a cryptic message that he left behind: "Beware the Seven Blessings." Sally finds herself on a terrifying journey through the dark side of life in Victorian England aided by a young photographer, his sister, and their assistant.

Rules of the Road by **Joan Bauer**   RL: 6

Putnam, 1998   IL: 7–10
Physically challenged: alcoholism

Jenna is sixteen: she is working at a job she loves, selling shoes, and saving money
for a car. She lives with her mom and sister and tries to avoid contact with her alcoholic father. When the owner of the shoe-store chain asks Jenna to drive her
from Chicago to Texas, Jenna embarks on a journey that is much more than she
anticipated.

Running Loose by **Chris Crutcher**   RL: 5.5

Greenwillow Books, 1983   IL: 8+
Grief/loss

In Trout, Idaho, Louis Banks is in great shape for football and in a happy daze that
Becky Sanders has chosen him as the object of her love. In a small town, however, everyone knows everyone else's business, so when Louis commits some
outrageous acts, the whole town judges him while he simply tries to survive the
upheavals of life. This story includes mature themes.

Running Out of Time by **Margaret P. Haddix**   RL: 5

Simon and Schuster Books for Young Readers, 1995   IL: 6–8
Physically challenged

Jesse lives in Clifton, Indiana, in 1840—or so she believes. When an outbreak of
diphtheria creates a crisis in her town, Jesse's mother reveals that it is really 1996,
that the town is a "tourist attraction," and that she must smuggle Jesse out of the
compound to get the medicine they need to save lives.

SOS Titanic by **Eve Bunting**   RL: 6

Harcourt Brace, 1996   IL: 6–8
Irish

The story of the voyage of the Titanic is entwined here with the story of Barry
O'Neill who is leaving Ireland to go live in Brooklyn with his parents, but he is
terribly sad to leave Ireland. The presence of his archenemies, the Flynns, on the
boat, makes Barry think about many aspects of life, as does his cabin steward
Watley.

Sadako and the Thousand Paper Cranes by **Eleanor Coerr**   RL: 5

Putnam, 1977   IL: 3–8
Japanese

Beautiful, moving, and simply told, this book is probably too brief for novel circles,
but excellent as a read-aloud or supplementary book. A young Japanese girl who

loves to run suddenly collapses and is diagnosed with "bomb-disease" (leukemia). Her friends start folding paper cranes so that she will not die.

Safe at Second by Scott Johnson   RL: 6

Philomel Books, 1999   IL: 6+
Physically challenged

Todd Bannister's desk overflows with letters from colleges and major league scouts: he and his fastball are destined for great things, and his best friend Paulie watches it all in awe. But when a line drive smacks Todd in the face, everything changes, and Paulie wonders how he can help Todd now.

Samir and Yonatan by Daniella Carmi, translated by
Yael Lotan   RL: 6

Arthur Levine Books, 2000   IL: 6–9
Israeli, Palestinian

Samir, a young man from the West Bank, lies uneasily in a Jewish hospital in Israel amid four other young people, as he awaits an operation on his shattered knee. He is amazed that he is fed three wonderful meals a day, but he worries about why he is alive when his younger brother has been shot dead, and wonders if his family will ever truly recover. He also wonders about the other children on the ward, especially Yonatan, who reads about the stars and invites him on a journey to Mars where no one worries about differences.

Sammy Keyes and the Skeleton Man by Wendy VanDraanen   RL: 5

Knopf: Distributed by Random House, 1998   IL: 4–7
Nontraditional family

Seventh-grade sleuth Sammy Keyes already has her hands full with trying to live undetected at her grandmother's home (where children aren't allowed) and trying to fend off verbal assaults from Heather at school, when she stumbles onto a mystery at Bush House on Halloween night. Someone has tied up Chauncy LeBard and stolen from him, so Sammy is determined to unravel the mystery. This is part of a strong series featuring Sammy who is a spunky, delightful heroine.

Sang Spell by Phyllis Reynolds Naylor   RL: 6

Atheneum Books for Young Readers, 1998   IL: 6–9
Grief/loss

Josh is in a haze of grief after his mother's sudden death, and decides to hitchhike to Texas, where he will live with his aunt instead of going on the three-week backpacking trip he had scheduled. But somehow he ends up in a strange place, Canara, that seems to be nowhere: a place where the rest of the world does not exist, and where there seems to be no way out. The elder of Canara tells a very frustrated Josh: "To go forward, you must go back."

Sarny: A Life Remembered by **Gary Paulsen**   RL: 5

Delacorte, 1997   IL: 6–10
African American

In this sequel to *Nightjohn*, Sarny is now ninety-four and takes out a tablet to write the story of her days after Nightjohn left. Sarny's story is told in her own distinctive, strong voice as she tells of leaving the plantation to find her children when the Civil War ends, and how she carries on the work of Nightjohn despite terrible backlash.

Saturnalia by **Paul Fleischman**   RL: 6

Harper & Row, 1990   IL: 7–12
Native American

After his family is wiped out in a raid in 1775, a Narragansett boy is taken in by a printer and his family as an apprentice. But the Puritan town is harsh in its rule, and William works hard to keep a low profile as he learns all he can and searches by night for his lost twin brother.

Say Goodnight, Gracie by **Julie R. Deaver**   RL: 6

Harper & Row, 1988   IL: 7+
Grief/loss

Seventeen-year-old Morgan has a best friend, Jimmy, who is always there to laugh with, talk to, fight with. When Jimmy is killed by a drunken driver, Morgan has a hard time both dealing with his death and finding a way to continue without him.

The Schernoff Discoveries by **Gary Paulsen**   RL: 5.1

Delacorte, 1997   IL: 5–8
Physically challenged: alcoholism

Harold and his best friend are misfits: Harold is too bright, and his narrator friend is too poor and struggling with his alcoholic parents. So the two of them blunder through experiments that Harold deems necessary, discovering much together in this funny and poignant story.

Scorpions by **Walter Dean Myers**   RL: 6

Harper & Row, 1988   IL: 7–10
African American

Jamal Hicks is only twelve when his older brother sends him word from prison that he should be the new leader of his gang, the Scorpions. Crazy Mack gives him a gun, and Jamal and his best friend, Tito, know it means trouble, but with so many troublesome things happening at school and on the streets, Jamal is confused as to what to do.

Searching for Candlestick Park by Peg Kehret   RL: 5

Cobblehill Books, Dutton, 1997   IL: 5–7
Nontraditional family

It's been tough for Spencer and his mom since his dad left three years ago, but his cat, Foxy, has always been there for him. So when the aunt they live with decides the cat must go, Spencer runs off with Foxy from Seattle to try to find his dad, whom he is sure is working for the San Francisco Giants.

The Second Bend in the River by Ann Rinaldi   RL: 6

Scholastic, 1997   IL: 7+
Native American

When Rebecca Galloway first glimpses Tecumseh, the Shawnee chief, he is standing by the river looking over land that used to be his home. During the next fifteen years, friendship develops between Rebecca and Tecumseh while the Ohio territory struggles with the "Indian problem" and the Indians struggle to hold on to what was once theirs.

The Secret Diary of Adrian Mole, Age 13 3/4 by Sue Townsend RL: 7

Methuen, 1985   IL: 7+
English

This fictional diary deals hilariously with the self-absorbed Adrian Mole who rattles on endlessly about the things he is obsessed with: sex, his "spots" (pimples), and his parents' irresponsible antics.

The Secret Journey by Peg Kehret   RL: 4.5

Pocket Books, 1999   IL: 4–7
English

In 1834, Emma's mother has consumption, so her father wants to take her to France with the hope she will get better. Emma is to stay in Liverpool with her aunt and a cousin whom she despises. Desperate to be with her mother, Emma decides to stow away on her parents' ship, but is misdirected to an illegal slaving ship bound for Africa. Author notes at the end are an interesting look at the research the book required her to do.

The Secret of Gumbo Grove by Eleanora Tate   RL: 5

F. Watts, 1987   IL: 5–9
African American

Raisin Stackhouse loves history. She just doesn't understand why all the history she learns is about white people. Raisin turns the small town on its ear when she makes some important discoveries about her people in the local cemetery.

Seedfolks by Paul Fleischman   RL: 5

HarperCollins, 1997   IL: 6+
Multiethnic

One by one, neighbors turn a vacant lot from a garbage dump into a living garden: each plot represents a person and his or her story. From the Vietnamese girl who wants to plant beans in memory of her father, to the African American woman who makes the contacts to get the garbage on the lot hauled away, each person has a special part of the story in these interwoven tales.

Sees Behind Trees by Michael Dorris   RL: 4

Hyperion Books for Children, 1996   IL: 3–7
Native American

Walnut cannot see clearly no matter how hard he tries, until his mother suggests he close his eyes and use his other senses. Honing these talents earns him the name Sees Behind Trees, and these talents eventually take him on a trip with an elder, Gray Fox, which changes everything for Sees Behind Trees.

The Serpent's Children by Laurence Yep   RL: 6

Harper & Row, 1984   IL: 7–9
Chinese

This pre-sequel to *Dragon's Gate* is the story of Foxfire's family. We learn of Foxfire's upbringing and of why he went to the demon's golden mountains.

Seven Daughters and Seven Sons by Barbara Cohen and
Bahija Lovejoy   RL: 6

Atheneum, 1982   IL: 6–10
Iraqi: Ancient

Based on a folk tale from Iraq, this is the story of one of seven daughters, Buran, who decides to disobey tradition and disguise herself as a boy to help her family, whose fortunes are floundering. In a distant city, she becomes a successful merchant in her disguise, but also realizes she has fallen in love with a prince who is also her best friend.

Shabanu, Daughter of the Wind by Suzanne Fisher Staples   RL: 7

Knopf: Distributed by Random House, 1989   IL: 7–12
Pakistani

This is a story of a young woman coming of age in Pakistan. One daughter of a camel herder is reaching the age (thirteen) when she will have to consider marrying and leaving her nomadic family. But Shabanu is caught between wanting to continue in her father's footsteps and honoring her parents' wishes. Everything comes to a head when she catches the eye of a rich older merchant.

The Shadow Children by Steven Schnur   RL: 4

Morrow Junior Books, 1994   IL: 4–8
French

Etienne loved to visit his grandparents' home in the French countryside during the summers following World War II. He loved it until he began to hear the trains and see the ghosts of children who hid in the woods from the Nazis. Etienne began to ask his grandparents about the children and learned more than he bargained for about secrets and guilt.

Shadow Like a Leopard by Myron Levoy   RL: 6

Harper & Row, 1981   IL: 5–9
Latino American

Ramon has problems: his father's in prison, his mother had a breakdown, and he is trying to decide on a life as a gang member or a life as a writer. How can a wheelchair-bound artist help him decide?

Shadow of a Bull by Maia Wojciechowska   RL: 6

Atheneum, 1964   IL: 6–9
Spanish

Manolo Olivar will soon turn twelve. His father was the most famous bullfighter in Spain until his death on the horns of a bull. Everyone in Manolo's village expects him to follow in his father's footsteps and fight his first bull when he turns twelve. Everyone, that is except Manolo.

The Shadow Spinner by Susan Fletcher   RL: 6

Atheneum Books for Young Readers, 1998   IL: 6+
Iraqi: Ancient

Marjan loves to tell stories, and one day when she is with her Auntie in the Sultan's harem to sell wares, she weaves a story for the children who come find her. Her story catches the ears of the sister of the famous Shahrazad, who arranges for Marjan to come live in the harem to help Shahrazad weave more tales that will keep her and others alive.

Shakedown Street **by Jonathan Nasaw**   RL: 6

Delacorte, 1993   IL: 7–10
Nontraditional family
Fourteen-year-old Caro and her mother are on the streets: the last guru her mother
followed ran with all their money, and now the streets of San Francisco are home.
Caro meets fellow panhandlers, as she tries to survive and find a way to get back
off of the streets; mature themes are discussed.

The Shakespeare Stealer **by Gary Blackwood**   RL: 6

Dutton Children's Books, 1998   IL: 5–9
English: Elizabethan
Widge has been in an orphanage for years when he's taken in by a rector and trained
in a strange shorthand so he can borrow other rector's sermons. But one day a
stranger comes to take him to London, where his job is to write down all the
words of a very popular play: *Hamlet.*

Shark Bait **by Graham Salisbury**   RL: 5

Delacorte, 1997   IL: 6–8
Hawaiian/Polynesian
Mokes lives in a small Hawaiian village where his father is police chief. When a
Navy ship is ready to drop anchor in the harbor, Mokes's father tells him to get
home so he will stay out of trouble. But a young man Mokes admires is spoiling
for a fight that Mokes has to watch—or does he?

Shark Beneath Reef **by Jean Craighead George**   RL: 5.5

Harper & Row, 1989   IL: 6–9
Latino: Mexican
Fourteen-year-old Tomas has a dream of catching a whale shark and a decision to
make about whether to study marine biology or follow his father's steps to become a fisherman. But officials start to complicate the lives of the Sea of Cortez's
fishermen, and Tomas's whale shark is not what it seems.

The Shark Callers **by Eric Campbell**   RL: 6

Harcourt Brace, 1994   IL: 6–10
New Guinean
The earth is ready to explode in the volcanoes in New Guinea. So Andy and his
family get their boat ready to sail away, unreliable engine and all. Meanwhile,
learning the ancient secrets of the shark callers, Keleku gets ready for his first

shark hunt. As the two boats leave their ports, neither can imagine what is in store for them, or what will happen to them after the earthquake and the tsunami that follows.

Shizuko's Daughter by Kyoko Mori   RL: 5+

H. Holt, 1993   IL: 6–10
Japanese
Grief/loss

Yuki is a talented young woman, strong in mind and body, and she has a special relationship with her mother. But her mother kills herself, and Yuki has a terrible time finding balance or happiness with anyone. She wonders if it's ever worth it to love somebody who will either hurt her or die. This episodically told tale is well-crafted.

Sign of the Beaver by Elizabeth George Speare   RL: 6

Houghton Mifflin, 1983   IL: 5–9
Native American

Left alone to guard his family's cabin and garden newly carved out of the wilderness in eighteenth century Maine, twelve-year-old Matt is hard-pressed to survive when a wanderer steals his gun. But local Indians help him, then teach him skills.

Sing Down the Moon by Scott O'Dell   RL: 5

Houghton Mifflin, 1970   IL: 7–12
Native American: Navaho

Bright Morning is a young Navaho women living peacefully in her settlement with her family and their sheep. She believes she will marry a warrior named Tall Boy. Then one day as she is tending the sheep, she and her friend are stolen away by Spanish slavers. This story is based on two years (1863–1865) in the Navaho history, the time of the Long Walk.

The Skin I'm In by Sharon G. Flake   RL: 6

Jump at the Sun/Hyperion Books for Children, 1998   IL: 6–8
African American

Maleeka Madison is dark black, dirt poor, and picked on. In self-defense, she throws in with Charlene who makes her do terrible things, but brings her clothes to wear at school. A new teacher, Miss Sanders, who has a large facial birthmark, tries to show Maleeka a different way. Even so, the peer pressure and harassment make Maleeka wonder which way to jump.

Slake's Limbo by Felice Holman   RL: 5

Scribner, 1974   IL: 6–9
Nontraditional family

Aremis Slake is thirteen, and his life is full of fear and misfortune. Without glasses
to see, the world is a blur around him, and the blurs chase and harass him un-
mercifully. So, one day he escapes to the subways and a small subway cave that
becomes his home for 121 days. How he survives, what he learns, and how the
lives of others affect him is told simply and movingly.

Slam! by Walter Dean Myers   RL: 6

Scholastic, 1996   IL: 7–10
African American

Seventeen-year-old "Slam" Harris is darned good on the basketball court: he has the
moves and does the slam like nobody's business. But how is his life off the court?
And what does it take to make it to the future he can imagine so clearly? *Slam!*
includes mature themes.

The Slave Dancer by Paula Fox   RL: 6

Bradbury Press, 1973   IL: 5–9
African American

A young colonist is kidnapped by sailors on a slave ship. He is forced to make the
long journey to Africa where the ship takes on its human cargo. He is then forced
to play the flute to "exercise" the slaves.

Slave Day by Rob Thomas   RL: 7

Simon and Schuster Books for Young Readers, 1997   IL: 7–10
Multiethnic

Slave Day is an annual fund-raiser at Robert E. Lee High School. This year, though,
the day starts with a letter to the editor in the morning paper protesting the day as
racist. From there the day goes on and we follow it through the eyes of a teacher,
a football player, a cheerleader, the mayor's daughter, a computer geek, and others. This book includes mature themes.

Slot Machine by Chris Lynch   RL: 6

HarperCollins, 1995   IL: 7–9
Physically challenged: weight issues

The summer before going to ninth grade, Elvin is sent to camp with the rest of the
boys in Christian Brothers Academy. It is the summer the boys are put to the test
to find the sport they are best suited for. Elvin hates camp. He hates sports and is

bad at every one they put him in. He knows there is no way out and so seeks out a place where he can fit in.

Small Steps: The Year I Got Polio by **Peg Kehret**   RL: 6

Albert Whitman, 1996   IL: 6–8
Physically challenged: polio

Author Peg Kehret relates the story of the year she was a seventh grader and contracted polio. This is a clear and interesting account, which covers seven months in Kehret's life and is also an interesting chapter in history before polio vaccines.

Snail Mail No More by **Paula Danziger and Ann Martin**   RL: 6

Scholastic, 2000   IL: 6–8
Physically challenged: alcoholism

Continuing their correspondences from *P.S. Longer Letter Later,* Tara*Starr and Elizabeth continue their stories of family and school life in their different states. Tara*Starr struggles with her feelings about her parents expecting a baby, and Elizabeth wishes her father would leave the family alone. Both come to realizations about family, friendships, and themselves in this strong sequel.

So Far from the Bamboo Grove by **Yoko Kawashima Watkins**   RL: 5

Lothrop, Lee & Shepard, 1986   IL: 6–9
Japanese

This excellent, moving story is set in 1945. A Japanese family is living in North Korea, and they are warned to leave quickly. A mother and her two daughters must travel to South Korea, then to Japan where they are met by fearsome results of the war and try to find their father and brother. This is a true account based on Watkins's own childhood.

Soldier's Heart: A Novel of the Civil War by **Gary Paulsen**   RL: 5.5

Delacorte, 1998   IL: 6–8
Grief/loss

Charlie Goddard leaves Minnesota in June 1861 to join up for the "great shooting war." He's fifteen, and this is an adventure he doesn't want to miss. Based on actual accounts, Charlie's experiences show the physical and mental anguish of the war with horrifying clarity.

Someone Like You by **Sarah Dessen**   RL: 6

Viking, 1998   IL: 8+
Nontraditional family
Grief/loss

High schoolers Halley and Scarlett are best friends. So when Scarlett calls Halley at camp to say Scarlett's boyfriend Michael has been killed in an accident, Halley comes home to stand by her. She continues to stand strong by Scarlett who soon discovers she is pregnant with Michael's child. In the midst of this, Halley begins her own first serious relationship and has a host of problems with her mother.

Someone to Count On by **Patricia Hermes**   RL: 5

    Little, Brown, 1993   IL: 6–9
    Nontraditional family

Samantha's mom gets bored easily, so she packs up and is on the move again so very often. Suddenly, Sam's mom tells her they are going to visit Sam's grandfather on a ranch in Colorado. This will be a different way of life with some of the stability Sam longs for. Will this be the final move for Sam with someone to count on at last?

Something Terrible Happened by **Barbara Ann Porte**   RL: 6

    Orchard Books, 1994   IL: 6–9
    Physically challenged: AIDS
    African American

Eleven-year-old Gillian is sent away from her mother, of West Indian heritage, to stay with the "all-white" relatives of her deceased father, because her mother is dying of AIDS. But the struggle to adapt is hard for Gillian, and she struggles to survive emotionally amid the upheaval.

Somewhere in the Darkness by **Walter Dean Myers**   RL: 6

    Scholastic, 1992   IL: 6+
    African American

Jimmy is at loose ends—undecided about what to do with his life as a teenager of above-average intelligence in New York City—when his father suddenly appears to take him with him, allegedly to Chicago and a new start. Jimmy's father, Crab, who has been in jail for the past eight years, doesn't really have a job in Chicago, didn't really get released from jail, and doesn't have long to live. The painful journey of the two, as they try to get to know one another, is told well and realistically.

Song of Be by **Lesley Beake**   RL: 6

    Maskew Miller Longman, 1991   IL: 6–9
    African

A young Bushman girl, Be, moves from her small village in Namibia to a white man's farm where her grandfather works. Be becomes the center of attention for the farmer's wife, but she has difficulty adjusting to the new life where people of her culture are considered less than fully human.

Song of the Buffalo Boy by Sherry Garland   RL: 7

Harcourt Brace Jovanovich, 1992   IL: 7+
Vietnamese

A young Amerasian girl, Loi, and her mother are the objects of much prejudice and hate because of Loi's mixed heritage. Her mother's brother has let the two of them live with his family in a small village twenty-four hours' drive from Ho Chi Minh City (Saigon). Loi is torn between wanting to stay in the village near the boy she loves and taking a chance to go to America to find her father.

Song of the Magdalene by Donna Jo Napoli   RL: 6

Scholastic, 1996   IL: 6+
Israeli: Ancient

When her first "fit" comes at age twelve, Miriam is certain she is now possessed by a demon and is unclean. Unwilling to tell her father what has happened, she finds companionship with the servant Hanna's son, Abraham. Abraham is a "crippled boy" whom all treat as an unfortunate thing. The relationship between Miriam and Abraham grows as he teaches her to read and think. But their happiness is shattered, and Miriam is exiled from home.

Songs of Faith by Angela Johnson   RL: 5

Orchard Books, 1998   IL: 6+
African American
Grief/loss

The Vietnam War is over, but its scars are apparent in the summer of '75 in Harvey, Ohio. Doreen tells the story of her father leaving, of Jolette coming to live next door, of Jeff, a Vietnam veteran who looks after the families of other vets, and of her brother Robert who is angry and sad. Johnson writes lyrically of love and life, and of the importance of family and friends.

Sons of Liberty by Adele Griffin   RL: 6

Hyperion Books for Children, 1997   IL: 6–8
Living with abuse

Rock Kindler's family is different: they live in a cottage that is freezing during New England winters; his mother never leaves the house and seems obsessed with cooking; his father believes he knows more than anyone else and wakes his sons in the middle of the night to patch their roof. Rock's not sure if all of this is as it should be.

Sounder by William Armstrong   RL: 5

Harper & Row, 1969   IL: 5–7
African American

When his sharecropper father is jailed for stealing food for his family, a young black
boy is humiliated and angry. With the help of his dog Sounder, he grows in
courage and in understanding.

Sparrow Hawk Red by Ben Mikaelsen   RL: 6

Hyperion Books for Children, 1993   IL: 6–9
Latino American

Ricky is a thirteen-year-old who is different from many others because of two things:
his mother is dead, and he knows how to fly airplanes. His father, a former DEA
agent and stunt pilot, has been his teacher. When Ricky discovers that his mother
has been murdered, he crosses the Mexican border disguised as a street kid, determined to steal a high-tech radar plane to avenge his mother's death.

Speak by Laurie Halse Anderson   RL: 7

Farrar, Straus, Giroux, 1999   IL: 8+
Living with abuse

Melinda is entering ninth grade as an outcast after a devastating event at an end-
of-the-summer party she attended, which culminated in Melinda calling the cops,
much to her classmates' disgust. Melinda stops speaking almost completely. Her
grades collapse, and only in her art class does she feel comfortable. What will it
take to get Melinda to speak?

Spindrift by Colby Rodowsky   RL: 5.5

Farrar, Straus, Giroux, 2000   IL: 5–7
Nontraditional family
Grief/loss

Cassie sees herself as a fixer of everything from lopsided sand castles to hurt feelings. But the summer after seventh grade finds her amid situations beyond her
fixing. Her sister and beloved brother-in-law's marriage is falling apart, and her
grandmother has decided to sell Spindrift, the bed-and-breakfast where she and
her mother have always lived.

Spud in Winter by Brian Doyle   RL: 5.5

Douglas & McIntyre, 1995   IL: 7–10
Canadian

Spud Sweetgrass is back along with his friends Connie Pan and Dink the Thinker.
This time, Spud is witness to a murder. He's frightened to come forward,

because he may endanger himself and Connie, but is also reluctant to remain silent.

Spud Sweetgrass by Brian Doyle   RL: 5.5

> Douglas & McIntyre, 1992   IL: 6–9
> Canadian

John "Spud" Sweetgrass has good things in his life: his job selling french fries; his friend Dink the Thinker; his girlfriend, Connie Pan; and ESL volleyball. But there are hard parts in his life, too: his father has died, his mom is so sad, and his favorite beach seems to be polluted by—french fry grease?

Star Fisher by Laurence Yep   RL: 5

> Morrow Junior Books, 1991   IL: 5–9
> Chinese American

A Chinese American family moves to a small town in the Midwest to start a laundry. They are met with fear and even hatred by many people in the town. One neighbor, however, reaches out to the family in friendship, and the town and the family begin to adjust to each other.

The Starplace by Vicki Grove   RL: 5.5

> Putnam, 1999   IL: 6–8
> African American

Quiver, Oklahoma, in 1961 was already challenging enough for Frannie Driscoll because she and her friends were about to start eighth grade. But when Celeste Chisholm and her father move to town, Celeste becomes the only black student in the junior high. Her presence creates even more questions, challenges, and worries for Frannie, who suddenly sees mean behavior and prejudice in a new light. This is a superb coming-of-age story.

Stay True: Short Stories for Strong Girls edited by Marilyn Singer   RL: 6

> Scholastic, 1998   IL: 6–9
> Multiethnic

A strong collection of short stories about young women of various cultures, their problems, their determination, and the paths they chose to follow.

Staying Fat for Sarah Byrnes by Chris Crutcher   RL: 8

> Greenwillow Books, 1993   IL: 7–10
> Physically challenged: weight issues
> Living with abuse

When Sarah was three, she was in an accident that left her hands and face horribly burnt. The scars produced mockery from classmates through the years. Eric "Moby" Calhoune has also endured taunts about his obesity, so Sarah and Eric unite as outcasts. Their friendship is tested, however, when Eric loses weight on the swim team and Sarah's past starts to be unveiled. This engaging story contains mature themes.

Stones in Water by Donna Jo Napoli   RL: 6

Dutton Children's Books, 1997   IL: 6–9
Italian: World War II

Roberto and his friends are excited to get to see an American western movie in their Italian town, as few amusements are available during the war. But German troops storm the movie theater and herd the boys to train cars to take them to German labor camps.

Stop Pretending: What Happened the Year My Big Sister Went Crazy by Sonya Sones   RL: 7

HarperCollins, 1999   IL: 7+
Mentally challenged

In free verse poems, thirteen-year-old Cookie tells about her older sister's mental breakdown. As she and her parents struggle with grief, anger, guilt, and resentment, Cookie's poems clearly and honestly show the tumult caused by the mental illness of a family member.

Storyteller's Beads by Jane Kurtz   RL: 6

Harcourt Brace, 1998   IL: 5+
African: Ethiopian
Grief/loss

Set in Ethiopia in the 1980s this is the story of two young women from different backgrounds, each fleeing for her life in a time of famine and political upheaval. Each must overcome prejudice in order to help each other survive their grueling journey of escape.

Stotan! by Chris Crutcher   RL: 7

Greenwillow Books, 1986   IL: 7+
Nontraditional family

A high school swim coach invites the members of his team to test their stamina and moral fiber in a way that teaches each about himself, his teammates, and life.

Stranded by Ben Mikaelsen   RL: 5.5

Hyperion Books for Children, 1995   IL: 5–8
Physically challenged

Twelve-year-old Koby loves the ocean out in her dinghy where she's away from her quarreling parents and the kids she glares at because she has one leg that ends in a stump because of a bicycle accident. When Koby helps two whales, things begin to change—at home, at school, at the water's edge—as she becomes part of the "Pod Squad." Koby learns that opening up your bagful of problems sometimes helps sort them out until there's only a pocketful left.

Stranded in Harmony by **Barbara Shoup**   RL: 7

Hyperion Books for Children, 1997   IL: 8+
Grief/loss

Lucas is a senior in high school in Harmony, Indiana. He's feeling trapped by his life, his football team, his girlfriend, and his family. The only person he enjoys talking to is his strange older cousin, Ronnie Dale. When a writer comes to visit Ronnie, her stories spark a deeper interest for Lucas in the '60s, Vietnam, and life.

Striking Out by **Will Weaver**   RL: 6

HarperCollins, 1995   IL: 6–9
Grief/loss

Billy Baggs has the arm, the talent, and the desire to play baseball, but his father says sports aren't for farm kids like Billy who have to work hard. Billy is torn by his desire to play and his dedication to the work he believes he owes his father, especially since the death of his older brother.

Stuck in Neutral by **Terry Trueman**   RL: 6

HarperCollins, 2000   IL: 7+
Physically challenged: cerebral palsy

In so many ways, Shawn McDaniel is a typical fourteen-year-old boy. He loves rock music and thinks about girls a lot of the time. He also thinks his father wants to kill him to take the pain away. Shawn has cerebral palsy: he has no control over his muscles at all, so he cannot let anyone know there is a very bright, thoughtful person inside his helpless body which is wracked by severe seizures several times a day. In this compelling story told from Shawn's point of view, we get a glimpse into a world we can only imagine.

Summer of My German Soldier by **Bette Greene**   RL: 6

Dial Press, 1973   IL: 6–10
Jewish
Living with abuse

Twelve-year-old Patty Bergen is Jewish. During World War II, that leaves no question as to where her loyalties should lie in respect to Germans and Nazis. But

Patty is unloved by her family and beaten by her father. When a young German man, Anton, a prisoner at a nearby camp offers her the hand of friendship, what is Patty willing to risk? This is a moving story of love and hatred.

The Summer of the Swans by Betsy Byars   RL: 6

Viking Press, 1970   IL: 5–8
Mentally challenged

Sara has what she considers to be a lot of problems during her fourteenth summer: her feet are too big, she hates her hands, her best friend is invited to a party that she isn't invited to, and people tease her younger brother, Charlie, who is mentally challenged. When Charlie disappears one night, Sara makes several discoveries about herself and her problems.

Summer on Wheels by Gary Soto   RL: 5

Scholastic, 1995   IL: 5–9
Latino American

The adventures of Hector and Mando (*Crazy Weekend*) continue. This time they ride their bikes from East L.A. to the beaches of Santa Monica. A fun and lively book, these two boys are real and likable characters.

The Sunita Experiment by Mitali Perkins   RL: 6

Little, Brown and Company, 1993   IL: 7–9
East Indian American

Sunita Sen is in the eighth grade, and this is going to be her year to totally fit in. Her parents both have good jobs and have adapted to American ways, until her grandparents come to live with them and bring the traditions of Calcutta. Sunita doesn't want to be different, and doesn't want her home and family to change. It takes the perseverance of her friends and the love of her parents to help Sunita see the value of combining both worlds.

Sunshine Rider: The First Vegetarian Western by Ric Hardman   RL: 6

Delacorte, 1998   IL: 7–10
Nontraditional family

1881: Odessa, Texas. Seventeen-year old Wylie Jackson sets out for his first cattle drive as an assistant cook. He promises Alice Beck he will take a side trip to deliver her cattalo (half buffalo, half cow), Roselle, to Alice's aunt. But Wylie's journey is interrupted quickly, and his side trips become a long path to self-discovery amid a colorful cast of characters.

Swallowing Stones by Joyce McDonald   RL: 6

Delacorte, 1997   IL: 7+
Grief/loss

A bullet shot into the air on July 4 finds a man repairing his roof more than a mile
away and kills him. This is the story of the aftermath told through the eyes of the
teenage shooter, Michael, and the dead man's daughter, Jenna. Both are devastated and struggle to deal with the death of a man, and how his death drastically
affects their lives.

Tae's Sonata by Haemi Balgassi   RL: 5

Clarion Books, 1997   IL: 5–8
Korean American

Tae misses her former home in Korea, but when her history teacher assigns her
South Korea as the country she must write a report on, along with the popular
Josh Morgan, she is horrified, wanting to minimize rather than accent the idea she
is "different." As she works with Josh, she becomes confused about how she feels
about him, quarrels with her best friend Meg, and wonders just how she fits into
life in the eighth grade.

Take It Easy by David Hill   RL: 5

Mallinson Rendel Publishers Ltd., 1995   IL: 7–9
New Zealander

Six teens set out for a wilderness hike in the rugged New Zealand mountains led by
an older man, Harvey. Two days into the hike, Harvey dies, leaving the six to survive on their own. Injuries, bad weather, panic, and lost gear all hinder the teens'
struggle to survive.

Taking Sides by Gary Soto   RL: 6

Harcourt Brace Jovanovich, 1991   IL: 6–9
Latino American

This is a story of two young boys who live in the barrio and play basketball on the
same high school team. One of the boys moves to a more affluent part of town
and finds himself the only Latino member of the new school's basketball team.
This is also a story about friendship and growth.

Tangerine by Edward Bloor   RL: 6

Harcourt, 1997   IL: 6–8
Physically challenged

Twelve-year-old Paul lives behind coke-bottle thick glasses and in the shadow of
uneasiness because of the amoral actions of his older brother Erik who is a foot-

ball hero. In a new home where weird weather phenomena overshadow each day, Paul tries to establish himself on the soccer team and figure out why he fears his own brother.

Taste of Salt: A Story of Modern Haiti by Frances Temple   RL: 7

Orchard Books, 1992   IL: 7–12
Caribbean

Djo is a young man who was born into poverty in Haiti. He was "adopted" by Father Jean-Bertrand Aristide and became a strong political supporter of Aristide. Djo tells his story to Jeremie from his hospital bed after being seriously injured in a bombing aimed at Aristide supporters. In return, Jeremie, too, tells her story about life in Haiti. The dialect in which this story is written makes it challenging for many students.

The Tears of a Tiger by Sharon Draper   RL: 6

Maxwell Macmillan International, 1994   IL: 8+
African American
Grief/loss

Andy Jackson is driving a car with three of his best friends as they celebrate a sweet basketball victory with beer—but suddenly there's a fiery crash that kills Andy's best friend Rob. Told in various viewpoints, this is the story of the aftermath, and Andy's struggle to deal with a death he has caused.

Tell Me How the Wind Sounds by Leslie D. Guccione   RL: 6

Scholastic, 1989   IL: 7–10
Physically challenged: deaf

Amanda Alden doesn't want to be on this small New England island for the summer: she'd rather be home with her friends. When she meets another teenager on the island, he frightens and confuses her until he is finally able to explain that he is deaf. The relationship that develops between Amanda and Jake is a meeting of two different worlds, one Jake is hesitant to bridge.

The Terrorist by Caroline Cooney   RL: 6

Scholastic, 1997   IL: 7–9
Multiethnic

While their parents are in London for a year for her father's job, Laura and Billy attend the London International Academy where political concerns and tensions confuse Laura. But one day as Billy is getting off a subway, he is handed a plain wrapped package containing a bomb, and suddenly terrorism and international tensions have a new meaning for Laura.

Thank You, Dr. Martin Luther King, Jr.! by Eleanora E. Tate   RL: 4

F. Watts, 1990   IL: 4–7
African American

In this second book set in Gumbo Grove, Mary Elouise hates being black. She
wants blond hair and blue eyes like the most popular girl in the class. She hides
the dark skinned dolls her grandmother gives her. And she can't stand it when she
has to take part in the annual Martin Luther King Day program until her grandmother helps her find her pride in her own heritage.

These Are the Rules by Paul Many   RL: 6

Walker & Company, 1997   IL: 6–8
Nontraditional family

Colm isn't particularly happy with the way the summer is shaping up: his parents
are splitting, his dad forgot to get him a summer job, he wants to learn how to
drive, and he is trying to figure out girls. But, as Colm's Rule No. 4 points out,
"It's hard to steer when you don't know where you're going."

Thief of Hearts by Laurence Yep   RL: 5.5

HarperCollins, 1995   IL: 5–8
Chinese American

Besides being the story of a strange set of thefts at a middle school, and being the
sequel to *Child of the Owl* (Casey is now married and this is her daughter's story),
this is also a look at having a mixed heritage, of roots or lack of roots, and of finding a place to truly belong.

Thunder Cave by Roland Smith   RL: 6

Hyperion Books for Children, 1995   IL: 6–9
African: Maasai

After his mother's accidental death, Jacob is determined to go find his wildlife biolo-
gist father who is somewhere in Kenya battling drought conditions and aggressive
poachers. Jacob embarks on a journey that turns out to be much more than he had
ever anticipated, including encounters with the Maasai, elephants, and poachers.

Thunder Rolling in the Mountains by Scott O'Dell/ Elizabeth Hall   RL: 6

Houghton Mifflin, 1992   IL: 8–12
Native American

O'Dell worked on this manuscript in the hospital until two days before he died, so
strongly did he feel about this story of Chief Joseph and his Nez Perce people.
Told through the eyes of Chief Joseph's daughter, the story traces the route of the

Nez Perce as they are ordered from their homeland, through five months and horrible battles, including the Battle of Little Bighorn.

A Time of Angels by **Karen Hesse**   RL: 5

Hyperion Books for Children, 1995   IL: 6–9
Russian-American
Physically challenged: epidemic

Hannah's father is fighting in the Great War and her mother is in Russia, unable to return because of the war, so Hannah and her sisters are with her Tanta Rose trying to survive. But when influenza grips Boston, Hannah's life begins to further unravel. Only a girl with violet eyes is able to guide her through the nightmarish weeks that follow.

Timothy of the Cay by **Theodore Taylor**   RL: 6

Harcourt Brace, 1993   IL: 5–9
Caribbean

A prequel/sequel to *The Cay,* this novel traces Timothy's childhood as well as his growing interest in sailing and owning his own ship. In alternate chapters, we follow Phillip's journey after his experiences with Timothy through his blindness, his memories of Timothy, and his anxiety over the operation on his eyes.

Tisha: The Story of a Young Teacher in the Alaska Wilderness by **Anne Purdy as told to Robert Specht**   RL: 6

St. Martin's Press, 1976   IL: 6+
Native American

"Tisha . . . you one helluva good white woman." This is the true account of a young woman who travels north to Chicken, Alaska, to teach. She encounters many problems, including prejudice of the townspeople who object when she welcomes an Indian into her classroom.

To Walk the Sky Path by **Phyllis Reynolds Naylor**   RL: 5.4

Follett Publishing Co., 1973   IL: 6–8
Native American: Seminole

Billie Tommie is a Seminole boy who lives in a *chickee* on a mangrove island in the Everglades. His life there is so different from the one he sees at school and at his friend Jeff's house. Billie wonders how he can walk in both the world of his ancestors and in that of the white man.

Tomorrow, When the War Began by **John Marsden**   RL: 6.5

Houghton Mifflin, 1995   IL: 7+
Australian

Ellie and her friends decide to go to the bush for a camping trip during Christmas
vacation. When they come out, they find that their country has been invaded, and
their families captured and imprisoned. Do they go back to the bush to hide, or
try to be heroic? This is the first in a series of books about Ellie and her friends.

Tomorrowland: Ten Stories about the Future edited by Michael Cart   RL: 7

> Scholastic, 1999   IL: 7+
> Multiethnic

In stories that look at "tomorrow" from many different time periods, including
Neanderthal, medieval, present, and future, this collection pays tribute to our
turn of the millennium. Nine other authors joined Cart in writing stories for this
collection, including Rodman Philbrick, Jacqueline Woodson, and James Cross
Giblin.

Tonight, by Sea by Frances Temple   RL: 6

> Orchard Books, 1985   IL: 6–9
> Haitian

Paulie helps her uncle build a boat. Actually, all the people in the village Belle
Heuve helped, bringing bits of plastic or cloth for the sail, wood for the boat.
There is no work, little food, and no real life here, but the people would like to
stay in Haiti—or must they sail for Mee-ya-mee? When a crisis strikes, Paulie
makes a brave decision and a hard journey, only to be faced with a still more difficult decision when she returns.

Toning the Sweep by Angela Johnson   RL: 7

> Orchard Books, 1993   IL: 7–10
> African American

Grandmama Ola is dying of cancer. So her granddaughter Emily and her daughter
Diane go down to the desert to help Ola pack up her life, her friendships, and her
memories. This story is a lyrical examination of three women's lives, memories,
and thoughts on life and death.

Torn Away by James Heneghan   RL: 6

> Viking, 1994   IL: 6–9
> Irish

Dangerous Declan Doyle: that's who he is at thirteen; he is also smart and strong
and determined to be a terrorist. Sent for by his uncle in Canada, Declan fights
tooth and nail to remain in Ireland, and once in Canada, only plots his return. But
his uncle's family tries to turn his taste for vengeance with love.

Trapped! edited by Lois Duncan

RL: 7

Simon & Schuster, 1998

IL: 7+

Multiethnic

Traps can come in many shapes and forms: many are mental, some are emotional, and others are physical. This is an interesting collection of stories by strong young adult writers examining traps of different types, from out-of-wedlock pregnancy to a raging forest fire.

Tribute to Another Dead Rock Star by Randy Powell

RL: 6

Farrar, Straus, Girioux, 1999

IL: 7+

Grief/loss

Physically/mentally challenged

Grady's been invited back to Seattle, Washington, to speak at a rock concert that is a tribute to his rock star mom who died at thirty-six. He stays with his half-brother's family and struggles to figure out how he feels about many things: his mom, his half-brother who is mentally challenged, his half-brother's family, himself, and what to do with his life.

Trino's Choice by Diane Gonzales Bertrand

RL: 6

Piñata Books, 1999

IL: 7–10

Latino American

Trino lives in a Texas trailer park with his mom, younger stepbrothers and his alcoholic uncle. Frustrated by his poverty and lacking adult supervision, he makes some bad choices which lead to tragedy. Along the way, he meets Lisanna who offers him some hope.

Trouble on the Tracks by Donna Jo Napoli

RL: 5

Scholastic, 1997

IL: 4–7

Australian

Zach and Eve are traveling by train from Alice Springs to Adeline to stay with their aunt while their anthropologist mom is working. Eve knows a lot about birds and is curious when two men bring one aboard the train. When Eve and Zack discover the men are part of a bird-smuggling ring, they're suddenly over their heads in trouble.

The Trouble with Lemons by Daniel Hayes

RL: 6

D. R. Godine, 1991

IL: 6–9

Physically challenged: asthma

Because of his bouts with allergies and asthma, Tyler has always considered himself the "lemon" of his famous family. When he and his best friend find a dead body at a local quarry, they set out to solve the mystery, and Tyler hopes to find some self-confidence for himself as well.

The Trouble with Mothers by **Margery Facklam**   RL: 5.3

Clarion Books, 1989   IL: 6–8
Nontraditional family

Eighth grader Luke has his hands full—living with his mom, a high school teacher; his grandma, an active woman; and his little sister is tough enough. When a book that his mother has written comes under an attack by a visiting "Clean Up America" zealot, things get really complicated.

Troubling a Star by **Madeline L'Engle**   RL: 5.6

Farrar, Straus, Giroux, 1994   IL: 6–9
Antarctic

Vicky Austen is growing up and believes she can take the challenges presented by the gift of a trip to Antarctica to see the fragile ecosystem she finds fascinating. But the trip tosses her into the middle of an intrigue involving drugs, nuclear waste, and a threat to her life.

Tru Confessions by **Janet Tashjian**   RL: 5

H. Holt, 1997   IL: 5–7
Mentally challenged

Tru's journal, written on her mom's computer, is a refreshing, honest look at a real problem. Tru's twin brother is mentally challenged, and she wants people to appreciate him for who he is, and not make fun of him.

True North: A Novel of the Underground Railroad by **Kathryn Lasky**   RL: 6

Blue Sky Press, 1996   IL: 6–9
African American

In 1858, Lucy is tired of the societal swirl around her older sisters and prefers spending time with her grandfather who seems to be preoccupied with some mysterious business. The business, Lucy finds by accident, deals with the Underground Railroad. Soon she, too, becomes very involved.

Tuesday Cafe by **Don Trembath**   RL: 6

Orca Book Publishers, 1996   IL: 7–10
Canadian

Harper didn't want to burn the school down: he just wanted to set a small fire to create a stir and get someone to notice him—maybe even his parents. So when the judge assigns him forty hours of community service and a two-thousand-word essay titled "How I Plan to Turn My Life Around," Harper ends up at a writing class that's like no other he's ever been to.

Tusk and Stone by Malcolm J. Bosse   RL: 8

Front Street, 1995   IL: 8+
Indian: Medieval

Arjin, a young member of the Brahmin caste, is captured from the caravan in which his family is traveling. His father and uncle are killed but his sister escapes. Arjin is put in shackles and put into service as an elephant driver. He becomes known as the best at his work and looks far and wide for his sister, and becomes something of a legend in seventh century India.

Ultimate Sports edited by Donald Gallo   RL: 6.5

Delacorte, 1995   IL: 8+
Multiethnic

An excellent collection of stories about sports of all types from some of today's strongest young adult writers, including Chris Crutcher, Harry Mazer, David Klass, and Graham Salisbury. Stories include both male and female protagonists.

Under the Blood-Red Sun by Graham Salisbury   RL: 4.7

Delacorte, 1994   IL: 6+
Japanese American

Tomi considers himself an American; he was born in Hawaii, loves baseball, and really hopes the Dodgers can beat the Yankees in the '41 World Series. Tomi's parents and grandfather have a Japanese flag, which his grandfather waves on occasion. When Pearl Harbor is bombed by the Japanese, suddenly Tomi and his family are viewed with suspicion, especially his father, whose fishing boat does not have a U.S. flag flying. How will Tomi and his family survive?

Under the Mermaid Angel by Martha Moore   RL: 6

Delacorte, 1995   IL: 6–9
Physically challenged

Thirteen-year-old Jesse is pragmatic about her life: Ida, Texas, is boring, her little sister drives her crazy, and she wishes she would mature faster. But when thirty-year-old Roxanne moves into the trailer next door, she becomes Jesse's friend and confidant, and life in Ida becomes a little bit better.

Unfinished Portrait of Jessica by Richard Peck   RL: 5.6

Delacorte, 1991   IL: 7–9
Nontraditional family

Jessica is almost fourteen and trying her best to live in her room and ignore her mother whom she believes drove away her beloved father, a handsome and talented photographer. So when her mother says Jessica may go spend the holidays in Mexico with her father, Jessica is thrilled. But neither Mexico nor her father turns out to be what she expects.

Until Whatever by Martha Humphreys   RL: 6

Clarion Books, 1991   IL: 7+
Physically challenged: AIDS

Connie Tibbs has AIDS: the news is all over the school before the second day of the school year has started. For Karen, this brings back memories of a day Connie helped her, and this also complicates her life when Connie is assigned as her lab partner in biology. As a campaign to oust Connie from school escalates, Karen tries to decide where her beliefs and loyalties lie.

Up Country by Alden R. Carter   RL: 6

Putnam, 1989   IL: 7–10
Nontraditional family
Physically challenged: alcoholism

Carl's mom is a drunk. So Carl makes The Plan. Sure, it involves repairing and re-selling stolen car radios, but he'll never get caught. But when his mom gets arrested again, she's sent to a detox program, and Carl is sent to the boonies with some relatives. What will he find in the frozen North?

Utterly Yours, Booker Jones by Betsy Duffey   RL: 4.5

Viking, 1995   IL: 4–6
Nontraditional family

Booker Jones, writer, has lost his room to his ninety-two-year-old grandfather who fell and broke his hip. Banished to the dining room, Booker continues to try to write his books and the letters to the publisher he has queried (twenty-three times!) as he works under the dining room table.

The View from Saturday by E. L. Konigsburg   RL: 5

Atheneum Books for Young Readers, 1996   IL: 5–7
Multiethnic
Physically challenged

As a sixth-grade Academic Bowl team sits down to a final round contest, the stories of each of the team's members, as well as their advisor, are told in turn. How four different individuals came to work so well together and answer more than the academic questions that they are presented makes a beautifully woven story.

The Voices of Silence by **Bel Mooney**   RL: 6

Dell, 1997   IL: 6–9
Romanian

Flora is thirteen-years-old and living under the horribly harsh regime of Ceausescu,
  whose dictatorship no one dares to criticize. But revolutionary ideas begin to surface around Flora and frightening changes begin to occur all around her as she
  tries to understand what is true, and what she must do to help those she loves.

Waiting for the Rain: A Novel of South Africa by **Sheila Gordon**   RL: 6

Orchard Books, 1987   IL: 7+
African: South African

Frikki is white, Tengo is black: Frikki is the farmer's nephew who will one day in-
  herit the family's South African farm. It's Frikki's dream. Tengo's family works
  on the farm and Tengo begins questioning why things are as they are. His hunger
  for knowledge and learning sends him to the city of Johannesburg where the fires
  of rage over apartheid burn fiercely. Tengo's fiercest wish, however, is for an education. As the boys' lives take very different directions, both struggle to understand the inevitable changes their worlds are undergoing.

Walk Two Moons by **Sharon Creech**   RL: 5

HarperCollins, 1994   IL: 6+
Grief/loss

A long car trip is the vehicle for Salamanca Tree Hiddle to tell her story. In the company of her lovable, eccentric grandparents, she unfolds her own life story and
  that of her mother, who left suddenly for Idaho one morning, and has not returned. A story rich with laughter, tears, mystery, and discovery.

Walkabout by **James Marshall**   RL: 6

Sundance, 1959   IL: 7+
Australian

A young girl and her brother learn to communicate with an Aborigine youth when
  they are thrown together in an effort to survive the wilderness of the Australian
  Outback.

Walking up a Rainbow by **Theodore Taylor**   RL: 5.4

Delacorte, 1986   IL: 7–10
Nontraditional family

Susan Carlisle is not your average fourteen-year-old. In 1852 she finds herself an
  orphan and in debt, so she decides to take her three-thousand sheep overland from

Iowa to California. With Drover Petit and his crew, Susan sets off on an amazing journey. Clay Carmen who is also on the drive tells his viewpoint of the adventure in some chapters as well.

The Wall by Elizabeth Lutzeier   RL: 6

Holiday House, 1992   IL: 7+
German

Hannah has to identify the body of her mother who was shot and killed trying to cross the Berlin Wall. She sticks to the story she has been given: her mother had left her and her father six months before. Meanwhile a girl named Steffe continually gets kicked out of schools for rebellious actions. When the two become friends, they work to find truth and trust on the eve of the opening of the Berlin Wall.

The Wanderer by Sharon Creech   RL: 5.5

HarperCollins, 2000   IL: 6–9
Grief/loss
Nontraditional family: adoption

This story is told through dual journal entries: Sophie hears the call of the sea loudly. Her journal of her sailing voyage from the East Coast to England with three uncles and two male cousins portrays that this is an important journey for her on many levels. Meanwhile, Cody's "dog-log" shows that this is a time of thought and growth for him, too, despite the fact that his father thinks he is a knuckleheaded doofus.

Wandering Girl by Glenyse Ward   RL: 6

Virago Press, 1988   IL: 6–10
Australian: Aboriginal

Glenyse was a year old when she was taken from her mother. She was raised at a mission, then sent out for her first job as a teenager. Although the year was 1965, the woman who takes her in refers to her as her "dark servant," disinfects the car seat Glenyse has sat on, then treats her like a slave. Told in a candid, calm manner, Glenyse's story of her year of servitude is a sad commentary on deep-seated prejudice against the Aborigines.

The War Between the Classes by Gloria Miklowitz   RL: 5.6

Delacorte, 1985   IL: 6–12
Multiethnic

Amy and her classmates find themselves questioning the use of power, humiliation, and punishments as a high school class experiment assigns "social classes" to each student along with sets of harsh rules that threaten friendships and loyalties. This is a school assignment that none of the students is likely to forget.

The War in Georgia by Jerrie Oughton   RL: 6

Houghton Mifflin, 1997   IL: 6+
Nontraditional family

Shanta lives with her grandmother and her bedridden Uncle Louie. Life is pretty ordinary and the family works hard at keeping love and humor in their home. When
a "normal" family moves in across the street, one with a mom and dad, Shanta
wishes she could belong until she learns there are dark secrets there.

The Watcher by James Howe   RL: 5

Atheneum, 1997   IL: 7+
Living with abuse

A girl sits daily on the stairs to the beach, watching a family of four and a young
man who is a lifeguard. And as she sits, she writes a story about a girl captured
by a beast who longs to find and be reunited with her real family.

The Watsons Go to Birmingham–1963 by Christopher
Paul Curtis   RL: 6

Holt Reinhart & Winston, 1995   IL: 6–9
African American

Kenny Watson tells the story of his family: the Weird Watsons of Flint, Michigan,
who plan a trip to Birmingham in the tumultuous times of the Civil Rights movement. The story is filled with fun, laughter, unforgettable characters, and also the
sad events in the summer of 1963 in Birmingham, Alabama.

West Against the Wind by Liza K. Murrow   RL: 6

Holiday House, 1987   IL: 6–10
Grief/loss

Abigail's father left to join the California gold rush in the 1850s. His family has received only one letter asking that his family come join him. This is fourteen-
year-old Abby's story as she, her family, and a rather mysterious young man journey across the land from Independence, Missouri, to California.

The Westing Game by Ellen Raskin   RL: 6

Dutton, 1978   IL: 6–10
Multiethnic

Sixteen people gather for the reading of a very unusual will: a document that is the
directions for the Westing Game, which, if played properly, will lead one of the
participants to find out who murdered Samuel Westing and make that person a
millionaire.

What Are They Saying About Me? by Maureen Wartski   RL: 6

Fawcett Juniper, 1996   IL: 6–9
Mentally challenged

This is a compelling story that deals with several issues: Meg is already struggling
   with being at a new, big high school when she is targeted by a group of girls who
   get their kicks by tormenting others. Meanwhile, Meg's beloved grandmother
   seems to be slipping away mentally.

What Hearts by Bruce Brooks   RL: 6

Harper Collins, 1992   IL: 6–9
Nontraditional family

Asa's life seems to be a perfect one as he hurries home on the last day of first
   grade. But suddenly his world crumbles: his mother is waiting for him on the
   front steps, sitting on her suitcase. She has called a cab, and they are leaving his
   father. Not only that, but another man is waiting for them, someone from his
   mother's past. Asa will soon have a stepdad, one who doesn't particularly like
   him! Visit Asa's ever-changing world in four different times: first grade, fourth
   grade, sixth grade, and seventh grade.

What Jamie Saw by Carolyn Coman   RL: 4

Front Street, 1995   IL: 5–9
Living with abuse

Jamie is a third grader when he sees Van pick up his baby sister and throw her across
   the room. Miraculously, Jamie's mom catches her. But then they are on the run,
   away from Van. The thoughts that run through Jamie's mind, thoughts of confusion, fear, hope, are ours to follow in this brief but powerful story. Jamie's voice
   is the strongest aspect of this book about domestic violence.

What You Don't Know Can Kill You by Fran Arrick   RL: 6

Bantam, 1992   IL: 7+
Physically challenged: AIDS

Ellen's life and future seem great. Her younger sister can't believe how fortunate
   Ellen is: college next year, marriage to the perfect boyfriend—but a blood test
   shows that Ellen is HIV positive, and both her world and her family's world start
   crashing around them.

What's in a Name by Ellen Wittlinger   RL: 7

Simon and Schuster Books for Young Readers, 2000   IL: 8+
Multiethnic
Gay/lesbian

Told in ten chapters, one for each character, these interwoven stories shed light on the lives and conflicts of a group of Scrub High School students. Each is involved in examining his or her own life and identity while the town is in the midst of an identity crisis as well. Should the town remain plain Scrub Harbor, or a more exotic Folly Bay?

When Zachary Beaver Came to Town by **Kimberly W. Holt**   RL: 5

Holt, 1999   IL: 5–8
Grief/loss
Physically challenged: weight issues
During the summer of '71, Toby is having a slow, hot summer in a small Texas town where not much happens. Then a trailer pulls into town, and for $2, you can see "the fattest boy in the world," Zachary Beaver. Zachary ends up staying for weeks, while Toby's mom ends up staying away for weeks, and Toby's summer is one of learning about life.

Where Do I Go from Here? by **Valerie Wilson Wesley**   RL: 6

Scholastic, 1993   IL: 7–10
Nontraditional family
African American
Nia is not comfortable at the Endicott Academy: she's black, and she's not rich, unlike most of the students there. She's a scholarship kid from Newark. But Marcus is her friend, and he makes it bearable, much better. So when he suddenly disappears, Nia is lost. Now it's important for her to find Marcus and, along the way, herself.

Whirligig by **Paul Fleischman**   RL: 7

H. Holt, 1998   IL: 7+
Grief/loss
Brent Bishop just wants to fit in with the cool crowd at his new school. But things go horribly wrong at a party, and a drunken Brent tries to kill himself as he drives home. Instead, he kills a young woman whose mother has a request of Brent that sends him on a journey of repentance and self-discovery.

White Lilacs by **Carolyn Meyer**   RL: 6

Harcourt Brace Jovanovich, 1993   IL: 6–8
African American
Freedom was part of the town of Dillon where the black community lived. When Dillon's white residents plan to raze Freedomtown, things change. Young Rose Lee Jefferson finds herself at the center of the debate on how to respond.

Who Is Eddie Leonard? by Harry Mazer   RL: 5

Delacorte, 1993   IL: 6–9
Nontraditional family

Eddie's grandmother, who is the only caretaker he's ever known, has just died. What now? Who are Eddie's mom and dad? Eddie sees a face on a "missing" poster, and decides that it must be his face. Determined to find a family he can call his own, Eddie sets off to find the place he hopes he belongs.

The Window by Michael Dorris   RL: 5

Hyperion Press for Children, 1997   IL: 6+
Native American
African American

In this prequel to *Yellow Raft on Blue Water* we find Rayona having to wait more and more often for her mother to come home after staying out all night. Finally her father comes and finds her alone, and decides its time for a foster family for Rayona while her mother goes through detox. But foster families fall through, and Rayona ends up in the arms of her father's Irish mother, grandmother, and aunt.

The Window by Jeanette Ingold   RL: 7

Harcourt Brace, 1996   IL: 7–10
Physically challenged

Mandy is blinded in an accident that kills her mother, and Mandy ends up with relatives whom she hadn't known existed in a new state at a new high school with challenges she's never faced. As she tries to cope, she also seems to hear voices from the past—but whose past? Listening to voices from the past and in the present, Mandy begins to come to terms with her life.

Winter Camp by Kirkpatrick Hill   RL: 5

Maxwell Macmillan International, 1993   IL: 4–7
Native American

Eleven-year-old Toughboy and his nine-year-old sister are living with the oldest Indian woman in their village, Natasha, now that their parents have died. She decides to take them out of school to her trapping camp where they learn lessons about the land and survival—especially when a friend of Natasha's comes to visit and is injured so badly that Natasha must go for help.

Wish Me Luck by James Heneghan   RL: 6.5

Farrar, Straus, Girioux, 1997   IL: 7–9
Irish/British

Jamie is almost thirteen at the beginning of World War II. He's tired of carrying a gas mask to school and tired of the air raid sirens. But when the bombing starts in earnest, his parents book him a passage on the City of Benares, a luxury liner bound for Canada that has agreed to take one hundred British evacuees along. This story is based on historical accounts.

Witch of Blackbird Pond by Elizabeth George Speare   RL: 5

Houghton Mifflin, 1958   IL: 7–9
Puritan

Kit Tyler had been raised by her grandfather in the West Indies in a setting of luxury and freedom. When he dies, she suddenly finds herself on her way to Puritan New England, where everyone is plain and God-fearing, and where everyone looks upon Kit and her beautiful clothes with suspicion. When Kit makes friends with a woman whom some suspect of witchcraft, she finds herself in more trouble than she can handle.

With Every Drop of Blood by James Collier and Christopher Collier   RL: 5

Delacorte, 1994   IL: 6–9
African American

Johnny's father makes him promise not to go fight in the war between the states: one family member's life is enough for the Confederate rebel cause. But Johnny wants vengeance, and when he can join a food train with his mule and wagon to earn money for his family and maybe kill a blue coat, away he goes. However, he is captured by the Union, by a black Union soldier his own age (fourteen), who shows him many things about people and the war.

Woman of Her Tribe by Margaret A. Robinson   RL: 7

Maxwell Macmillan International, 1990   IL: 7+
Native American

Annette was raised in her father's Nootka Indian village while her English mother traveled. Suddenly, Annette received a scholarship to an exclusive private school where she learns about the other side of her cultural heritage.

Won't Know Till I Get There by Walter Dean Myers   RL: 5

Viking Press, 1982   IL: 5–10
African American

Steve and his family decide they are comfortable enough to share their home with a second child. Earl moves into the home, a foster brother for Steve, bringing with him his past criminal record and attitude hardened by many years of moving from one foster home to another. Steve and Earl get into trouble and are sentenced to community service in a retirement home.

Words by Heart by Ouida Sebestyen   RL: 5

Little, Brown, 1979   IL: 6–9
African American

Set in the cotton country of the West in 1910, this is the story of Lena and her family who are share-croppers. Lena wants her classmates to notice her for her "magic mind" rather than her black skin, but when she wins a Scripture-quoting contest, the results are unexpected violence and death, teaching Lena she must also learn forgiveness.

Words of Stone by Kevin Henkes   RL: 5

Greenwillow Books, 1992   IL: 5–7
Grief/loss

Blaze is an introspective ten-year-old who is more at ease with imaginary friends than with real people. He misses his mom who has died. Joselle is a strong-willed, eccentric ten-year-old girl who is fighting mad that her mother has deserted her again. When the paths of these two very different children cross, both have much to learn.

The World of Daughter McGuire by Sharon Dennis Wyeth   RL: 4.5

Delacorte, 1994   IL: 5–7
Multiethnic

Daughter McGuire and her brothers and mom have just moved, which means adjustments of all sorts, including being without her father who has not made the move with them. Daughter struggles with understanding her parents' relationship, with some students at school, with a boy who calls her "zebra," and with an assignment dealing with her ancestry: African, Italian, Irish, Jewish, Russian, American.

Year of Impossible Goodbyes by Sook Nyul Choi   RL: 6

Houghton Mifflin, 1991   IL: 6–10
Korean

It is 1945. Ten-year-old Sookan and her mother, brother, grandfather, aunt, and cousin pray to their Buddha and Christian God that the war will finally end and the harsh rule of the Japanese will end as well. First the Japanese police, then the communists from Russia do all they can to break the spirits and wills of Sookan and her family. Their only hope lies in a dangerous escape to South Korea. This vividly written story makes compelling reading.

The Year of the Leopard Song by **Eric Campbell**   RL: 6

Harcourt Brace Jovanovich, 1992   IL: 6–10
African

Told from alternating points of view, this is the story of the time when the Chagga tribespeople reaffirm their connection to their animal brothers: a time of the Song. Alan Edwards's family owns the Kenyan coffee plantation that the Chagga work on, and when something seems to be amiss, none of the Edwards family understands the true implications of a very important ritual.

Zebra and Other Stories by **Chaim Potok**   RL: 6

Knopf, 1998   IL: 7–10
Multiethnic

In this collection of six stories, teens experience life changing events that include peer harassment, sexuality issues, intense anger, and separation of parents. Beautifully and thoughtfully written, this book contains mature themes.

Zlata's Diary by **Zlata Filipovic**   RL: 6

Viking, 1994   IL: 6+
Croatian

Zlata describes her everyday life in this diary, which covers the early months of war as her hometown in Sarajevo is ravaged.

APPENDIXES AND INDEXES

Sample Literary Circles

Before starting literary circles, identify a theme around which to set them, and then select books around that theme. Ideally, we like to find books that represent different cultures around a particular theme, books that have a variety of reading levels, and books that have both strong male and strong female protagonists. What follows are sample literary circle themes with a selection of possible titles: use them as a jumping-off point. Before you begin a circle, we strongly recommend that you read each of the books you will booktalk to students. (Titles marked with an asterisk indicate science fiction/fantasy titles from appendix E.)

ADOLESCENT STRUGGLES

Besides the struggles that young adults have with their families, they also have struggles of their own that range from mental instability, to questions of sexuality, to peer pressures of various types.

Angus, Thongs, and Full Frontal Snogging (Rennison)
Another Way to Dance (Southgate)
Babcock (Cottonwood)
Bloomability (Creech)
Buried Onions (Soto)
Cages (Kehret)
Changes in Latitude (Hobbs)
Dakota Dream (Bennett)
Dancing on the Edge (Nolan)
Danny Ain't (Cottonwood)
Darnell Rock Reporting (Myers)
Dean Duffy (Powell)
Do Angels Sing the Blues? (LeMieux)
Dogwolf (Carter)

Don't You Dare Read This, Mrs. Dunphrey (Haddix)
Dreams in the Golden Country: The Diary of Zipporah Feldman (Lasky)
The Eclipse of Moonbeam Dawson (Okimoto)
The Facts Speak for Themselves (Cole)
Farm Team (Weaver)
Finding My Voice (Lee)
Girl Named Disaster (Farmer)
Hannah in Between (Rodowsky)
Hard Love (Wittlinger)
Hero (Rottman)
Holes (Sacher)
Homeless Bird (Whelan)
The House You Pass on the Way (Woodson)
Humming Whispers (Johnson)
I Can Hear the Mourning Dove (Bennett)
Ice (Naylor)
I Hate Being Gifted (Hermes)
Imani All Mine (Porter)
Language of Goldfish (Oneal)
The Long Season of Rain (Kim)
The Luckiest Girl in the World (Levenkron)
Make Lemonade (Wolff)
Monster (Myers)
Necessary Roughness (Lee)
Out of Control (Mazer)
Out of Nowhere (Sebestyn)
The Rainy Season (Griffin)
Shark Bait (Salisbury)
The Skin I'm In (Flake)
Slake's Limbo (Holman)
Slam! (Myers)
Someone Like You (Dessen)
Someone to Count On (Hermes)
Speak (Anderson)
Stop Pretending (Sones)
Tae's Sonata (Balgassi)
Tribute to Another Dead Rock Star (Powell)
Tuesday Cafe (Trembath)
The World of Daughter McGuire (Wyeth)

ADVENTURE STORIES

Although adventure can have different nuances, each of these stories has one or more strong male protagonists and a hefty dose of action.

Beardance (Hobbs)
Between a Rock and a Hard Place (Carter)
Canyons (Paulsen)
Countdown (Mikaelsen)
Dogsong (Paulsen)
Downriver (Hobbs)
Far North (Hobbs)
Ghost Canoe (Hobbs)
Green Thumb (Thomas)
Hatchet (Paulsen)
Hawk Moon (MacGregor)
The Maze (Hobbs)
Place of Lions (Campbell)
Prophecy Rock (MacGregor)
Rescue Josh McGuire (Mikaelsen)
The Righteous Revenge of Artemis Bonner (Myers)
Scorpions (Myers)
Take It Easy (Hill)
Thunder Cave (Smith)
The Thief (Turner)*

CIRCLE ON CENSORSHIP

What is censorship? Why do we need to be aware of it? These are titles that explore some ramifications of censorship and losses of individual rights.

Fahrenheit 451 (Bradbury)*
The Giver (Lowry)*
A Handful of Stars (Schami)
The Last Safe Place on Earth (Peck)
Memoirs of a Bookbat (Lasky)
Places I Never Meant to Be (ed. Blume)

Red Scarf Girl (Jiang)
The Trouble with Mothers (Facklam)

COMING-OF-AGE STORIES

Rites of passage take many shapes and forms in life. While some are de-
liberate and ritual, others simply happen as we journey along the path of
life. The protagonists in these titles face events or moments that change
them profoundly in some way, so that each views life in a different light afterward.

Armageddon Summer (Yolen/Coville)
Babcock (Cottonwood)
Between a Rock and a Hard Place (Carter)
Bloomability (Creech)
Countdown (Mikaelsen)
Danger Zone (Klass)
Dogwolf (Carter)
Downriver (Hobbs)
For the Life of Laetitia (Hodge)
A Girl Named Disaster (Farmer)
The Giver (Lowry)
Holes (Sacher)
Is Kissing a Girl Who Smokes Like Licking an Ashtray? (Powell)
Jesse (Soto)
Make Lemonade (Wolff)
Marisol and Magdalena (Chambers)
The Maze (Hobbs)
Moon Dancer (Rostkowski)
The Moves Make the Man (Brooks)
One Bird (Mori)
Parrot in the Oven: Mi Vida (Martinez)
The Rain Catchers (Thesman)
Rules of the Road (Bauer)
The Secret Diary of Adrian Mole, Age 13 3/4 (Townsend)
Shadow Like a Leopard (Levoy)
Slam! (Myers)
Song of Be (Beake)
Stranded in Harmony (Shoup)

Toning the Sweep (Johnson)
Tribute to Another Dead Rock Star (Powell)
Unfinished Portrait of Jessica (Peck)

DEALING WITH PREJUDICE

This circle opens up broad channels of discussion. We have started by using a quote attributed to Mother Teresa: "If you judge people, then you have no time to love them."

Another Way to Dance (Southgate)
Buried Onions (Soto)
Burning Up (Cooney)
Chain of Fire (Naidoo)
Children of the River (Crew)
Color Me Dark: The Diary of Nellie Lee Love (McKissack)
Come a Stranger (Voigt)
Crazy Lady (Conley)
Danger Zone (Klass)
Deliver Us from Evie (Kerr)
Dragon's Gate (Yep)
The Drowning of Stephen Jones (Greene)
Earthshine (Nelson)
Finding My Voice (Lee)
From the Notebooks of Melanin Sun (Woodson)
Home Boy (Hansen)
If I Should Die Before I Wake (Nolan)
If It Hadn't Been for Yoon Jun (Lee)
If You Come Softly (Woodson)
Jack (Homes)
Jip: His Story (Paterson)
Jubilee Journey (Meyer)
Lasso the Moon (Covington)
A Long Way Home (Wartski)
Maniac Magee (Spinelli)
Monster (Myers)
Music from a Place Called Half Moon (Oughton)
My Louisiana Sky (Holt)
Necessary Roughness (Lee)

Prank (Lasky)
Probably Still Nick Swanson (Wolff)
The Skin I'm In (Flake)
Star Fisher (Yep)
The Starplace (Grove)
Stop Pretending (Sones)
Storyteller's Beads (Kurtz)
Torn Away (Heneghan)
Under the Blood-Red Sun (Salisbury)
Until Whenever (Humphreys)
The War Between the Classes (Miklowitz)
The Watsons Go to Birmingham, 1963 (Curtis)
When Zachary Beaver Came to Town (Holt)
White Lilacs (Meyer)
Words by Heart (Sebestyen)

DISPLACED OR HOMELESS PEOPLE

What is it like to have to leave your home for a completely new country? Who are those people out on the streets, and how did they get there? Not all stories are the same, and some are more sympathetic than others, but these titles put realistic faces on those who are without homes, or even without countries.

Beggar's Ride (Nelson)
A Boat to Nowhere (Wartski)
The Clay Marble (Ho)
The Crossing (Paulsen)
Darnell Rock Reporting (Myers)
Goodbye, Vietnam (Whelan)
Grab Hands and Run (Temple)
Homecoming (Voigt)
Homeless Bird (Whelan)
Kiss the Dust (Laird)
Lasso the Moon (Covington)
Maniac Magee (Spinelli)
My Brother, My Sister, and Me (Watkins)
Out of Nowhere (Sebestyn)
The Pickle Song (DeClements)

Shakedown Street (Nasaw)
Slake's Limbo (Holman)
So Far from the Bamboo Grove (Watkins)
Sparrow Hawk Red (Mikaelsen)
Storyteller's Beads (Kurtz)

FAMILY CONFLICTS

Adolescent struggles are so often tied to problems at home, or worries about problems with alcohol, abuse, divorce. This theme for circles opens possibilities for discussion that can center on characters in books rather than personal issues. This is also a great set of books to supplement lessons in a health class, or for school counselors who are running support groups.

Amazing Gracie (Cannon)	parental depression
Nightfather (Friedman)	parental depression
Cages (Kehret)	alcoholism
Bill (Reeves)	alcoholism
Hannah in Between (Rodowsky)	alcoholism
Heart of a Champion (Deuker)	alcoholism
Up Country (Carter)	alcoholism
What Jamie Saw (Coman)	abuse
Staying Fat for Sarah Byrnes (Crutcher)	abuse
Chinese Handcuffs (Crutcher)	abuse
Sons of Liberty (Griffin)	abuse
I Hadn't Meant to Tell You This (Woodson)	abuse
Bruises (deVries)	abuse
The Watcher (Howe)	abuse
The 3 NB of Julian Drew (Deem)	abuse
Boomer's Journal (Kelly)	abuse
Prank (Lasky)	abuse
Danny Ain't (Cottonwood)	Vietnam vet father
Charlie Pippin (Boyd)	Vietnam vet father
Freak the Mighty (Philbrick)	criminal father
It's a Matter of Trust (Byalick)	criminal father
Somewhere in the Darkness (Myers)	criminal father
Dog Years (Warner)	criminal father

Leaving Fishers (Haddix)	criminal father
Up Country (Carter)	mother in rehabilitation
My Louisiana Sky (Holt)	mentally challenged parents
Changes in Latitude (Hobbs)	divorce/separation
Flour Babies (Fine)	divorce/separation
Letters to Julia (Holmes)	divorce/separation
These Are the Rules (Many)	divorce/separation
Don't You Dare Read This, Mrs. Dunphrey (Haddix)	divorce/separation
Night Hoops (Deuker)	divorce/separation
One Bird (Mori)	divorce/separation
What Hearts (Brooks)	divorce/separation
Missing Pieces (Mazer)	divorce/separation
Searching for Candlestick Park (Kehret)	divorce/separation
Frozen Stiff (Shahan)	divorce/separation
Unfinished Portrait of Jessica (Peck)	divorce/separation

FINDING FRIENDS TO COUNT ON

Another theme of central importance to teens is friendship: making connections with the right person in a time when there are so many questions and so many changes is vital. Each of the following stories has a protagonist who finds a relationship to count on or cements a friendship in a special way, and in doing so learns more about him or herself.

Another Way to Dance (Southgate)
Babcock (Cottonwood)
Bloomability (Creech)
Confess-O-Rama (Koertge)
Dave at Night (Levine)
Diving for the Moon (Bantle)
Far North (Hobbs)
For the Love of Venice (Napoli)
Freak the Mighty (Philbrick)
Holes (Sacher)
Ironman (Crutcher)
Love Among the Walnuts (Ferris)
Make Lemonade (Wolff)
Maniac Magee (Spinelli)

My Louisiana Sky (Holt)
One Bird (Mori)
Out of Nowhere (Sebestyen)
Safe at Second (Johnson)
Shadow Like a Leopard (Levoy)
Shakespeare Stealer (Blackwell)
Someone Like You (Dessen)
Sparrow Hawk Red (Mikaelsen)
The View from Saturday (Konigsburg)
Won't Know Till I Get There (Myers)

FITTING IN

So many times teens find themselves in new situations: a new town, a new school, a new country. Trying to fit in to the new situation inevitably involves having to ascertain what behaviors are correct and which ones are unacceptable. Other times teens are simply trying to adapt to a change in their lives, and want to fit in to an existing situation: what is the lie of the land, and how does one do the right thing to fit in now that something in life is different? Fitting in is a tough part of teen existence, and sometimes involves compromises that turn out to be too much to handle. These titles involve teens struggling to fit in to all sorts of different situations.

Bloomability (Creech)
The Captive (Hansen)
Children of the River (Crew)
Dave at Night (Levine)
Dog Years (Warner)
A Gathering of Pearls (Choi)
Go and Come Back (Abelove)
Holes (Sacher)
Home Boy (Hansen)
In the Year of the Boar and Jackie Robinson (Lord)
Izzy, Willy Nilly (Voigt)
Kiss the Dust (Laird)
Leaving Fishers (Haddix)
A Long Way From Home (Wartski)
Midwife's Apprentice (Cushman)
Necessary Roughness (Lee)

One More River (Banks)
Out of Nowhere (Sebestyn)
Pacific Crossing (Soto)
Pickle Song (DeClements)
Pinballs (Byars)
Probably Still Nick Swanson (Wolff)
Sees Behind Trees (Dorris)
The Skin I'm In (Flake)
Slot Machine (Lynch)
Someone to Count On (Hermes)
Speak (Anderson)
The Sunita Experiment (Perkins)
The Star Fisher (Yep)
The Starplace (Grove)
Tangerine (Bloor)
Where Do I Go From Here? (Wesley)
Whirligig (Fleischman)

GENERATION TO GENERATION

What do we learn from those who are older and wiser? How are generations
different in their values, in the way they see things? What causes dissention
among generations of families? How are traditions passes down? These are
stories of interaction between different generations of people who are trying to find answers to some of life's challenges.

April and the Dragon Lady (Namoika)
Backwater (Bauer)
Bud, Not Buddy (Curtis)
Child of the Owl (Yep)
Cookcamp (Paulsen)
The Dragon's Gate (Yep)
The Education of Little Tree (Carter)
The Glory Field (Myers)
Holes (Sacher)
Life's a Funny Proposition, Horatio (Polikoff)
Love Among the Walnuts (Ferris)
Marisol and Magdalena (Chamber)
Marked by Fire (Thomas)

Mind's Eye (Fleischman)
Missing May (Rylant)
Over the Water (Casey)
Raincatchers (Thesman)
Seedfolks (Fleischman)
Someone to Count On (Hermes)
Toning the Sweep (Johnson)
True North (Lasky)
The Window (Dorris)
The Window (Ingold)
Won't Know Till I Get There (Myers)

GRIEF/LOSS

Students who are dealing with grief or loss of any type can use titles such
as the following in order to find a way to discuss their own grief. These titles deal with different types of losses, from death, to loss of health, to loss
of a homeland, to loss through divorce or separation. At different times we
have provided a list like this one to school counselors, and have recommended various titles to families.

Belle Prater's Boy (White)
Bridge to Terabithia (Paterson)
The Broken Bridge (Banks)
Chasing Redbird (Creech)
Chinese Handcuffs (Crutcher)
Confess-O-Rama (Koertge)
Dave at Night (Levine)
Dive (Griffin)
Earthshine (Nelson)
Freak the Mighty (Philbrick)
Getting Near to Baby (Couloumbis)
The Islander (Rylant)
Kiss the Dust (Laird)
Letters to Julia (Holmes)
Life's a Funny Proposition, Horatio (Polikoff)
A Long Way from Home (Wartski)
May I Cross Your Golden River? (Dixon)
Mick Harte Was Here! (Park)

Missing May (Rylant)
My Brother Has AIDS (Davis)
Necessary Roughness (Lee)
The Other Shepards (Griffin)
Out of the Dust (Hesse)
Peeling the Onion (Orr)
Phoenix Rising (Hesse)
The Return (Levitin)
Running Loose (Crutcher)
Say Goodnight, Gracie (Deaver)
Scorpions (Myers)
Shizuko's Daughter (Mori)
Somewhere in Darkness (Myers)
Something Terrible Happened (Porte)
Swallowing Stones (McDonald)
Tears of a Tiger (Draper)
Toning the Sweep (Johnson)
Walk Two Moons (Creech)
The Wanderer (Creech)
Whirligig (Fleischman)
Words of Stone (Henkes)

THE HERO'S JOURNEY

If you have not explored Joseph Campbell's ideas about the hero cycle, his ideas make for fascinating reading, and the cycle he describes ties together so many of the stories and legends we have read, as well as many movies we have seen. Campbell poses the ideas that heroes have companions, go on quests, and must face great trials and tribulations, emerging from them as wiser individuals. The following stories may not fit Campbell's hero cycle perfectly, but they are stories of individuals on important journeys— physical or mental—from which each learns valuable life lessons.

Between a Rock and a Hard Place (Carter)
The Borning Room (Fleischman)
Deep Dream of the Rain Forest (Bosse)
Dogwolf (Carter)
The Dove and the Sword (Garden)
The Ear, the Eye, and the Arm (Farmer)*

Elske (Voigt)*
The Examination (Bosse)
Maniac Magee (Spinelli)
Sabriel (Nix)*
The Thief (Turner)*
A Time of Angels (Hesse)
Tomorrow, When the War Began (Marsden)
Whirligig (Fleischman)
Zel (Napoli)

JOURNALS/DIARIES/EPISTOLARY NOVELS

Through the years, our students have loved reading journal, letter, or diary forms of books to see what other young adults, like themselves, might write about their lives.

Absolutely Normal Chaos (Creech)
Among Friends (Cooney)
Angus, Thongs, and Full-Frontal Snogging (Rennison)
Boomer's Journal (Kelly)
The Diary of a Young Girl (Frank)
Don't You Dare Read This, Mrs. Dunphrey (Haddix)
Catherine, Called Birdy (Cushman)
Fat Chance (Newman)
From the Notebooks of Melanin Sun (Woodson)
Handful of Stars (Schami)
Ironman (Crutcher)
Journal of Joshua Loper: A Black Cowboy (Myers)
Journal of Won Ming-Chung: A Chinese Miner (Yep)
Letters from the Inside (Marsden)
Letters from Rifka (Hesse)
Letters to Julia (Holmes)
Out of the Dust (Hesse)
P.S. Longer Letter Later (Danziger and Martin)
The Secret Diary of Adrian Mole, Age 13 3/4 (Townsend)
Snail Mail No More (Danziger and Martin)
The Wanderer (Creech)
Won't Know Till I Get There (Myers)
Zlata's Diary (Filipovic)

LISTENING TO THE BEAT OF A DIFFERENT DRUMMER

While many teens struggle to fit in and be a part of the crowd, there are many others who prefer their unique and different styles. These are titles that feature teens who, for one reason or another, go in a direction different from others: from their culture, from their family, or from their peers.

Alias (Ryan)
Among the Volcanoes (Castaneda)
Babcock (Cottonwood)
Backwater (Bauer)
Crazy Jack (Napoli)
Dakota Dream (Bennett)
Dive (Griffin)
The Eclipse of Moonbeam Dawson (Okimoto)
Freak the Mighty (Philbrick)
A Girl Named Disaster (Farmer)
Hard Love (Wittlinger)
The House You Pass on the Way (Woodson)
The Islander (Rylant)
Love Among the Walnuts (Ferris)
Out of Control (Mazer)
Plain City (Hamilton)
Shadow of a Bull (Wojciechowska)
Song of Magdalene (Napoli)
Speak (Anderson)
Stranded (Mikaelsen)
Tangerine (Bloor)

MYSTERIES FROM DIFFERENT CULTURES AND TIMES

Beyond the series of mysteries that so many young adults read, there are other mysteries that explore different times, places, and cultures.

Another Kind of Monday (Coles Jr.)
Bad News Travels Fast (Haywood)
The Ear, the Eye, and the Arm (Farmer)
Ghost Canoe (Hobbs)
Ghosts of Stony Clove (Charbonneau)

Green Thumb (Thomas)
Hawk Moon (MacGregor)
A Man Named Poe (Avi)
Net Bandits (Coleman)
Never Trust a Dead Man (Vande Velde)
Prophecy Rock (MacGregor)
Ruby in the Smoke (Pullman)
Running Out of Time (Haddix)
Spud in Winter (Doyle)
Spud Sweetgrass (Doyle)
The Trouble with Lemons (Hayes)
Troubling a Star (L'Engle)
The Westing Game (Raskin)

PHYSICALLY AND/OR MENTALLY CHALLENGED PEOPLE

The Native Americans remind us not to judge people until we have walked for two moons in their moccasins. Until we take the time to visit the lives of those with physical or mental challenges, we tend to judge their lives without true understanding. Each of the following stories provides a visit to a life that has a special challenge.

The Acorn People (Jones)
After the Dancing Days (Rostkowski)
Amazing Gracie (Cannon)
The Bus People (Anderson)
Crazy Lady (Conley)
Dancing on the Edge (Nolan)
Dovey Coe (Dowell)
Fat Chance (Newman)
Freak the Mighty (Philbrick)
Hero of Lesser Causes (Johnston)
Humming Whispers (Johnson)
I Can Hear the Mourning Dove Sing (Bennett)
Izzy, Willy-Nilly (Voigt)
Kissing Doorknobs (Hesser)
Language of Goldfish (Oneal)
Lisa, Bright and Dark (Neufeld)
The Luckiest Girl in the World (Levenkron)

The Man Who Loved Clowns (Wood)
Mind's Eye (Fleischman)
My Louisiana Sky (Holt)
Peeling the Onion (Orr)
Petey (Mikaelsen)
Picking Up the Pieces (Calvert)
Probably Still Nick Swanson (Wolff)
Radiance Descending (Fox)
Safe at Second (Johnson)
Sees Behind Trees (Dorris)
Small Steps (Kehret)
Stuck in Neutral (Trueman)
Stop Pretending (Sones)
Stranded (Mikaelsen)
Summer of the Swans (Byars)
Tell Me How the Wind Sounds (Guccione)
The Trouble with Lemons (Hayes)
Tru Confessions (Tashjian)
The Window (Ingold)

SPORTS STORIES

Although these stories are certainly deal with sports, the main characters deal with many other issues as well.

Bull Catcher (Carter)	baseball
Choosing Sides (Ritter)	baseball
Dean Duffy (Powell)	baseball
Farm Team (Weaver)	baseball
Hard Ball (Weaver)	baseball
Heart of a Champion (Deuker)	baseball
Honus and Me (Gutman)	baseball
Painting the Black (Deuker)	baseball
Safe at Second (Johnson)	baseball
Striking Out (Weaver)	baseball
Danger Zone (Klass)	basketball
The Moves Make the Man (Brooks)	basketball
Night Hoops (Deuker)	basketball
Slam! (Myers)	basketball
Tangerine (Bloor)	soccer

Downriver (Hobbs)	white-water rafting
River Thunder (Hobbs)	white-water rafting
Frozen Stiff (Shahan)	kayaking
Stotan! (Crutcher)	swimming
Ironman (Crutcher)	triathalon
Necessary Roughness (Lee)	football
Crash (Spinelli)	football
Slot Machine (Lynch)	sports camp
Ultimate Sports (ed. Gallo)	multiple sports
Athletic Shorts (Crutcher)	multiple sports

SET IN AFRICA

While these books are set in very different times, this circle might be done concurrently with a social studies unit on Africa.

AK (Dickinson)
Beduins' Gazelle (Temple)
Beyond the Mango Tree (Zemser)
Chain of Fire (Naidoo)
Countdown (Mikaelsen)
The Ear, the Eye, and the Arm (Farmer)*
A Girl Named Disaster (Farmer)
Journey to Jo'burg (Naidoo)
Mara, Daughter of the Nile (McGraw)
A Place of Lions (Campbell)
The Return (Levitin)
Thunder Cave (Smith)
Song of Be (Beake)
Storyteller's Beads (Kurtz)
Waiting for the Rain (Gordon)
Year of the Leopard Song (Campbell)

TEENS ENGAGING IN LITERATE BEHAVIOR

The books we use in our classrooms serve in many capacities: as models for good writing and as impetus for discussion, among others. They can also model behavior we wish to encourage in teens, such as engaging in writing. These titles are about teens who write—to help themselves sort through events in their lives, or to have an audience who will "listen" as only paper can. They also talk about the importance of reading to teen protagonists: how important is the ability to read, and to read what we want?

Adam and Eve and Pinch Me (Johnston)
Among Friends (Cooney)
Boomer's Journal (Kelly)
Catherine, Called Birdy (Cushman)
Diary of a Young Girl (Anne Frank)
Don't You Dare Read This, Mrs. Dunphrey (Haddix)
For the Life of Laetitia (Hodge)
Freak the Mighty (Philbrick)
From the Notebooks of Melanin Sun (Woodson)
Handful of Stars (Schami)
Hard Love (Wittlinger)
Ironman (Crutcher)
Letters from the Inside (Marsden)
Letters from Rifka (Hesse)
Letters to Julia (Holmes)
The Library Card (Spinelli)
Maniac Magee (Spinelli)
Memoirs of a Bookbat (Lasky)
Nightjohn (Paulsen)
Out of the Dust (Hesse)
P.S. Longer Letter Later (Danziger and Martin)
Picture of Freedom: The Diary of Clotee, a Slave Girl (McKissack)
Rio Grande Stories (Meyer)
The Secret Diary of Adrian Mole, Aged 13 3/4 (Townsend)
Snail Mail No More (Danziger and Martin)
Tru Confessions (Tashjian)
Tuesday Cafe (Trembath)
Wanderer (Creech)
Words by Heart (Sebestyen)
Zlata's Diary (Filipovic)

YOUNG WOMEN THROUGH THE AGES

How have young women's roles changed over the centuries? How have their roles remained constant? What challenges have they faced throughout the years?

Mara, Daughter of the Nile (McGraw)	Ancient Egyptian Empire
Seven Daughters and Seven Sons (Cohen/Lovejoy)	Ancient Persia
Song of Magdelene (Napoli)	Time of Christ
Catherine, Called Birdy (Cushman)	Middle Ages
Matilda Bone (Cushman)	Middle Ages
Midwife's Apprentice (Cushman)	Middle Ages
The Ramsay Scallop (Temple)	Middle Ages
Forestwife (Tomlinson)	Middle Ages
Morning Girl (Dorris)	European exploration of America
Beyond the Burning Time (Lasky)	Salem witch trials
Witch of Blackbird Pond (Speare)	Salem witch trials
Walking Up a Rainbow (Taylor)	Westward expansion
The Ballad of Lucy Whipple (Cushman)	California gold rush
Lyddie (Paterson)	Industrial Revolution
Sing Down the Moon (O'Dell)	Navaho's Long Walk
Ruby in the Smoke (Pullman)	Victorian England
Words by Heart (Sebestyen)	Turn of the century
Tisha (Purdy)	Turn of the century
A Time of Angels (Hesse)	World War I
White Lilacs (Meyer)	Post–World War II
Roll of Thunder, Hear My Cry (Taylor)	Depression era
Out of the Dust (Hesse)	Depression era/Dust Bowl
So Far from the Bamboo Grove (Watkins)	World War II
The Year of Impossible Goodbyes (Choi)	World War II
Cage (Sender)	World War II—Holocaust
Devil's Arithmetic (Yolen)	World War II—Holocaust
Music from a Place Called Half Moon (Oughton)	Post–World War II
The Road Home (White)	Vietnam War
Chain of Fire (Naidoo)	South Africa apartheid
Shabanu, Daughter of the Wind (Staples)	Pakistan
Where Do I Go from Here? (Wesley)	modern

Imani All Mine (Porter)	modern
The Wanderer (Creech)	modern
Don't You Dare Read This, Mrs. Dunphrey (Haddix)	modern
The House You Pass on the Way (Woodson)	modern
Make Lemonade (Wolff)	modern
Speak (Anderson)	modern
Shade's Children (Nix)*	future

Books to Use Across the Curriculum and in Other Reading Groups

As discussed in chapter 4, young adult literature is reaching out to embrace such a wide range of issues and topics that many of the titles available now are appropriate to use in venues other than a traditional English or language arts class. Science, health, and social studies classes seem especially appropriate for books that could be used as supplementary reading to support many topics. Counselors can use these books as a means of opening discussions in groups or with individuals. Mother/daughter or father/son book groups are another appropriate place for discussions on issues such as the ones that follow. These might also be used as the basis for more specifically targeted literary circles. (Titles followed by an asterisk indicate science fiction/fantasy titles from the appendix E.)

HEALTH

Health issues are covered in a number of ways in schools: through separate health classes, as part of science classes, through special presentations, or in home and family-life classes. Wherever it is taught, the following issues are possibilities for inclusion in the health curriculum.

AIDS

Whenever we have booktalked any of these titles about people who have AIDS, we have had a variety of responses. Amid those responses have come many students who say things such as, "I would like to borrow that book: my aunt is dying of AIDS." Somehow the books are comforting to those students who know people with AIDS, because it helps them know they are not alone in the world.

Baby Alicia Is Dying (McDaniel)
Diving for the Moon (Bantle)

Eagle Kite (Fox)
Earthshine (Nelson)
It Happened to Nancy (Anonymous)
My Brother Has AIDS (Davis)
Something Terrible Happened (Porte)
Until Whatever (Humphreys)
What You Don't Know Can Kill You (Arrick)

Sexuality

Teenage years are fraught with difficulties, and one of those certainly deals with sexual identity. As Marion Bauer points out in her introduction to the superb anthology *Am I Blue*, teens who are confused and without support or resources can become at risk for suicide. The following titles deal with gay and lesbian issues. While having a literature circle of these selections might not be feasible, having these titles as supplementary reading for a health class is certainly reasonable, as is having them as a part of a library or classroom collection.

Am I Blue? Coming Out from the Silence (ed. Bauer)
Deliver Us from Evie (Kerr)
The Drowning of Stephen Jones (Greene)
Eagle Kite (Fox)
Earthshine (Nelson)
From the Notebooks of Melanin Sun (Woodson)
Hard Love (Wittlinger)
The House You Pass on the Way (Woodson)
Jack (Homes)
My Brother Has AIDS (Davis)
Name Me Nobody (Yamanaka)
No Big Deal (McClain)
What's in a Name? (Wittlinger)

Alcoholism

Alcoholism is a huge issue for adolescents for many reasons. Some are already experimenting with alcohol, while others are trying to decide whether they should try it. Some adolescents know people with alcohol problems, some of whom they may live with. These books can provide a means of talking about the huge effect of alcohol in their lives.

Bill (Reaver)
Boomer's Journal (Kelly)
Cages (Kehret)
Do Angels Sing the Blues? (LeMieux)
Dogwolf (Carter)
Hannah in Between (Rodowsky)
Heart of a Champion (Deuker)
Parrot in the Oven: Mi Vida (Martinez)
Rats Saw God (Thomas)
Rules of the Road (Bauer)
Schernoff Discoveries (Paulsen)
Up Country (Carter)

Depression/Suicide

Teenage years also are fraught with emotional upheavals. Peer and family relationships can cause so many of our children to struggle with depression. These titles deal with teens who are dealing with depression and suicide.

Amazing Gracie (Cannon)
Among Friends (Crutcher)
Chinese Handcuffs (Crutcher)
I Can Hear the Mourning Dove (Bennett)
Language of the Goldfish (Oneal)
Lisa, Bright and Dark (Neufeld)
Shizuko's Daughter (Mori)
Speak (Anderson)
Tears of a Tiger (Draper)

Living with Abuse

Abuse in any form—physical, mental, emotional—changes the patterns of daily life in any family. The cyclical nature of abuse is also very real. These are stories where abuse of some sort is occurring.

Boomer's Journal (Kelly)
Bruises (deVries)
Bull Catcher (Carter)
Chinese Handcuffs (Crutcher)
Don't You Dare Read This, Mrs. Dunphrey (Haddix)

Ellen Foster (Gibbons)
I Hadn't Meant to Tell You This (Woodson)
Letters from the Inside (Marsden)
The Luckiest Girl in the World (Levenkron)
Parrot in the Oven: Mi Vida (Martinez)
Prank (Lasky)
Rescue Josh McGuire (Mikaelsen)
Sons of Liberty (Griffin)
Staying Fat for Sarah Byrnes (Crutcher)
3NB of Julian Drew (Deem)
The Watcher (Howe)
What Jamie Saw (Coman)

Weight Issues

In our modern society, which seems to send so many messages about what looks good and what does not, one of the issues that hits very close to home with teens is weight. These are books whose protagonists are worried about being thin or fat; about anorexia and bulimia; about being judged by one's appearance.

The Best Little Girl in the World (Levenkron)
Fat Chance (Newman)
I Am an Artichoke (Frank)
Life in the Fat Lane (Bennett)
One Fat Summer (Lipsyte)
Slot Machine (Lynch)
Staying Fat for Sarah Byrnes (Crutcher)
When Zachary Beaver Came to Town (Holt)

Mental-Health Issues

Fortunately our society no longer cages people who do not fit in the "normal" mental category, yet our understanding and tolerance of those with mental diseases, illnesses, or other challenges are still not where they need to be. Teens, like others, may still be harsh critics of those who are struggling with mental-health issues. These books shed light on different types of mental-health issues and create opportunities for good discussion, more awareness, and better tolerance.

Adam Zigzag (Barrie)
Crazy Lady (Conley)
Dancing on the Edge (Nolan)
Humming Whispers (Johnson)
I Can Hear the Mourning Dove Sing (Bennett)
John Riley's Daughter (Matthews)
Kissing Doorknobs (Hesser)
Language of Goldfish (Oneal)
Lisa, Bright and Dark (Neufeld)
Stop Pretending (Sones)

HOME AND FAMILY LIFE

As with the health section, these titles address a variety of issues that are important no matter in what class they are addressed.

Divorce/Separation

Two-parent families are more the exception than the rule for a vast number of our teens. Many of them live in homes that have been affected by divorce or separation of parents. Each of the following stories features a protagonist dealing in some way with parental separation.

Changes in Latitude (Hobbs)
Don't You Dare Read This, Mrs. Dunphrey (Haddix)
Eagle Kite (Fox)
Flour Babies (Fine)
Frozen Stiff (Shahan)
Hard Love (Wittlinger)
Hawk Moon (MacGregor)
Ice (Naylor)
Ironman (Crutcher)
Letters to Julia (Holmes)
Missing Pieces (Mazer)
Searching for Candlestick Park (Kehret)
These Are the Rules (Many)
Unfinished Portrait of Jessica (Peck)
What Hearts (Brooks)

Orphans/Adopted Children/Foster Children

Many of the adolescents we encounter are living with someone other than their birth parents. As they grow older, some have questions about being adopted, living as foster children, or being an orphan. The characters in these books can open avenues of discussion and understanding.

Adam and Eve and Pinch Me (Johnston)
Anne of Green Gables (Montgomery)
A Blessing in Disguise (Tate)
Bud, Not Buddy (Curtis)
The Crossing (Paulsen)
Dakota Dream (Bennett)
Dave at Night (Levine)
Find a Stranger, Say Goodbye (Lowry)
Heaven (Johnson)
Home for a Stranger (Weiss)
If It Hadn't Been for Yun Joon (Lee)
Pinballs (Byars)
Torn Away (Heneghan)
The Wanderer (Creech)
Winter Camp (Hill)
Won't Know Till I Get There (Myers)

SOCIAL STUDIES

Social studies classes are rich with opportunities for providing literature links. Whether a teacher wants to read excerpts from a book aloud or do literary circles, these are categories of books that are appropriate for inclusion.

Exploration/Expansion/Immigration

What is it like to go somewhere very different? To a new country, or a new part of the country? These are stories of young adults setting out for new places—voluntarily in some cases, or fleeing for their lives in others.

The Ballad of Lucy Whipple (Cushman)
Call Me Ruth (Sachs)
Children of the River (Crew)

Dragon's Gate (Yep)
Dragonwings (Yep)
Dreams in the Golden Country: The Diary of Zipporah Feldman (Lasky)
The Gentleman Outlaw and Me—Eli (Hahn)
Goodbye, Vietnam (Whelan)
Jason's Gold (Hobbs)
Journal of Joshua Loper: A Black Cowboy (Myers)
Journal of Wong Ming-Chung: A Chinese Miner (Yep)
Letters from Rifka (Hesse)
Morning Girl (Dorris)
One More River (Banks)
The Righteous Revenge of Artemis Bonner (Myers)
Sunshine Rider: The First Vegetarian Western (Hardman)
Walking up a Rainbow (Taylor)
West Against the Wind (Murrow)

Questions of Ethical Behavior

Weighty issues lead to tremendous discussions. Each of these books deals with issues which raise questions of what is and is not ethical behavior. We have created mock trials based on some of these titles, to explore the good or bad, right or wrong of historical or fictional decisions. Others simply open the avenues for excellent questions and discussion.

Adem's Cross (Mead)
Armageddon Summer (Yolan/Coville)
Asylum for Nightface (Brooks)
The Bomb (Taylor)
Galax-Arena (Rubinstein)*
Gathering Blue (Lasky)
Green Thumb (Thomas)
I Hadn't Meant to Tell You This (Woodson)
The Last Safe Place on Earth (Peck)
Leaving Fishers (Haddix)
Memoirs of a Bookbat (Lasky)
Out of Control (Mazer)
Painting the Black (Deuker)
Running Out of Time (Haddix)
Shade's Children (Nix)*
Star Split (Lasky)

What Jamie Saw (Coman)
What You Don't Know Can Kill You (Arrick)

Holocaust

Stories of the Holocaust are difficult to read at any age. These are books—some fact, some fiction—dealing with young adults who find themselves in the midst of a terrible and bleak time, or dealing with the aftermath of the Holocaust.

Anna Is Still Here (Vos)
Briar Rose (Yolen)
The Cage (Sender)
The Devil's Arithmetic (Yolen)
The Diary of a Young Girl (Frank)
Escape from Warsaw (Serraillier)
Gentlehands (Kerr)
I Have Lived a Thousand Years (Jackson)
If I Should Die Before I Wake (Nolan)
Night (Wiesel)
Nightfather (Friedman)
Number the Stars (Lowry)
Shadow Children (Schnur)

Incarceration

The following stories deal directly or peripherally with someone who is incarcerated in some way. In one case (*Monster*), a young man writes a screenplay of his murder trial. In others, youths are in detention facilities or are trying to cope with a parent or sibling who is in jail. These are titles we have handed to individuals who have a similar situation in their own lives to open an avenue for discussion. Sometimes it works.

Bearstone (Hobbs)
Dog Years (Warner)
Farm Team (Weaver)
Freak the Mighty (Philbrick)
Hero (Rottman)
Holes (Sacher)
It's a Matter of Trust (Byalick)

Leaving Fishers (Haddix)
The Maze (Hobbs)
Monster (Myers)
Scorpions (Myers)

Life in Another Nation's Culture

Books are trusty frigates that can land us in the middle of another country and another culture without requiring that we leave our homes. These stories help us understand what living in a country other than our own might be like.

Adem's Cross (Mead)	Albania
Among the Volcanoes (Castaneda)	Guatemala
Beduins' Gazelle (Temple)	Medieval North Africa: Beduins
The Bomb (Taylor)	Pacific Islanders: Bikini Atoll
The Broken Bridge (Banks)	Israel: kibbutz
Dissidents (Shusterman)	American in Russia in 1989
Echoes of the White Giraffe (Choi)	Post–World War II South Korea
The Fall of the Red Star (Szablya)	Hungary: 1956
Forbidden City (Bell)	Canadian in China
For the Love of Venice (Napoli)	American in Italy
Go and Come Back (Abelove)	Peru: Amazon rainforest
A Handful of Stars (Schami)	Syria
Journey to Jo'burg (Naidoo)	South Africa
Kiss the Dust (Laird)	Iraq, Iran
Over the Water (Casey)	Ireland
The Rainy Season (Griffin)	Americans in Panama
Red Scarf Girl (Jiang)	China: Cultural Revolution
Samir and Yonatan (Carmi)	Israel, Palestine
Shabanu (Staples)	Pakistan
Shadow of a Bull (Wojciechowska)	Spain
Song of Be (Beake)	Africa
Storyteller's Beads (Kurtz)	Africa
Taste of Salt (Temple)	Haiti
The Voices of Silence (Mooney)	Romania
Waiting for the Rain (Gordon)	South Africa
The Wall (Lutzeier)	Germany
The Year of the Leopard Song (Campbell)	Kenya

Arranged Marriages

Most of our students value their independence tremendously. The thought of others running their lives, even to the point of telling them who they will marry, is mind-boggling to most teens living in America. These titles are wonderful for exploring the ramifications of arranged marriages as well as looking at the cultures in other times and places.

A Coal Miner's Bride: The Diary of Anetka Kaminska (Bartoletti)
A Girl Named Disaster (Farmer)
Homeless Bird (Whalen)
Shabanu, Daughter of the Wind (Staples)

The Middle Ages

Beduins' Gazelle (Temple)
Catherine, Called Birdy (Cushman)
The Forestwife (Tomlinson)
Matilda Bone (Cushman)
The Midwife's Apprentice (Cushman)
Never Trust a Dead Man (Vande Velde)
A Proud Taste for Scarlet and Miniver (Konigsburg)
Ramsay Scallop (Temple)
Tusk and Stone (Bosse)

Migrant Workers/Illegal Aliens

Blue Willow (Gates)
A Boat to Nowhere (Wartski)
The Circuit (Jiminez)
Grab Hands and Run (Temple)
Journey of the Sparrows (Buss)
Lasso the Moon (Covington)
Lupita Mañana (Beatty)
Tonight, by Sea (Temple)

Slavery

Amos Fortune, Freeman (Yates)
The Captive (Hansen)

Jump Ship to Freedom (Collier)
Nightjohn (Paulsen)
Slave Dancer (Fox)
True North (Lasky)

Cults

Armageddon Summer (Yolen/Coville)
Asylum for Nightface (Brooks)
Leaving Fishers (Haddix)

War/Revolution

Often stories set during the time of war make wars seem more real than the pages of a textbook. These are stories not only set during wars and revolutions, but have teenage protagonists.

The Dove and the Sword (Garden)	Hundred Years War
My Brother Sam Is Dead (Collier)	American Revolution
War Comes to Willy Freeman (Collier)	American Revolution
With Every Drop of Blood (Collier)	Civil War
Bull Run (Fleischman)	Civil War
Soldier's Heart (Paulsen)	Civil War
A Time of Angels (Hesse)	World War I
After the Dancing Days (Rostkowski)	Post–World War I
The Endless Steppe (Hautzig)	World War II
House of Sixty Fathers (De Jong)	World War II
Stones in the Water (Napoli)	World War II
Wish Me Luck (Heneghan)	World War II
Under the Blood-Red Sun (Salisbury)	World War II
Year of Impossible Goodbyes (Choi)	World War II
So Far from the Bamboo Grove (Watkins)	World War II
The Girl with the White Flag (Higa)	World War II
Summer of My German Soldier (Greene)	World War II
Heroes (Cormier)	World War II
The Moved Outers (Means)	World War II internment camp
Farewell to Manzanar (Watson)	World War II internment camp
The Cage (Sender)	World War II/Holocaust

I Have Lived a Thousand Years (Jackson)	World War II/Holocaust
Diary of a Young Girl (Frank)	World War II/Holocaust
Devil's Arithmetic (Yolen)	World War II/Holocaust
Night (Wiesel)	World War II/Holocaust
Briar Rose (Yolen)	World War II/Holocaust
If I Should Die Before I Wake (Nolan)	World War II/Holocaust
Number the Stars (Lowry)	World War II/Holocaust
Sadako and the Thousand Paper Cranes (Coerr)	World War II aftermath
The Bomb (Taylor)	World War II aftermath
Red Scarf Girl (Jiang)	China's Cultural Revolution
The Road Home (White)	Vietnam
Fallen Angels (Myers)	Vietnam
The Clay Marble (Ho)	Cambodia
Little Brother (Baillie)	Cambodia
Kiss the Dust (Laird)	Iran, Iraq
One More River (Banks)	Israeli/Arab conflict
The Broken Bridge (Banks)	Israeli/Arab conflict
Fall of the Red Star (Szablya)	Hungarian Revolution
The Forty-Third War (Moeri)	Central America
Grab Hands and Run (Temple)	Central America
Taste of Salt (Temple)	Haiti
Tonight, by Sea (Temple)	Haiti
Forbidden City (Bell)	Tiananmen Square
Zlata's Diary (Filipovic)	Croatia
Adem's Cross (Mead)	Kosovo
The Voices of the Silence (Mooney)	Romania

Witch Trials

Beyond the Burning Time (Lasky)	Salem witch trials
The Burning Time (Matas)	French witch trials
The Witch of Blackbird Pond (Speare)	Salem witch trials

Other Social Studies Titles

War Between the Classes (Miklowitz)	Class experiment about social divisions
Color Me Dark: The Diary of Nellie Lee Love (McKissack)	The Great Migration

SCIENCE

Science classes also seem full of opportunities to include literature. Below are categories of books, as well as separate titles that are appropriate for including in science curriculum.

Nuclear Power/Bombs

Once we have learned to split the atom, we have learned that we can unleash an amazing amount of power. What responsibility does that power bring? These are all books, some fiction, others nonfiction, that provide avenues for discussion on this ethics-laden topic.

The Bomb (Taylor)
Hiroshima (Hersey)
Fall-Out (Pausewang)
Phoenix Rising (Hesse)
Sadako and the Thousand Paper Cranes (Coerr)

Environmental Issues

The Ancient One (Barron)*
The Ear, the Eye, and the Arm (Farmer)
Green Thumb (Thomas)
Phoenix Rising (Hesse)
Spud Sweetgrass (Doyle)

Endangered Species

Along the Tracks (Napoli)
Beardance (Hobbs)
California Blue (Klass)
The Maze (Hobbs)
Thunder Cave (Smith)

Other Titles Dealing with Science Issues

Star Split (Lasky)	Genetics
Among the Volcanoes (Castenada)	Modern medicine versus folk remedies

Troubling a Star (L'Engle)	Antarctic ecosystem
Stranded (Mikaelsen)	Pilot whales
Bone from a Dry Sea (Dickinson)	Evolution theories
Running Out of Time (Haddix)	Using people for medical experiments
Music of the Dolphins (Hesse)	Language development
Countdown (Mikaelsen)	Space program
Kokopelli's Flute (Hobbs)	Seed development
Fever 1793 (Anderson)	Yellow fever epidemic in Philadelphia

PARENT/CHILDREN BOOK GROUPS

What better way to open channels of discussion between parents and their offspring than to discuss a book they have both read? Parents have at various times come to us and asked for ideas for mother/daughter book groups, and we would like to encourage father/son book groups as well. During adolescent years, there are so many gender-based issues that many books would benefit vastly from discussions these groups would create. Obviously, any parent/child group would be appropriate and wonderful. The lists below are jumping off places for parent/child book groups.

Mother/Daughter Book Group Titles

The Ballad of Lucy Whipple (Cushman)
Forestwife (Tomlinson)
Go and Come Back (Abelove)
Homeless Bird (Whelan)
Ice (Naylor)
Imani All Mine (Porter)
Kissing Doorknobs (Hesser)
Language of Goldfish (Oneal)
Leaving Fishers (Haddix)
Letters to Julia (Holmes)
Long Season of Rain (Kim)
Luckiest Girl in the World (Levenkron)
Make Lemonade (Wolff)
Mama, I Want to Sing (Higginsen and Bolden)

Memoirs of a Bookbat (Lasky)
Midwife's Apprentice (Cushman)
One Bird (Mori)
Out of Control (Mazer)
Over the Water (Casey)
P.S. Longer Letter Later (Danziger and Martin)
Phoenix Rising (Hesse)
Rain Catchers (Thesman)
Shabanu, Daughter of the Wind (Staples)
Someone to Count On (Hermes)
Something Terrible Happened (Porte)
Speak (Anderson)
Spindrift (Rodowsky)
Starplace (Grove)
Stay True: Short Stories for Strong Girls (ed. Singer)
Tisha (Purdy)
Toning the Sweep (Johnson)
The Wanderer (Creech)

Father/Son Book Group Titles

Babcock (Cottonwood)
Bud, Not Buddy (Curtis)
Countdown (Mikaelsen)
Crash (Spinelli)
The Crossing (Paulsen)
Danger Zone (Klass)
Dragon's Gate (Yep)
Dragonwings (Yep)
Far North (Hobbs)
Harris and Me (Paulsen)
Holes (Sacher)
Ironman (Crutcher)
Jason's Gold (Hobbs)
A Long Way From Home (Wartski)
Parrot in the Oven: Mi Vida (Martinez)
The Place of Lions (Campbell)
Prophecy Rock (MacGregor)
Radiance Descending (Fox)
Rats Saw God (Thomas)

Scorpions (Myers)
Searching for Candlestick Park (Kehret)
Shark Bait (Salisbury)
Shark Callers (Campbell)
Somewhere in Darkness (Myers)
Sparrow Hawk Red (Mikaelsen)
Stuck in Neutral (Trueman)
Tears of a Tiger (Draper)
These Are the Rules of the Road (Many)
Thunder Cave (Smith)
Under the Blood-Red Sun (Salisbury)

Story Collections

Today's story collections, like other young adult literature, have blossomed in diverse directions, taking on subjects that are challenging and thought-provoking. Sometimes, teen attention spans are such that wading through anything that seems like expository writing or explanation in the early chapters of a story has them setting a book aside before the "good part." Short stories are good to have on hand for those teens: they begin quickly and are short, to the point. Those that are selected around themes are some of our favorite collections. Sometimes after reading a captivating short story, teen readers will ask the magical question, "Did _____ write anything else?" Below are some of the story collections that we have found to be excellent compilations of well-written tales by some of today's top writers of young adult fiction.

STORY COLLECTION (EDITOR/AUTHOR)	THEME/TOPIC
Am I Blue? Coming Out from the Silence (ed. Bauer)	Gay and lesbian characters
American Dragons (ed. Yep)	Asian American stories
An Island Like You (Cofer)	Puerto Rican American barrio
Athletic Shorts (Crutcher)	Sports stories
Baseball in April (Soto)	Latino Americans
The Circuit (Jimenez)	Migrant worker family
Doing Time (Thomas)	Service projects
Join In (ed. Gallo)	Multiethnic teen stories
Leaving Home (ed. Rochman and McCampbell)	Going out into the world
Living Up the Street (Soto)	Barrio stories
No Easy Answers (ed. Gallo)	Teens making choices
Places I Never Meant to Be (ed. Blume)	Stories by censored writers

Rio Grande Stories (Meyer)	Each student in a class gathers a story
Tomorrowland (ed. Cart)	Looking at tomorrow in various aspects
Trapped (ed. Duncan)	Mental, physical traps
Ultimate Sports (ed. Gallo)	Sports stories
What's in a Name? (Wittlinger)	Interconnected stories of high school students
Zebra and Other Stories (Potok)	Multiethnic, multiple themes

Good Read-Aloud Books

Reading aloud to our students is a great way to share our love of books and a good story at the same time. We have used all or parts of these as read-alouds with great success.

Babcock (Cottonwood)
Cages (Kehret)
Darnell Rock Reporting (Myers)
Freak the Mighty (Philbrick)
The Giver (Lowry)
Harris and Me (Paulsen)
Harry Potter and the Sorcerer's Stone by J. K. Rowling*
Holes (Sacher)
Ironman (Crutcher)
Journey to Jo'burg (Naidoo)
Kokopelli's Flute (Hobbs)
Maniac Magee (Spinelli)
Phoenix Rising (Hesse)
Quake (Cottonwood)
Running Out of Time (Haddix)
Seedfolks (Fleischman)
Slake's Limbo (Holman)
Sparrow Hawk Red (Mikaelsen)
Taking Sides (Soto)
Tangerine (Bloor)
Walk Two Moons (Creech)
The Wanderer (Creech)
The Watsons Go to Birmingham—1963 (Curtis)
Whirligig (Fleischman)
Won't Know Till I Get There (Myers)

Science Fiction and Fantasy

These works are listed first by author, then series where appropriate, and then in order of the date of publication. Series as well as single titles are briefly annotated for your convenience. This is by no means an exhaustive list of all the great works in this genre, these are the ones we have read and have shared with our students.

Alexander, Lloyd   Chronicles of Prydain
   Taran, the Assistant Pig Keeper, finds himself playing a key role as he works with new friends, and enemies, to keep Prydain from falling into the hands of the forces of evil that threaten to take over this land.
   The Book of Three   Holt, Rinehard and Winston, 1964
   The Black Cauldron   Holt, Rinehard and Winston, 1965
   The Castle of Llyr   Holt, Rinehard and Winston, 1966
   Taran Wanderer   Holt, Rinehard and Winston, 1967
   The High King   Holt, Rinehard and Winston, 1968

   Time Cat   Holt, Rinehard and Winston, 1963
   Gareth, a time-traveling cat that can talk, takes Jason on unforgettable journeys.

Anthony, Piers   Xanth Series
   This is a light but satisfying fantasy series full of puns, humor, and magic. The series has more than twenty titles. These are the first six.
   A Spell for Chameleon   Ballantine Publishing Groups, 1977
   The Source of Magic   Ballantine Publishing Groups, 1978
   Castle Roogna   Ballantine Publishing Groups, 1979
   Centaur Aisle   Ballantine Publishing Groups, 1981
   Night Mare   Ballantine Publishing Groups, 1982
   Ogre, Ogre   Ballantine Publishing Groups, 1982

Barron, T. A.   Merlin Series
   In this exciting and well-written Arthurian fantasy series, readers will follow the life of a young man destined to become one of the greatest magicians of all time.

The Lost Years of Merlin	Philomel Books, 1996
The Seven Songs of Merlin	Philomel Books, 1997
The Fires of Merlin	Philomel Books, 1998
The Mirror of Merlin	Philomel Books, 1999
The Wings of Merlin	Philomel Books, 2000

The Ancient One   Philomel Books, 1992

Set in the Oregon old timber regions, this is the story of a thirteen-year old girl who is taken back five-hundred years and learns about the connections between nature and humans.

Bradbury, Ray

Fahrenheit 451   Ballantine Books, 1953

Bradbury paints a grim vision of the future where firefighters burn books.

The Illustrated Man   Doubleday, 1951

In a classic Bradbury tale, people watch as the tattooed man moves and the marks on his body reveal many tales.

The Martian Chronicles   Doubleday, 1950

Human beings leave an Earth close to destruction to conquer Mars, only to find they are unable to let go of the past—especially past mistakes.

Britain, Kristen

The Green Rider   DAW Books, 1998

Karigan has been booted out of school for battling with another student. As she starts for home, out of the forest comes a horse carrying a dying rider who has a vital message for the king. The rider makes Karigan swear to carry the message through a journey of peril.

Brooks, Terry   The Shannara Series

In the Four Lands there is very little that is free from evil, and in this well-loved series the reader will meet druids, elves, gnomes, warlocks, trolls, dwarves, and many other beings who live in this land. This is a classic good-versus-evil series.

The Sword of Shannara	Ballantine Books, 1977
Elfstones of Shannara	Ballantine Books, 1982
Wish Song of Shannara	Ballantine Books, 1985
Scions of Shannara	Ballantine Books, 1990
Druid of Shannara	Ballantine Books, 1991
Elf Queen of Shannara	Ballantine Books, 1992
Talismans of Shannara	Ballantine Books, 1993
First King of Shannara	Ballantine Books, 1996
Star Wars: The Phantom Menace	Del Rey Books, 2000

In a galaxy far, far away, young Skywalker makes the choice to leave his mother and his pod-racing to begin training as a Jedi warrior. This story is the beginning of the Star Wars stories.

Card, Orson Scott   Ender Quartet (plus one)
In this futuristic series about computerized wars, annihilation of alien races, and the consequences of that action, readers are confronted with ethical questions that will be debated for a long time. *Ender's Game* is the most popular for middle school students of this set, as the others are more complex in theme. The newer *Ender's Shadow* is also popular.

Ender's Game	T. Doherty Associates, 1985
Speaker for the Dead	TOR, 1986
Xenocide	TOR, 1991
Children of the Mind	TOR, 1996
Ender's Shadow	T. Doherty Associates, 1999

A parallel story to *Ender's Game*, this is the story of Bean.

Clarke, Arthur C.
Childhood's End   Ballantine, 1953
The Overlords appear one day in shiny spaceships over all the major cities on Earth. With them comes an end to poverty and disease. But there is a price to pay.

Rama Quartet
Out of nowhere, coming toward Earth at an alarming speed, appears a gigantic metallic cylinder. As it nears Earth, scientists prepare to intersect its path and determine what it is and where it comes from. Thus begins a great adventure with alien beings, landscape, and architecture.
Rendezvous with Rama   Harcourt Brace Jovanovich, 1973

w/Gentry Lee

Rama II	Bantam Books, 1989
The Garden of Rama	Bantam Books, 1991
Rama Revealed	Bantam Books, 1994

Cooney, Caroline   Time Travel Trilogy
When Annie Lockhart wishes she had a more romantic boyfriend, she falls through a time portal to Victorian times, becoming involved not only in romance, but also strange customs and plots of murder and mayhem.

Both Sides of Time	Delacorte Press, 1995
Out of Time	Delacorte Press, 1996
Prisoners of Time	Delacorte Press, 1998

Cooper, Susan   The Darkover Series
Will Stanton is the last of the Old Ones, the immortals dedicated to keep-
ing the world from domination by the Dark.
Over Sea, Under Stone   Harcourt Brace Jovanovich, 1965
The Dark Is Rising   Atheneum, 1973
Greenwitch   Atheneum, 1974
The Grey King   Atheneum, 1975
Silver on the Tree   Atheneum, 1977

Crichton, Michael
Sphere   Knopf, 1987
Civilization scientists are co-opted by the United States military to go
underwater to explore an American ship that has come back from the future carrying an alien sphere.
Jurassic Park   Knopf: distributed by
                                     Random House, 1990
Through the wonder of cloning, scientists are able to create several
species of dinosaurs, once extinct, but things go terribly wrong when a
large corporation wants to create a park where families can roam with
these magnificent, but sometimes deadly, creatures.
Lost World   Knopf: distributed by
                                     Random House, 1995
In this sequel to *Jurassic Park*, it is six years later, the park is dismantled,
and all the dinosaurs are dead. Or are they?

Dickinson, Peter
Eva   Delacorte Press, 1989
Following a tragic accident that leaves Eva all but dead, scientists in this futuristic world are able to transplant her brain into the body of a chimpanzee
from the preserve her father oversees. As Eva learns to integrate her two
selves, she becomes involved in the plight of her nonhuman primate relatives whose natural habitats have been destroyed in the name of progress.

Eddings, David   The Belgariad
Garion, a farm boy, is caught up in the quest to fulfill a prophecy to cap-
ture and return the Orb that protects the West from the evil god Torak.
This series is filled with magic, adventure, humor, mystery, and a host of
interesting characters.
Pawn of Prophesy   Random House, 1982
Queen of Sorcery   Random House, 1982
Magician's Gambit   Random House, 1983

Castle of Wizardry	Random House, 1984
Enchanter's End Game	Random House, 1984

The Malloreon

In this sequel series to the Belgariad, Garion has slain evil Torak but another prophecy arises and more evil is brewing. Once again, Garion finds the world's fate in his hands.

Guardians of the West	Random House, 1988
King of Murgos	Random House, 1989
Demon Lord of Karanda	Random House, 1989
Sorceress of Darshwa	Ballantine Books, 1990
The Seeress of Kell	Random House, 1992

Farmer, Nancy

The Ear, the Eye, and the Arm   Orchard Books, 1994

Set in a futuristic Zimbabwe, this is the story of three upper-class children who leave home for a brief adventure and find themselves captured by the leader of a large underground gang of people who live outside the government.

Goldman, William

Princess Bride   Harcourt Brace Jovanovich, 1973

Before the movie, there was the book—full of fun, word-play, swordplay, and more.

Haddix, Margaret Peterson

Among the Hidden	Simon and Schuster Books for Young Readers, 1998

Luke has met only four people in his life: his parents and two brothers. Luke is a third child, forbidden by the Population Police. When he unexpectedly finds another like himself, he is challenged to terrifying risks.

Herbert, Frank   Dune Saga

This series has become a must-read for all science fiction lovers. Planet Arrakis is a desert world of the future. Spice, the key to immortality, is the most valuable asset of the planet and people will do anything to get it.

Dune	Chilton Books, 1965
Dune Messiah	Putnam, 1969
Children of Dune	Berkley Pub. Corp: distributed by Putnam, 1976
God Emperor of Dune	Putnam, 1981
Heretics of Dune	Putnam, 1984

Jacques, Brian   The Redwall Series
Mice, stoats, rats, birds, and a host of others visit the legendary Redwall
Abby in a Medieval world. (Books are listed in order of publication; the
numbers after them represent an approximate chronological order for the
stories.)

Redwall (9)	Philomel Books, 1986
Mossflower (3)	Philomel Books, 1988
Mattimeo (10)	Philomel Books, 1990
Mariel of Redwall (6)	Philomel Books, 1992
Salmandastron (8)	Philomel Books, 1993
Martin the Warrior (2)	Philomel Books, 1994
The Bellmaker (7)	Philomel Books, 1995
Outcast of Redwall (5)	Philomel Books, 1996
The Pearls of Lutra (11)	Philomel Books, 1997
The Long Patrol (12)	Philomel Books, 1998
Marlfox (13)	Philomel Books, 1998
The Legend of Luke (4)	Philomel Books, 2000
Lord Brocktree (1)	Philomel Books, 2000

Kindl, Patricia
  Owl in Love   Houghton Mifflin, 1993
Being a shapeshifter with the appetite of an owl is tough: how can you
politely bring mice to school for lunch? Having witches for parents is
also a challenge, and then falling in love with your science teacher makes
it all the more complicated!

Lackey, Mercedes
  Brightly Burning   DAW Books
In the newest tale of Valdemar, Lackey tells the tale of Lavan Chitwal,
one of the most intriguing characters in her earlier series. This is a story
of love, honor and sacrifice.

                            The Mage Storms
Old enemies, Valdemar and Karse, must now work together to fight the
Mage Storms that threaten to destroy all of their lands. This series brings
together magic, religion, and science as they are all needed to fend off
the threat.

Storm Warning	DAW Books, 1994
Storm Rising	DAW Books, 1995
Storm Breaking	DAW Books, 1996

Lasky, Kathryn
> *Star Split*   Hyperion Books for Children, 1999
> Thirteen-year-old Darci is fortunate. She was born into a family that
> could afford genetic enhancement, which means she is a valued person
> in society. As she discovers an underground movement to stop this ge-
> netic manipulation, she joins in their attempt to save humanity.

LeGuin, Ursula   The Earthsea Quartet
> A young mage has released a terrible evil into the world and he must set
> it right. This series is about his quest and his rise to become the Arch-
> mage of all of Earthsea.
> *The Wizard of Earthsea*   Parnassus Press, 1968
> *The Tombs of Atuan*   Atheneum, 1971
> *The Farthest Shore*   Atheneum, 1972
> *Tehanu*   Atheneum, 1990

L'Engle, Madeleine   Wrinkle in Time Series
> In this classic series, a family is separated when the father disappears and
> the children must cross time and space to try to find out why.
> *A Wrinkle in Time*   Farrar, Straus & Giroux, 1962
> *Wind in the Door*   Farrar, Straus & Giroux, 1973
> *A Swiftly Tilting Planet*   Farrar, Straus & Giroux, 1978

Lewis, C. S.   Chronicles of Narnia
> In this well-loved series, good and evil are sorted out by a wonderful cast
> of human and animal characters.
> *The Lion, the Witch and the*   Macmillan, 1950
>   *Wardrobe*
> *Prince Caspian*   Macmillan, 1951
> *The Voyage of the Dawn Trader*   Macmillan, 1952
> *The Silver Chair*   Macmillan, 1953
> *The Horse and His Boy*   Macmillan, 1954
> *The Magician's Nephew*   Macmillan, 1955
> *The Last Battle*   Macmillan, 1956

Lowry, Lois
> *The Giver*   Houghton Mifflin, 1993
> This is a powerful story set in a perfect world, where there are no worries,
> no disease, and no choice. The story focuses on Jonas as he reaches the time
> when his life work is announced, and he learns he is to be the Receiver of
> Memory. But those memories hold ideas that Jonas cannot accept.

Gathering Blue   Houghton Mifflin, 2000
Kira has lost her mother and her father and the women of the village
want her put out to die, but the leaders have another plan for her. Kira
has the ability to create wonderful pictures with thread and her skill is
needed to mend a valuable artifact of the community, and to add new stories with her thread weaving.

McCaffrey, Anne   The Dragon Lizards Trilogy
A subset of the Pern books, these are geared for younger readers, who
may then feel compelled to tackle the whole *Dragonriders of Pern* series,
which is long and rich.
Dragonsong   Atheneum, 1976
Dragonsinger   Atheneum, 1977
Dragondrums   Atheneum, 1979

McKillip, Patricia   Riddle Master Trilogy
This old favorite series is now out of print but Penguin Putnam has re-
leased a one-volume collection of all these titles. This is the classic story
about a prince and a land awaiting the rebirth of magic.
The Riddle-Master of Hed   Atheneum, 1976
Heir of Sea and Fire   Atheneum, 1977
Harpist in the Wind   Atheneum, 1979

McKinley, Robin
The Hero and the Crown   Greenwillow Books, 1985
Aerin, the daughter of the King, spends much of her time alone where
she makes magical discoveries, slays dragons, and eventually discovers
the truth of her parentage.
The Blue Sword   Greenwillow Books, 1982
Harry is kidnapped by a local ruler where she learns about her own psy-
chic powers while using the Blue Sword in battle.

Nix, Garth
Sabriel   HarperCollins, 1995
Sabriel is eighteen when her father does not arrive for his annual mystical moonlight visit, and thus begins her journey to try to find her father
and hold at bay dark destructive forces.
Shade's Children   HarperCollins, 1997
A dark haunting tale of the future, this is the story of four children who have
escaped from the Dorms where Overlords keep children until they harvest
their brains at fourteen. But one man—or his memory—provides a refuge
for the children and helps them to overthrow the Overlords—or does he?

Oldham, June
Found   Orchard Books, 1996
A strange tale set in the twenty-first century, this tells of a time when a
tax on extra children forces Ren into the wilds where she meets up with
three other young people and a baby.

Oppel, Kenneth
Silverwing   Simon and Schuster Books
                                     for Young Readers, 1997
This is the story of a young bat trying to prove to the elders that he is fit
and not just the runt of the litter. On a journey to the south he has a
chance to prove himself by defeating an evil cannibal bat and finding the
true location of his long missing father.
Sunwing   Simon and Schuster Books
                                     for Young Readers, 2000
This continues the adventures of Shade who persists on his journey of
self-discovery, with a remarkable cast of friends and foes. Redwall fans
will enjoy this series.

Pierce, Tamora   Song of the Lioness Quartet
Alanna's dream is to become a knight, so she trades places with her
brother and enters training disguised as a boy.
Alanna: The First Adventure   Atheneum, 1983
In the Hand of the Goddess   Atheneum, 1984
The Woman Who Rode Like
   a Man   Atheneum, 1986
Lioness Rampant   Atheneum, 1988

                                     Protector of the Small Series
Ten-year-old Keladry wants to be a page but has to overcome the objec-
tions of all the males. She has to go a long way to prove that she is wor-
thy to become a knight.
The First Test   Random House, 1999
The Page   Random House, 2000

                                     The Immortals
Thirteen-year-old Daine joins the Knights of Tortall in the battle to save
the kingdom from the immortal creatures who have found their way back
into the world of mortals.
Wild Magic   Maxwell Macmillan, 1992
Wolf-Speaker   Maxwell Macmillan, 1994
Emperor Mage   Atheneum Books for
                                     Young People, 1995

The Realm of the Gods	Atheneum Books for Young People, 1996

Circle of Magic Series

Four teenagers find themselves in the care of the craftspeople and mages at Winding Circle Temple. There they set out to learn their crafts and to perfect their own magical talents.

Tris's Book	Scholastic Press, 1997
Sandry's Book	Scholastic Press, 1998
Daja's Book	Scholastic Press, 1998
Briar's Book	Scholastic Press, 1999

Pullman, Philip   His Dark Materials Series

In this complex and riveting series dealing with souls, love, friendship, and parallel worlds, Lyra Silvertongue and Will move through a changing universe, attempting to find the source of the evil that is threatening all of their friends.

The Golden Compass	AAK: distributed by Random House, 1996
The Subtle Knife	AAK: distributed by Random House, 1997
The Amber Spyglass	Alfred A. Knopf, 2000

Regan, Dian Curtis

Princess Nevermore	Scholastic Press, 1995

Princess Quinnella lives in a magical world under the Earth where a wishing pool is her window to the world above. She longs to visit this other world, but suddenly her wish comes true, and she must adapt to a new and strange place.

Reiss, Kathryn

Pale Phoenix	Harcourt Brace, 1994

Miranda is confused about the orphan named Abby who suddenly joins her family. Abby says and does odd things, and seems to be able to disappear.

Rowling, J. K.   The Harry Potter Series

Harry doesn't remember how his parents died, although sometimes he has strange dreams about a blinding flash of light. He does know that his aunt and uncle don't like him, and he wishes he had somewhere else to live. Then a letter arrives that summons him to his true calling.

Harry Potter and the Sorcerer's Stone	Arthur A. Levine Books, 1998
Harry Potter and the Chamber of Secrets	Arthur A. Levine Books, 1999

Harry Potter and the Prisoner of Azkaban	Arthur A. Levine Books, 1999
Harry Potter and the Goblet of Fire	Arthur A. Levine Books, 2000

Rubinstein, Gillian

Galax-Arena   Simon and Schuster Books for Children, 1997

In this strange and haunting tale, three Australian children living in the twenty-first century are kidnapped and taken to Galax-Arena, where they and other children are trained to do death-defying stunts for the amusement of the inhabitants of the planet Vexak.

Shusterman, Neal

Dark Side of Nowhere   Little, Brown, 1997

Jason is confused when he finds out that the "normal" life he and his closest friends have been living is anything but. In fact, his parents and the parents of his friends are aliens from another planet who have been trying to blend in with human beings.

Silverberg, Robert

Lord Valentine's Castle   Harper & Row, 1980

This prequel to Silverberg's Majipoor series is filled with intrigue, treachery, and magic.

Stewart, Mary   The Merlin Trilogy

This series gives readers a unique look at life in fifth-century Britain through the eyes of Merlin, the magician of Arthurian legend.

The Crystal Cave	Morrow, 1970
The Hollow Hills	Morrow, 1973
The Last Enchantment	Morrow, 1979

Tolkien, J. R. R.

The Hobbit   Houghton Mifflin, 1937

Bilbo Baggins is living a happy life in his Hobbit hole when the powerful magician Gandalf comes to call and demands that he join the search for a magical ring. This is a classic tale of fantasy, adventure, and intrigue.

The Lord of the Rings Trilogy

Frodo Baggins leads a band of misfits in the search for the magic rings that have the power to overcome evil in the land. This series is a classic and should be reserved for higher level readers.

The Fellowship of the Ring	Houghton Mifflin, 1954
The Two Towers	Houghton Mifflin, 1955
The Return of the King	Houghton Mifflin, 1956

Turner, Megan

| *The Thief* | Greenwillow Books, 1996 |
| *The Queen of Attolia* | Greenwillow Books, 2000 |

These two books tell the story of Eugenides, or Gen, who is rescued from the dungeons, where he has been placed for thieving, only to find himself named Royal Thief of Eddis. His mission is to help overcome his ruler's rival queen.

Vande Velde, Vivian

| *Dragon's Bait* | Jane Yolen Books, 1992 |

Fifteen-year-old Alys is accused of witchcraft and is set out to become the local dragon's dinner but he takes an interest in her story and they set out to get revenge on her accusers.

Voigt, Cynthia   The Kingdom

The setting is what unites these four books set in a medieval kingdom where there are wars, slavery, and heroism. The protagonists are all young teens and the adventures are alluring.

Jackaroo	Atheneum Books, 1985
On Fortune's Wheel	Simon & Schuster, 1991
The Wings of a Falcon	Atheneum Books, 1993
Elske	Atheneum Books, 1999

Whitcher, Susan

| *The Enchanter's Glass* | Harcourt Brace, 1996 |

Thirteen-year-old Phoeby works against an enchanter who traps people's images in her glass.

Wrede, Patricia   The Enchanted Forest Chronicles

Queen Cimorene and Morwa the Witch work to spoil the wizards' plot to destroy the forest.

Book One: Dealing with Dragons	Jane Yolen Books, 1990
Book Two: Searching for Dragons	Harcourt Brace, 1991
Book Three: Calling on Dragons	Jane Yolen Books, 1993
Book Four: Talking to Dragons	Harcourt Brace, 1993

Mairelon the Magician   TOR Books, 1991
Kim lives as a street urchin in London until she falls in with a traveling magician called Mairelon. She joins forces with him in search of a valuable magical artifact.

Yep, Laurence   Dragon Series
Shimmer, a centuries old dragon princess, and a boy named Thorn try and free her clan from the evil Dragon King.
Dragon of the Lost Sea   HarperCollins, 1982
Dragon Steel   HarperCollins, 1985
Dragon Cauldron   HarperCollins, 1991
Dragon War   HarperCollins, 1992

Yolen, Jane   Young Merlin Series
A young boy is raised in the wilderness as a feral child. As he grows and begins to wonder who he is, he joins a company of traveling performers, where he learns many things. To escape from the evil he encounters, he takes refuge in the woods. This is the story of Merlin the Magician as a young boy.
Passenger   Harcourt, 1996
Hobby   Harcourt, 1996
Merlin   Harcourt Brace & Company, 1997

Boots and the Seven Leaguers:
A Rock and Troll Novel   Harcourt, 2000
In a rollicking story, teen troll Gog and his best magical friend Pook decide to pose as roadies to get tickets to see their favorite band's concert. Their plan seems to be working well until Gog's younger brother is kidnapped. Naturally, Gog and Pook have to go rescue him.

Zambreno, Mary Frances
Plague of Sorcerers   Harcourt Brace Jovanovich, 1991
Young Jermyn thinks he will never become a wizard because he cannot seem to attract a familiar. When he finally does, he has to fend off much taunting and doubts of his abilities because of the form his familiar takes.

Author Index

A

Abelove, Joan — *Go and Come Back*
Anderson, Laurie Halse — *Fever 1793*
Speak
Anderson, Peggy, and Helen M. Szablya — *Fall of the Red Star*
Anderson, Rachel — *Bus People*
Anonymous — *It Happened to Nancy*
Armstrong, William — *Sounder*
Arrick, Fran — *What You Don't Know Can Kill You*
Avi — *Man Who Was Poe*
Night Journeys

B

Baillie, Allan — *Little Brother*
Balgassi, Haemi — *Tae's Sonata*
Banks, Lynne Reid — *Broken Bridge*
One More River
Bantle, Lee F. — *Diving for the Moon*
Barrie, Barbara — *Adam Zigzag*
Barron, T. A. — *Lost Years of Merlin*
Bartoletti, Susan C. — *Coal Miner's Bride: The Diary of Anetka Kaminska*
Bauer, Joan — *Backwater*
Rules of the Road
Bauer, Marion Dane, ed. — *Am I Blue?*
Beake, Lesley — *Song of Be*
Beatty, Patricia — *Lupita Mañana*
Bell, William — *Forbidden City: A Novel of Modern China*
Bennett, Cherie — *Life in the Fat Lane*

E

Easley, Mary Ann	*I Am the Ice Worm*
Ewing, Lynne	*Drive-By*

F

Facklam, Margery	*Trouble with Mothers*
Farmer, Nancy	*Ear, the Eye, and the Arm*
	Girl Named Disaster
Ferris, Jean	*Love Among the Walnuts*
Filipovic, Zlata	*Zlata's Diary*
Fine, Anne	*Flour Babies*
Flake, Sharon	*Skin I'm In*
Fleischman, Paul	*Bull Run*
	Mind's Eye
	Saturnalia
	Seedfolks
	Whirligig
Fletcher, Susan	*Shadow Spinner*
Fox, Paula	*Eagle Kite*
	Radiance Descending
	Slave Dancer
Frank, Anne	*Diary of a Young Girl*
Frank, Lucy	*I Am an Artichoke*
Friedman, Carl	*Nightfather*
Fritz, Jean	*Homesick: My Own Story*

G

Gallo, Donald, ed.	*Join In*
	No Easy Answers
	Ultimate Sports
Garden, Nancy	*Dove and Sword*
Garland, Sherry	*Song of the Buffalo Boy*
Gates, Doris	*Blue Willow*
George, Jean Craighead	*Julie*
	Julie of the Wolves
	Julie's Wolf Pack
	Shark Beneath the Reef

I

Ingold, Jeanette   *Window*

J

Jackson, Livia Bitton   *I Have Lived a Thousand Years*
Jaffe-Gill, Ellen   *No Big Deal*
Jiang, Ji-Li   *Red Scarf Girl*
Jimenez, Francisco   *Circuit*
Johnson, Angela   *Heaven*
                                Humming Whispers
                                Songs of Faith
                                Toning the Sweep
Johnson, Lou Anne   *My Posse Don't Do Homework*
Johnson, Scott   *Safe at Second*
Johnston, Julie   *Adam and Eve and Pinch Me*
                                Hero of Lesser Causes
Jones, Ron   *Acorn People*

K

Kehret, Peg   *Cages*
                                Searching for Candlestick Park
                                Secret Journey
                                Small Steps
Keller, Beverly   *Amazon Papers*
Kelley, Ruth E.   *Boomer's Journal*
Kerr, M. E.   *Deliver Us from Evie*
                                Gentlehands
Keyes, Daniel   *Flowers for Algernon*
Killilea, Marie   *Karen*
Kim, Helen   *Long Season of Rain*
Klass, David   *California Blue*
                                Danger Zone
Koertge, Ron   *Confess-O-Rama*
Konigsburg, E. L.   *Proud Taste for Scarlet and Miniver*
                                View from Saturday
Kurtz, Jane   *Storyteller's Beads*

L

M

O

O'Dell, Scott	*Black Pearl*
	Black Star, Bright Dawn
	Island of the Blue Dolphins
	Sing Down the Moon
O'Dell, Scott and Elizabeth Hall	*Thunder Rolling in the Mountains*
Okimoto, Jean Davies	*Eclipse of Moonbeam Dawson*
Oneal, Zibby	*Language of Goldfish*
Orr, Wendy	*Peeling the Onion*
Oughton, Jerrie	*Music from a Place Called Half Moon*
	War in Georgia

P

Park, Barbara	*Mick Harte Was Here!*
Paterson, Katherine	*Bridge to Terabithia*
	Jip, His Story
	Lyddie
	Master Puppeteer
Paulsen, Gary	*Canyons*
	Cookcamp
	Crossing
	Dogsong
	Harris and Me
	Hatchet
	Night White Deer Died
	Nightjohn
	Sarny: A Life Remembered
	Schernoff Discoveries
	Soldier's Heart
Pausewang, Gudrun	*Fall-Out*
Peck, Richard	*Last Safe Place on Earth*
	Unfinished Portrait of Jessica
Peck, Robert Newton	*Day No Pigs Would Die*
Perkins, Mitali	*Sunita Experiment*
Philbrick, Rodman	*Freak the Mighty*
Polikoff, Barbara	*Life's a Funny Proposition, Horatio*
Porte, Barbara Ann	*Something Terrible Happened*
Porter, Connie	*Imani All Mine*

Potok, Chaim

I Am the Clay
Zebra and Other Stories

Powell, Randy

Dean Duffy
Is Kissing a Girl Who Smokes Like
  Licking an Ashtray?
Tribute to Another Dead Rock Star

Pullman, Philip

Broken Bridge
Ruby in the Smoke

Purdy, Anne

Tisha: The Story of a Young Teacher in
  the Alaskan Wilderness

R

Ransom, Candice F.

Between Two Worlds

Raskin, Ellen

Westing Game

Reaver, Chap

Bill

Rennison, Louise

Angus, Thongs, and Full-Frontal
  Snogging

Richter, Conrad

Light in the Forest

Richter, Hans Peter

I Was There

Rinaldi, Ann

Hang a Thousand Trees with Ribbons
Second Bend in the River

Ritter, John

Choosing Up Sides

Robinson, Margaret A.

Woman of Her Tribe

Rochman, Hazel, and
  McCampbell, Darlene

Leaving Home

Rodowsky, Colby

Hannah in Between
Spindrift

Rostkowski, Margaret

After the Dancing Days
Moon Dancer

Rottman, Susan L.

Hero

Ryan, Mary Elizabeth

Alias

Ryan, Pam Muñoz

Esperañza Rising

Rylant, Cynthia

Islander
Missing May

S

Sacher, Louis

Holes

Sachs, Marilyn

Call Me Ruth

T

U

V

Culture Index

African	*AK* *Bedouins' Gazelle* *Beyond the Mango Tree* *Bone from a Dry Sea* *Captive* *Chain of Fire* *Countdown* *Ear, the Eye, and the Arm* *Girl Named Disaster* *Journey to Jo'burg* *Magical Adventures of Pretty Pearl* *Mara, Daughter of the Nile* *Place of Lions* *Return* *Song of Be* *Storyteller's Beads* *Thunder Cave* *Waiting for the Rain: A Novel of South Africa* *Year of the Leopard Song*
African American	*Another Way to Dance* *Amos Fortune, Free Man* *Babcock* *Bad News Travels Fast* *Blessing in Disguise* *Bud, Not Buddy* *Burning Up* *Charlie Pippin* *Color Me Dark: The Diary of Nellie Lee Love* *Come a Stranger*

Cousins
Danger Zone
Dangerous Skies
Darnell Rock Reporting
Different Beat
Everywhere
Fallen Angels
From the Notebooks of Melanin Sun
Glory Field
Hang a Thousand Trees with Ribbons
Heaven
Hoops
House You Pass on the Way
Humming Whispers
I Hadn't Meant to Tell You This
If You Come Softly
Imani All Mine
Jip: His Story
Journal of Joshua Loper: A Black Cowboy
Jubilee Journey
Jump Ship to Freedom
Let the Circle Be Unbroken
M.C. Higgins, the Great
Make Lemonade
Mama, I Want to Sing
Marked by Fire
Melitte
Monster
Motown and Didi
Moves Make the Man
Nightjohn
Only Twice I've Wished for Heaven
Philip Hall Likes Me, I Reckon, Maybe
Picture of Freedom: The Diary of Clotee, a
  Slave Girl
Plain City
Righteous Revenge of Artemis Bonner
Roll of Thunder, Hear My Cry
Sarny: A Life Remembered
Scorpions